WHAT A FRIEND WE HAVE IN JESUS

TRADITIONS OF CHRISTIAN SPIRITUALITY SERIES

WHAT A FRIEND WE HAVE IN JESUS

The Evangelical Tradition

Ian Randall

SERIES EDITOR:
Philip Sheldrake

DARTON·LONGMAN+TODD

First published in 2005 by
Darton, Longman and Todd Ltd
1 Spencer Court
140–142 Wandsworth High Street
London SW18 4JJ

ISBN 0–232–52533–1

A catalogue record for this book is available from the British Library.

Phototypeset by Intype Libra Ltd
Printed and bound in Great Britain by CPI Bath

To Douglas McBain
with thanks.

CONTENTS

PREFACE TO THE SERIES

Nowadays, in the Western world, there is a widespread hunger for spirituality in all its forms. This is not confined to traditional religious people, let alone to regular churchgoers. The desire for resources to sustain the spiritual quest has led many people to seek wisdom in unfamiliar places. Some have turned to cultures other than their own. The fascination with Native American or Aboriginal Australian spiritualities is a case in point. Other people have been attracted by the religions of India and Tibet or the Jewish Kabbalah and Sufi mysticism. One problem is that, in comparison to other religions, Christianity is not always associated in people's minds with 'spirituality'. The exceptions are a few figures from the past who have achieved almost cult status such as Hildegard of Bingen or Meister Eckhart. This is a great pity, for Christianity East and West over two thousand years has given birth to an immense range of spiritual wisdom. Many traditions continue to be active today. Others that were forgotten are being rediscovered and reinterpreted.

It is a long time since an extended series of introductions to Christian spiritual traditions has been available in English. Given the present climate, it is an opportune moment for a new series which will help more people to be aware of the great spiritual riches available within the Christian traditions.

The overall purpose of the series is to make selected spiritual traditions available to a contemporary readership. The books seek to provide accurate and balanced historical and thematic treatments of their subjects. The authors are also conscious of the need to make connections with contemporary experience and values without being artificial or reducing a tradition to one dimension. The authors are well versed in reliable scholarship about the traditions they describe. However, their intention is that the books should be fresh in style and accessible to the general reader.

One problem that such a series inevitably faces is the word 'spirituality'. For example, it is increasingly used beyond religious circles and does not necessarily imply a faith tradition. Again, it could mean substantially different things for a Christian and a Buddhist. Within Christianity itself, the word in its modern sense is relatively recent. The reality that it stands for differs subtly in the different contexts of time and place. Historically, 'spirituality' covers a breadth of human experience and a wide range of values and practices.

No single definition of 'spirituality' has been imposed on the authors in this series. Yet, despite the breadth of the series there is a sense of a common core in the writers themselves and in the traditions they describe. All Christian spiritual traditions have their source in three things. First, while drawing on ordinary experience and even religious insights from elsewhere, Christian spiritualities are rooted in the Scriptures and particularly in the Gospels. Second, spiritual traditions are not derived from abstract theory but from attempts to live out gospel values in a positive yet critical way within specific historical and cultural contexts. Third, the experiences and insights of individuals and groups are not isolated but are related to the wider Christian tradition of beliefs, practices and community life. From a Christian perspective, spirituality is not just concerned with prayer or even with narrowly religious activities. It concerns the whole of human life, viewed in terms of a conscious relationship with God, in Jesus Christ, through the indwelling of the Holy Spirit and within a community of believers.

The series as a whole includes traditions that probably would not have appeared twenty years ago. The authors themselves have been encouraged to challenge, where appropriate, inaccurate assumptions about their particular tradition. While conscious of their own biases, authors have none the less sought to correct the imbalances of the past. Previous understandings of what is mainstream or 'orthodox' sometimes need to be questioned. People or practices that became marginal demand to be re-examined. Studies of spirituality in the past frequently underestimated or ignored the role of women. Sometimes the treatments of spiritual traditions were culturally one-sided because they were written from an uncritical Western European or North Atlantic perspective.

However, any series is necessarily selective. It cannot hope to do full justice to the extraordinary variety of Christian spiritual traditions. The principles of selection are inevitably open to question. I hope that an appropriate balance has been maintained between a sense of the likely readership on the one hand and the dangers of narrowness on the other. In the end, choices had to be made and the result is inevitably weighted in favour of traditions that have achieved 'classic' status or which seem to capture the contemporary imagination. Within these limits, I trust that the series will offer a reasonably balanced account of what the Christian spiritual tradition has to offer.

As editor of the series I would like to thank all the authors who agreed to contribute and for the stimulating conversations and correspondence that sometimes resulted. I am especially grateful for the high quality of their work which made my task so much easier. Editing such a series is a complex undertaking. I have worked closely throughout with the editorial team of Darton, Longman and Todd and Robert Ellsberg of Orbis Books. I am immensely grateful to them for their friendly support and judicious advice. Without them this series would never have come together.

PHILIP SHELDRAKE
University of Durham

ACKNOWLEDGEMENTS

I wish to express my gratitude to Philip Sheldrake, the editor of this series, who has encouraged me over a number of years to write on aspects of evangelical spirituality. Several people have helped me in the writing of this particular book. I have benefited from comments on my material from Joy Osgood, an Anglican minister who is one of my teaching colleagues at Spurgeon's College, from Martyn Groves, a former student at Spurgeon's, and from my wife, Janice. Herbert McGonigle, who was for many years Principal of the Nazarene Theological College, Didsbury, has given me much-valued help with my work on the contribution of John Wesley. Another colleague at Spurgeon's, John Colwell, lecturer in Christian Doctrine and Ethics, made a suggestion for a theme which proved to be crucial in determining the thrust of the book.

Much of the material in this book has been shaped through my teaching over the past thirteen years at Spurgeon's College, London and also at the International Baptist Theological Seminary, Prague. I am greatly indebted to the many students with whom I have had the privilege of discussing a wide range of issues connected to Christian spirituality. In addition, I worked on some of the themes included here for a lecture on evangelical spirituality and evangelical identity at a conference at King's College London in the summer of 2004, and for talks later that year at the London School of Theology.

I would like to thank Brendan Walsh and Helen Porter at DLT for their assistance and care in the production of this book, Sandy Waldron for her work as copy editor, and Sarah John for the lovely cover.

Finally, I am personally indebted in my spiritual journey to Douglas McBain, whose ministry included a number of years in which he served the Baptist denomination in a significant way through his superintendency of London Baptists. I have dedicated this study of evangelical spirituality to Douglas, a valued mentor and friend.

1. INTRODUCTION
'HOLY AFFECTIONS': EVANGELICAL SPIRITUALITY

In 1846 an Irishman, Joseph Scriven, who had studied at Trinity College, Dublin, emigrated to Ontario, Canada, following the tragic death of his fiancée just before their marriage. In Canada Scriven involved himself in helping people who were suffering and he became known locally as the 'Good Samaritan of Port Hope'. Previously a member of the Church of Ireland, he joined the Brethren, an evangelical movement that had begun in England and Ireland earlier in the century. Scriven's life and that of his family continued to be marked by pain. To comfort his mother, he wrote a hymn in 1855, 'What a Friend we have in Jesus'. The first verse reads:

> What a Friend we have in Jesus,
> All our sins and griefs to bear:
> What a privilege to carry
> Everything to God in prayer.
> Oh, what peace we often forfeit,
> Oh, what needless pain we bear,
> All because we do not carry
> Everything to God in prayer.

This story offers insights into evangelical spirituality. It is a spirituality which is not confined to one country or to one denomination. Evangelicals hold to orthodox Trinitarian doctrine, but an overriding theme, as expressed in this hymn, is a personal relationship with Jesus Christ, which is sometimes nurtured in difficult experiences. It is also a spirituality of ordinary people. Scriven was not a well-known evangelical leader, but *was* significant in his local setting. His sentiments

were spread by his very popular hymn. The American evan-
gelist/singer Ira D. Sankey added a tune. The hymn became so
well known that in the early twentieth century it was paro-
died by soldiers as 'When this bloody war is over/Oh, how
happy I will be'.[1] Hymn-singing has been integral to evangelical spirituality, and 'What a Friend we have in Jesus' is
still sung in many parts of the world.

The evangelical movement, of which Joseph Scriven was
a part, has its origins in the Evangelical Revival of the
eighteenth century. The impact on British Protestantism of
this Revival, led principally in England by two Church of
England clergymen, John Wesley and George Whitefield, has
been thoroughly analysed by David Bebbington. He describes
in his seminal work, *Evangelicalism in Modern Britain*,
how the decade beginning in 1734 'witnessed in the English-
speaking world a more important development than any
other, before or after, in the history of Protestant Christianity:
the emergence of the movement that became Evangelicalism'.[2]
Although some have queried the significance of the movement, it is difficult to write off its long-term effect. John Kent,
in *Wesley and the Wesleyans*, speaks about the 'so-called evangelical revival' as one of 'the persistent myths of modern
British history', but even he has to admit that Wesleyanism
grew because John Wesley 'responded to the actual religious
demands and hopes of his hearers'.[3] The influence of the
Revival was in fact widely felt, both within and beyond the
Church of England. Samuel Walker of Truro was one example
of an eighteenth-century Church of England clergyman who
was dramatically transformed by the evangelical message and
who hoped for widespread evangelical co-operation.[4] A
balanced introduction to the different facets of the
Evangelical Revival in Britain is found in G.M. Ditchfield's
book, *The Evangelical Revival*.[5]

Although evangelicalism emerged in the eighteenth century, it had strong links with the Protestant Reformation of
the sixteenth century and the English Puritan movement of
the seventeenth century. The evangelicals followed Martin

Luther and John Calvin in preaching the doctrine of justification by grace through faith and calling for adherence to the Scripture.[6] Like Calvin and the Puritans they stressed the practical outworking of faith in the sanctified life. However, the Puritans tended to see a 'settled, well-grounded' assurance of personal salvation as a blessing that was rare. J.I. Packer, in his book on Puritan theology and spirituality, shows that typically the Puritans believed such assurance was something for the few. Thomas Brooks wrote: 'God will only give it [assurance] to his best and dearest friends.' For another Puritan, Thomas Goodwin, assurance was to be seen as 'a reward for faith'.[7] R.T. Kendall, in his study of English Calvinism, argues that in the case of some of the Puritans, such as William Perkins, the way to assurance could be highly introspective. In this they differed significantly from Calvin, who warned against such introspection. According to some of the Puritans the exercise of discovering if one was among those whom God had elected to be saved meant a 'descending into our own hearts', as Perkins put it, in an attempt to find the answer to this crucial spiritual question. The result of this thinking was that a person's sanctification became the ground of assurance of salvation: it was necessary to do certain things and infer assurance from them.[8] By contrast, the evangelical leaders considered that for believers an assured sense of personal salvation through a relationship with God in Christ was normative.

Evangelicalism, while affirming certain central doctrines of the Christian faith, has always recognised other matters, particularly to do with understandings of the Church, as secondary. It has been transdenominational. Initially, John Wesley, who had High Church tendencies, showed relatively little interest in the activities of Dissenters. However, as he began to preach in places other than Church of England buildings, and as he founded his Methodist societies, he inevitably made more Dissenting contacts. Ultimately Methodism would become a Nonconformist denomination. Calvinistic Methodism flourished in Wales – indeed some of the earliest expressions of the eighteenth-century Revival in Britain were in Wales – and this to a considerable extent laid the foundation for the huge Nonconformist growth in the Principality. The Revival also took hold in parts of Presbyterian Scotland. John Wesley and George Whitefield both refused to be constrained by the traditions of the Church of England. Wesley followed both Whitefield's example and that of Howell Harris in Wales in preaching in the open air in Bristol in April 1739. In Wesley's famous words, 'At four in the afternoon I submitted to be more vile, and proclaimed in the highways the glad tidings of salvation ... to about three thousand people'.[9] Wesley never felt at ease with field preaching, but he believed that this was an important way to reach the people. Up to that point preaching outside one's parish had been a Dissenting activity, but Wesley insisted that the world was his mission field – 'I look upon all the world', he stated, 'as my parish.'[10]

This interest in the whole world has also been typical of evangelicalism. The transnational nature of the movement has been increasingly recognised. Jonathan Edwards, America's most notable theologian, was known across Europe as much for the powerful revivals or 'awakenings' that took place through his ministry as for his theological thought. Whereas Charles Chauncy, a New England minister who wrote in opposition to Edwards, represented a section of urbane New England society which despised emotion and enthusiasm, seeing them as forces that removed religion from the control of reason, Edwards brought reason and experience together. In so doing he was a primary shaper of evangelical spirituality. In Edwards' own phrase, 'holy affections' constituted a great part of true religion. 'The Holy Scriptures', he asserted, 'do everywhere place religion very much in the affections; such as fear, hope, love, hatred, desire, joy, sorrow, gratitude, compassion, zeal.'[11] Yet for Edwards evangelical spirituality was not a matter of feelings, however pious. As Edwards put it again: 'Holy affections are not heat without light; but evermore arise from the information of the understanding, some spiritual instruction that the mind receives, some light or actual knowledge.'[12] This kind of thorough evangelical instruction spread widely. Mark Noll, in *The Rise of Evangelicalism*, has contributed a fine analysis of the theological and spiritual roots of the powerful currents of transatlantic evangelicalism that developed in the eighteenth century.[13]

Both in Britain and America, as well as in other parts of the English-speaking world, evangelicalism saw very considerable growth in the nineteenth century, sometimes seen as the 'evangelical century'. In 1966, writing in his book *The Victorian Church*, Owen Chadwick concluded that throughout the mid-Victorian era 'the evangelical movement was the strongest religious force in British life'.[14] A decade later, Ian Bradley noted that historians were generally agreed that evangelicalism in Britain had been 'one of the most important forces at work in shaping the character of the Victorians'.[15] In 1994, John Wolffe's *God and Greater Britain* described the evangelical movement in the opening decades of Queen Victoria's reign as 'a dynamic and broadly based religious force, combining spiritual energy, institutional diversity and cultural sensitivity'.[16] Although the first avowedly evangelical bishop in the Church of England was not appointed until 1815 – when Henry Ryder became Bishop of Gloucester – by 1848 the evangelical John Bird Sumner had been appointed Archbishop of Canterbury. From 1800 to the mid-century the proportion of evangelical clergy in the Church of England grew significantly, and with Sumner as the primate a moderate Anglican evangelicalism came to occupy a central position in the life of the Established Church.[17]

In the twentieth century the growth of evangelicalism continued. There has also been a significant re-shaping of aspects of evangelical experience in the period since the early twentieth century, due to the massive influence on evangelical life world-wide of the Pentecostal and charismatic movements, with their emphasis on gifts of the Holy Spirit such as prophecy, speaking in tongues and healing. The international

Pentecostal community has seen phenomenal numerical growth since its beginnings about one hundred years ago. There has been debate about the exact number of people within the various Pentecostal denominations, and some earlier estimates have been revised. According to the *World Churches Handbook* there were 153 million Pentecostals in 1995.[18] There have also been debates about Pentecostal antecedents, with the dominant view having been that the roots of Pentecostalism lie in the American holiness movements of the nineteenth century.[19] A case has been made, however, for the significance of the more Reformed evangelical contribution to Pentecostal origins.[20] Crucially, Pentecostals themselves have normally insisted on their evangelical pedigree. Thus a leading and formative international Pentecostal spokesman from Britain, Donald Gee, who was at one stage in his life a member of a Baptist church, argued in 1933 that in its assent to the fundamentals of the Christian faith the Assemblies of God (his own denomination) were 'in agreement with all sections of the Church holding orthodox and evangelical views'.[21]

Studies of evangelicalism over the past few years have generally followed the argument advanced by David Bebbington in *Evangelicalism in Modern Britain* that evangelicalism is a movement comprising all those who stress the Bible, the cross, conversion and activism.[22] This thinking has been developed further through work that has been done on evangelical spirituality. In his significant study, *Trust and Obey: Explorations in Evangelical Spirituality*, David Gillett covers a number of the major features of evangelical spirituality – conversion, assurance, the cross of Christ, the Bible, holiness, active service and prayer.[23] In my own study of evangelical spirituality in England between the First and Second World Wars, I found that there were four main strands in evidence – Keswick holiness, the Wesleyan tradition, Reformed approaches and Pentecostal/charismatic spirituality. Each of these had significant internal variations.[24] In his book *Holiness in Nineteenth-Century England*,[25] David Bebbington considers three evangelical traditions (Calvinist, Wesleyan and Keswick) and also the High Church tradition, and he has a further analysis of holiness in a recent book edited by Stephen Barton, *Holiness Past and Present*.[26] Evangelical spirituality in Britain is receiving more attention than was previously the case.

A sustained attempt on the part of evangelicals to analyse their spiritual tradition has come from within Anglicanism. The Grove Booklets on spirituality, for instance, have been imaginative in their coverage.[27] In one of these John Cockerton shows that there have been sacramental and mystical strands within evangelicalism, and he is aware that holiness teaching has been remoulded over the last two centuries.[28] Philip Seddon has recently written *Gospel and Sacrament: Reclaiming a holistic evangelical spirituality*.[29] Joyce Huggett's writings, such as *Open to God*, have been widely read.[30] A leading evangelical Anglican theologian who has argued for a distinctive spirituality as an integral part of wider evangelical identity is Alister McGrath. Among his many books, McGrath wrote in 1991 a historical study in this area, *Roots that Refresh: A Celebration of Reformation Spirituality*, and he subsequently returned to the topic of evangelical spirituality in a lecture in 1993, substantially reproduced in a chapter in his *Evangelicalism and the Future of Christianity*.[31] McGrath, in the context of what he and others have called the evangelical renaissance, sees the potential for a creative partnership between theology and experience. For him, evangelicalism is 'the slumbering giant in the world of spirituality'.[32]

Significant work on evangelical spirituality has also been undertaken in the USA and Canada. In a call that Alister McGrath made for more evangelical institutions and more evangelical writing dedicated to promoting evangelical spirituality, McGrath instanced the example set by Regent College, Vancouver, Canada, which had two chairs of 'spiritual theology'. These were occupied by James Houston and by Eugene Peterson, whose books on spirituality, such as

Working the Angles and *The Contemplative Pastor*, became highly influential in Britain in the 1990s.[33] Evangelicals in the USA who have produced stimulating material in this area include Dallas Willard, for example through his *The Divine Conspiracy: Rediscovering our hidden life in God*,[34] and especially Richard Foster, an evangelical American Quaker, who has written a number of formative books such as *Celebration of Discipline, Prayer: Finding the Heart's True Home*, and *Streams of Living Water*.[35] At the interdenominational London Bible College (now the London School of Theology), Derek Tidball, the Principal from 1995, introduced small groups that utilised Foster's thinking. Tidball commented on his own vision for evangelical spirituality: 'It is easy in today's world to come up with a hybrid spirituality which is no longer evangelical or to transform the evangelical tradition so much that it ceases to be evangelical. The challenge then is so to breathe life into tradition that it does, as it can, answer the deepest inner searches of the contemporary seeker.'[36]

This volume is able, therefore, to draw on much good work that has already been done on the nature of evangelical spirituality. In my analysis I am using an analytical framework proposed by Philip Sheldrake in *Spirituality and History*, in which spirituality is seen as concerned with the conjunction of theology, communion with God and practical Christianity.[37] Thus I have devoted sections of the book to some of the theological concerns to be found among evangelicals, concerns which have shaped their spirituality. I have also looked at the way in which evangelicals have worked out their spiritual experiences in practice, both as individuals and communally. Evangelical spirituality is sometimes thought of as being highly individualistic, but it shares with other approaches to spiritual experience an awareness that the individual's relationship with God is translated into practice in the context of both spiritual tradition and the surrounding culture.[38] Evangelical individualism is, however, apparent in the way commanding personalities have exercised a profound influence on their followers. Indeed, one study from which I have drawn extensively, *Evangelical Spirituality* by James Gordon, has concentrated on some of the formative leaders within evangelical history.[39] To some extent I have followed this way of dealing with the history.

The major themes covered in this book show the breadth of evangelical spirituality. There has at times been an assumption that the daily devotional 'quiet time' – consisting of prayer and Bible reading – was the central and dominating feature of older evangelical devotion. In an article on evangelical spirituality in 1991, David Parker, writing from the Australian context, included Christian fellowship, Christian service and discipline as elements of evangelical spirituality, but he suggested that for evangelicals the personal quiet time had been the most basic of all spiritual disciplines.[40] Derek Tidball, in *Who are the Evangelicals?*, rightly questioned the close association of evangelical spirituality with the quiet time, and in examining evangelical spirituality he has dealt with such broader themes as grace, holiness and involvement in society.[41] I have included areas of evangelical spirituality that are normally covered – conversion, the Bible, prayer and holiness – but have also explored themes like the fellowship of the church and the place of the sacraments, topics that tend not to be so commonly dealt with on the grounds that they do not appear to form such a significant part of evangelical spirituality. The central theme of this strand of spirituality is a personal relationship with Christ.

Because evangelical spirituality is pan-denominational, I have drawn examples from different denominational streams within the evangelical movement. My references to the Wesleyan dimension should be read in conjunction with the forthcoming volume on Wesleyan spirituality in this series. At times quite conflicting views of spiritual experience are to be found in evangelicalism, not least over holiness. A collection of historico-thematic essays which highlights these differences well is *Five Views of Sanctification*, in which there is an outstanding contribution by M.E. Dieter on Wesleyan themes.[42] In terms of time period, I have given more attention to the eighteenth and nineteenth centuries, as these were the formative eras of evangelicalism. I have referred to some of the developments in the twentieth century, but have not dealt with Pentecostalism or charismatic renewal, since they will be analysed in another book in this series.[43] The geographical expansion of evangelicalism has been notable, and it is impossible in a short book to do justice to the movement's important global dimensions. I have concentrated primarily on British evangelicalism, although I have also drawn from the closely related evangelical story in North America and in the conclusion have made reference to global trends. Jonathan Edwards, arguably the principal shaper of American evangelicalism, set the agenda for such studies of spirituality with his treatment of the marks of 'truly gracious affections' or 'holy affections', that is, signs of authentic spirituality. True spiritual experience was to be seen in action when the living of the Christian way in fellowship with Christ was, as Edwards put it, the whole 'business of life'.[44] This understanding of evangelical experience is what we will seek to explore.

2. 'AMAZING GRACE': EVANGELICALS AND CONVERSION

John Wesley, who shaped much early evangelical thinking, recorded in his diary for 24 May 1738 the following words, which were to become among the most famous in the story of Christian experience:

> In the evening I went very unwillingly to a society in Aldersgate Street, where one was reading Luther's Preface to the Epistle to the Romans. About a quarter before nine, while he was describing the change which God works in the heart through faith in Christ, I felt my heart strangely warmed. I felt I did trust in Christ, Christ alone, for salvation; and an assurance was given me that He had taken away *my* sins, even *mine*, and saved *me* from the law of sin and death ... I then testified openly to all there what I now first felt in my heart.[1]

This account, describing as it does how John Wesley came to a point of personal reliance on God's grace and Christ's work on the cross for salvation, later came to be seen as a description of a typical experience of evangelical conversion, although there has been considerable discussion as to whether it should rather be seen as an expression of assurance of salvation.[2] In 1735, three years before this event in Aldersgate Street, London, George Whitefield, who with Wesley was central to the rise of the evangelical movement, had also experienced an evangelical conversion. At that point Whitefield, like Wesley, was an Oxford undergraduate.[3] John Wesley, his brother Charles and Whitefield had been members of a small group in Oxford in the early 1730s called Methodists, or the 'Holy

Club'. It was comprised of people who wanted to take their religion seriously. It is important in understanding their later evangelical experience – Charles Wesley had such an experience a few days before John – to trace a number of significant spiritual influences which led to their conversions. The reality of conversion, or turning to Christ and finding a relationship with him, is basic to evangelical spirituality, but the early evangelicals brought to that experience currents of spirituality they had known before.

Currents in conversion

John and Charles Wesley had been influenced by three differing traditions, largely through their family. One was the English Puritan tradition, which shaped English Dissent from the seventeenth century. Although this tradition had become increasingly inward-looking, the Puritans had spoken of the experience of conversion and of the preaching of the gospel and although John and Charles Wesley's parents were staunchly high Church of England, a gospel-centred Puritanism was an element in their piety. They came from Puritan stock. Among the Dissenters who were widely respected in the eighteenth century, were preachers such as the Congregationalist Philip Doddridge, who conducted an academy in Northampton which had a high reputation, and the outstanding hymn-writer Isaac Watts.[4] Doddridge wrote of the day of his own conversion in the famous hymn 'O happy day'. The second stream of influence on the Wesleys was Catholic and High Church devotion, which set out rigorous demands to be met by those taking up the spiritual life. In 1725 John Wesley read Jeremy Taylor's *Holy Living and Dying* (1651), which made a profound impact on him. He resolved to dedicate all his life to God. A year later he read the *Imitation of Christ*, by Thomas à Kempis, which directed him to 'the religion of the heart'. He was also affected by the writings of the high churchman William Law, *On Christian Perfection* (1726) and *A Serious Call to a Devout and Holy Life*

(1728), which helped to create within him moral longings. A final element in the mix was the more mystical stream of spirituality, such as that expressed in the book *The Life of God in the Soul of Man*, by Henry Scougal of Aberdeen, a Scottish Episcopalian.[5] The evangelical stress on a changed life and on spiritual vitality was not a new emphasis.

A variety of influences was typically present in the conversion of others who also became evangelical leaders in the early eighteenth century in England, Scotland, Wales and Ireland. William Law's work was particularly important.[6] George Whitefield's experience, like John Wesley's, offers a typical example of an evangelical expression of assurance. He commented that although he had fasted, prayed and taken the sacrament of Holy Communion, he 'never knew what true religion was' until he read Henry Scougal's *Life of God in the Soul of Man*, with its emphasis on Christ being formed within a person. Whitefield's search continued, and through repentance and personal faith in Christ his personal sense of the heavy load of sin was replaced by 'joy unspeakable'. As an example of how the message of the need for spiritual change was spread, Scougal's book was lent to Whitefield by Charles Wesley.[7] Whitefield utilised Scougal's concepts in his own preaching of the new birth. The new birth, or regeneration, was seen as God's activity in conversion. In 1737 Whitefield published a sermon, 'On the Nature and Necessity of Our Regeneration or New Birth in Christ Jesus', from the text 'If any man be in Christ, he is a new creature' (2 Corinthians 5:17), in which he spoke of conversion as 'an inward Change and Purity of Heart'. This became Whitefield's most widely circulated sermon and sums up much evangelical thinking. Whitefield argued that real religion meant being 'mystically united' to Christ by a 'lively Faith'. This relationship with Christ was in contrast to merely nominal religion.[8] It was an experience that was, for evangelicals, fundamental.

The same message was already being preached in North America. In Northampton, Massachusetts, a strong evangelical movement developed from 1734, with Jonathan

Edwards, a scholarly Congregational pastor in Northampton, becoming the foremost theological thinker exploring issues connected with conversion and revival.[9] 'Conversion', wrote Edwards, 'is a great and glorious work of God's power, at once changing the heart, and infusing life into the dead soul; though the grace then implanted more gradually displays itself in some than in others.'[10] Edwards' personal narrative confirms his view of conversion as a decisive change, although not necessarily something that took place instantaneously. In 1721 he experienced an 'inward, sweet delight in God', at the end of a period of spiritual struggle. This experience led him in a new direction. Edwards wrote: 'On January 12, 1723, I made a solemn dedication of myself to God, and wrote it down; giving up myself, and all that I had to God; to be for the future, in no respect, my own; to act as one that had no right to himself, in any respect.'[11] He saw those who had been 'truly converted' as having 'new hearts, new eyes, new ears, new tongues, new hands, new feet'.[12] After five years of ministry in Northampton, the 31-year-old Edwards decided in 1734 to preach a series of sermons on 'Justification by Faith Alone'. The effect on the community was dramatic. In his first report Edwards put it this way:

> And then a concern about the great things of religion began ... to prevail abundantly in the town, till in a very little time it became universal throughout the town, among old and young, and from the highest to the lowest. All seemed to be seized with a deep concern about their eternal salvation; all the talk in all companies, and upon occasions was upon the things of religion, and no other talk was anywhere relished; and scarcely a single person in the whole town was left unconcerned about the great things of the eternal world.[13]

The report by Edwards, which he revised and enlarged, was published as *A Faithful Narrative of the Surprising Work of God in the Conversion of Many Hundred Souls*.[14] Isaac Watts was one of the two editors of the British edition of this book, published in October 1737, and Philip Doddridge read it in the week that it appeared. The account by Edwards has never gone out of print and the content of this document, with its view of conversion as a 'great change', in which people's hearts are centred on God, would 'define the standard expectations for evangelical conversion'.[15]

A movement of spiritual renewal in central Europe was also highly influential in forging a concept of conversion. In 1722 a Saxon count who had been educated in a German pietist environment, Nicholas Ludwig von Zinzendorf, opened his estate in south-east Saxony to a group of Protestant refugees from Bohemia and Moravia.[16] This group, which was escaping from persecution by the Roman Catholic Habsburgs, was known as the Unity of the Brethren or the Moravians, but the community created was an ecumenical one. Zinzindorf's estate, Herrnhut (the Lord's Protection), became the scene in 1727 of a profound spiritual renewal. Four girls from the Moravian community, who had been struggling with doubts about their salvation, came to a powerful spiritual assurance. This kind of assurance was expected in Moravian circles, but the intensity of these experiences spread to the whole community at a subsequent Communion service and this was to lead to a significant Moravian missionary movement. Zinzendorf taught the immediate experience of the Spirit of God. He described how 'we must first hear the voice of the Son of God, then we begin to live', and spoke of this life as a new experience of the soul in which 'the Spirit of God overshadows her'.[17] It was at a Moravian-led meeting in Aldersgate Street in 1738 that John Wesley had his experience of assurance. Charles Wesley was similarly influenced by the Moravians and this contributed to his own conversion.[18] There were many links between evangelicals across the Atlantic and across Europe, as well as much variety between the different movements. Conversion was a vital part of the glue that held them together.

Understandings of conversion

The conversions that took place in the early evangelical movement were quite often rapid rather than gradual. By contrast with the commonly accepted view that conversion was a long process, Edwards recorded that in the town of Northampton God 'seemed to have gone out of his usual way in the quickness of his work'. None the less, Edwards insisted that there was great variety in people's spiritual experiences.[19] Whitefield, who knew exactly when and where he had experienced new birth himself, looked for instantaneous conversions to take place in response to his preaching. In Wales, a 24-year-old clergyman, Daniel Rowland, came to a more personal experience of Christ in 1735 through an evangelical minister, Griffith Jones, and Rowland immediately began to preach about conversion and to draw hundreds and then thousands of hearers.[20] The evangelical message of conversion spread rapidly under the dynamic preaching of Whitefield and Rowland, through writings such as those by Edwards, in the sustained ministry of John Wesley and the hymns of Charles Wesley, and through other leaders such as Howell Harris, in Wales, and an Irishman, Gilbert Tennett, who moved to New Jersey. For these evangelicals, the experience of conversion and the publicising of conversions as they took place were together seen as effective in producing even more changed lives. Two of the conversion stories told by Edwards, of a young woman and a young girl, became classic templates. Conversion involved a movement from sinful self-despair to a focus on Christ as the only Saviour, to a joyful response to God and a purpose to do good in the world.[21]

There were, however, divisions between evangelicals over aspects both of the experience and the theology of conversion. In England, George Whitefield and John Wesley were divided over the doctrines of predestination and divine election to salvation. Whitefield, although not a theologian, drew from the profound theological thinking of Edwards, who expounded a Calvinistic view that God had elected certain individuals to salvation. This view did not, however, hinder Whitefield's evangelistic preaching. In 1741 he said to Wesley: 'Though I hold to particular election, yet I offer Jesus freely to every individual soul.'[22] Wesley, for his part, expounded an evangelical Arminian position, believing that grace had opened a path to salvation for all, and that in turn it was open to all to choose Christ as Saviour.[23] There were huge debates in early Methodism and then later at the Wesleyan Conference of 1770 on these issues. Augustus Montagu Toplady, known for his fine hymn-writing, led the attack on Arminianism. The Countess of Huntingdon, who was a supporter of Whitefield, was so incensed by the anti-Calvinism of the Wesleyan Conference that she had the minutes of the Conference burned.[24] From 1778 the *Arminian Magazine* began to be published, whereas before that many Methodists read the Calvinistic *Gospel Magazine*. This difference of view has continued among evangelicals, as David Gillett notes: 'There are those who put most emphasis on the sovereignty of God and the work of the Spirit in individual believers, opening their hearts and minds to respond to the call of God to repentance and faith. Others place greater emphasis on the individual's decision and response.'[25]

Later in the eighteenth century, the common ground that evangelicals occupied with regard to the experience of conversion and of assurance was emphasised again. John Newton, who had experienced a dramatic conversion when he was a slave ship captain, and who later became a moderately Calvinistic Church of England clergyman, sought to draw evangelicals together around their shared belief in conversion as a response to divine love. He had a significant bridge-building role.[26] His own conversion was expressed in the very personal words of assurance in the most famous hymn that he wrote:

> Amazing grace! (how sweet the sound)
> That sav'd a wretch like me!
> I once was lost, but now am found;
> Was blind, but now I see.

'Twas grace that taught my heart to fear,
And grace my fears reliev'd;
How precious did that grace appear,
The hour I first believ'd.[27]

Leading evangelical lay people wanted to stress the importance of active Christian service by those who had been converted and had entered into a personal relationship with Christ. Evangelical lay people within the Church of England, for example, such as William Wilberforce and Hannah More, both of whom had been influenced by John Newton, became known for their practical expressions of evangelical faith. Wilberforce, who became an MP in 1780 at the age of twenty-one, read Philip Doddridge's *Rise and Progress of Religion in the Soul* in 1784–5 and experienced an evangelical conversion which dramatically changed the direction of his life.[28]

As well as the experiences of these shapers of evangelicalism, there were many others in the eighteenth century who experienced the 'new birth'. Mrs Platt, a poor woman in Oxford who was helped by Charles Wesley, wrote about her deep experience of Christ and of 'the Holy Ghost upon me, wherein I have sure pardon of my sins'. She concluded, with reference to her spiritual struggles: 'It is hard work to be born again.'[29] In 1779, William Black, a nineteen-year-old from Yorkshire who had emigrated to Nova Scotia, Canada, and who later became the leading Canadian Methodist of his period, wrote in his journal:

> We tarried ... singing and praying for about two hours when it pleased the Lord to reveal his free grace; his fulness and his suitableness as a Saviour: his ability and willingness to save *me* ... My burden dropped off: my guilt was removed: condemnation gave place to mercy: and a sweet peace and gladness were diffused through my soul.[30]

Ten years later Olaudah Equiano, an ex-slave, wrote about his story in his *Interesting Narrative*. As a freed slave he had

tried to find spiritual truth in many places and as part of his
search he began to attend evangelical services. The result was
that he had an instantaneous conversion, in which, as he put
it, he 'saw clearly, with the eye of faith, the crucified Saviour
bleeding on the cross on Mount Calvary'. This vision convinced him that he was 'a great debtor ... to sovereign free
grace'.[31] These testimonies express the classic evangelical
understanding of conversion as a personal encounter with
Christ.

The spread of 'conversionism'

Evangelical spirituality, with its stress on conversion, spread
in the nineteenth century in all the main Protestant denominations. Charles Simeon influenced many Cambridge
undergraduates and others throughout his long ministry at
Holy Trinity, Cambridge. He preached for fifty-three years,
steered evangelicals into parish ministry, and conducted an
enormous correspondence.[32] By contrast with this long
ministry, Robert Murray McCheyne, an evangelical Church of
Scotland minister, died at the age of twenty-nine, in 1843.[33]
Together with his friends, the brothers Horatius and Andrew
Bonar, McCheyne had a powerful spiritual impact on many
people within the national Church in Scotland. As an indica-
tion of his commitment to conversionism, McCheyne wrote
that the conversion of an individual soul was 'by far the most
remarkable event in the history of the world'.[34] The Baptist
denomination was also profoundly affected by this expression
of spirituality through energetic new leaders such as the
Arminian pastor and evangelist Dan Taylor, whose early
Christian experience was shaped by Wesley's preaching, and
the Calvinistic Baptist minister Andrew Fuller.[35] In 1785
Fuller wrote his ground-breaking theological work *The Gospel
Worthy of all Acceptation*, which argued for 'the free offer of
the gospel' to all sinners, and rejected the non-evangelistic
'high Calvinism' which had been prevalent in Baptist thinking in the earlier eighteenth century.[36] The nineteenth century

saw Baptists taking up the conversionist message with enthusiasm.

In America new thinking about conversion led to new practices in evangelism.[37] Charles Finney, who has been described as the first great professional evangelist of North America, introduced 'new measures' for those seeking to be converted – they were invited to come forward at the end of evangelistic meetings to the 'anxious seat' and to remain for the 'protracted meeting'. The call was for an immediate decision for Christ. One of Finney's earliest published sermons, 'Sinners Bound to Change Their Own Hearts' (1834), vividly highlights the emphasis that he brought. He rejected the idea that regeneration was the work of God alone and that conversion was the response from the human side, in which a person exercised repentance and faith. Finney wrote: 'Both conversion and regeneration are sometimes in the Bible ascribed to God, sometimes to man'.[38] Finney was a magnetic preacher, an educationalist, and an effective social reformer. Church growth, sometimes dramatic growth, was a feature of the campaigns of this early nineteenth-century period in America. The stress that Finney laid on free will was also to be a feature of much evangelical thinking about conversion in the twentieth century. Finney believed that 'God cannot do the sinner's duty, and regenerate him without the exercise of the sinner's own agency.'[39] Finney's 'new measures' were adopted by some Methodist and Baptist evangelists in Britain, although the approach to conversion in Britain and across the continent of Europe remained generally a somewhat more restrained one.

The work of nineteenth-century evangelists such as Finney, with their special campaigns, was important in highlighting conversion, but many people had an experience of coming to Christ in local church settings. Evangelical preachers – ordained ministers and lay preachers – regularly urged conversion. A study by Linda Wilson of the obituaries of one hundred women, which includes comparisons with men, from English Nonconformist denominations in the period 1825–75, found that among Methodists included in the sample 83 per

cent of male Wesleyans and 88 per cent of female Wesleyans
mentioned conversion explicitly. Among Primitive Methodists
the percentages were higher.[40] Charles Haddon Spurgeon, who
became known as the Prince of Preachers of the Victorian era,
described his own conversion in classic terms. He went to a
Primitive Methodist chapel one Sunday as a fifteen year old.
Spurgeon later wrote:

> In that chapel there may have been a dozen or fifteen
> people. I had heard of the Primitive Methodists, how they
> sang so loudly that they made people's heads ache; but
> that did not matter to me. I wanted to know how I might
> be saved, and if they could tell me that, I did not care how
> much they made my head ache ... a very thin-looking
> man, a shoemaker, or tailor, or something of that sort,
> went up into the pulpit to preach ... The text was 'LOOK
> UNTO ME, AND BE YE SAVED, ALL THE ENDS OF
> THE EARTH.' ... Just fixing his eyes on me, as if he knew
> all my heart, he said 'Young man, you look very miser-
> able ... but if you obey now, this moment, you will be
> saved' ... 'Young man, look to Jesus Christ' ... I looked
> until I could have almost looked my eyes away ... the
> cloud was gone ... I saw the sun.'[41]

Spurgeon was subsequently baptised by immersion and
became the most famous Baptist minister of the nineteenth
century. In his ministry at the Metropolitan Tabernacle,
Elephant and Castle, London, where he preached to 5,000
people every Sunday morning and evening until his death in
1892, the strongly evangelistic Spurgeon always stressed conversion.[42] He did not, however, insist that all conversions
should be instantaneous. Another Baptist minister of this
period, F.B. Meyer, who was a fervent advocate of Christian
devotion, could not pinpoint the exact time when he was converted, a fact which caused him some anxiety until he listened
to Spurgeon explaining (in a sermon at the Tabernacle) that
what mattered was for someone to be alive, even if his or her

birthday had been forgotten.[43] In evangelical terms, to be 'alive' spiritually means a personal relationship with Christ.

C.H. Spurgeon was the leading representative in Free Church life in England in the later nineteenth century of the strongly evangelistic Calvinist tradition. There were ministers in Independent and Baptist Chapels in the nineteenth century, such as William Huntington and William Gadsby, who held to a high Calvinism that maintained it was not the job of preachers to call people to repentance, but this was a minority view.[44] Within the Church of England, the foremost advocate of the Calvinistic theological position was J.C. Ryle, who became Bishop of Liverpool in 1880. Ryle was not so concerned about the terms used regarding conversion, as he was about the reality of the experience. He wrote: 'Call it what you please – new birth, regeneration, renewal, new creation, quickening, repentance – the thing must be possessed if we are to be saved: and if we have the thing it will be *seen*.'[45] Ryle was deeply unhappy that some people considered they were born again because they had been baptised, or went to church, or received the Lord's Supper. He looked, rather, for 'the marks of the new birth'. Ryle did not envisage that believers would be uncertain about whether or not they had the evidence of conversion. In a sermon on 'Assurance', he affirmed his belief that someone who was converted should in general 'feel entirely confident as to the pardon and safety of his soul'.[46] Here we have an explicit contrast with a major strand of Puritan thought. This conversionist Calvinist tradition was also to be found across Europe. The ministry of Johann Oncken, in Hamburg, paralleled that of Spurgeon. Oncken's conversion took place in a Methodist chapel in London, and he was instrumental in the spread of Baptist churches and evangelical experience across many parts of Northern and Eastern Europe in the second half of the nineteenth century.[47]

A decision for Christ

The Calvinist approach to conversion has continued to influence a section of evangelicalism, but among many evangelicals in the twentieth century the emphasis was much more on the human activity of making 'a decision for Christ' rather than on divine initiative. The leading American evangelist Dwight L. Moody, a Congregational layman, on his third visit to Britain in 1873–5, preached to between one and a half and two million people, and his proclamation of a 'simple gospel' was to have considerable influence. In his last sermon in London, preached in Camberwell Hall on 11 June 1875, Moody told his audience that he presumed they did not want to hear a sermon (on this last night of his campaign) so much as to have the answer to the question 'What must I do to be saved?' Moody's message was centred on the 'three R's' – 'ruin by sin, redemption by Christ, and regeneration by the Holy Spirit'. He believed in conversion as something that was by nature instantaneous. The person who was converted might not *necessarily* be able to identify an instant when he or she was born again, but Moody's own approach was to press home the importance of the moment and to call for immediate acceptance of Christ as Saviour and as Lord. Often he spoke of regeneration and conversion as the same thing. Records Moody kept showed that he preached on 'The New Birth' at least 184 times in the space of eight years, from 1881 to 1899.[48]

Many evangelists who became well known to evangelicals in the twentieth century followed Moody's thinking about the need to call for immediate decisions for Christ. Among these were Rodney (Gipsy) Smith from England,[49] and Billy Sunday and Reuben A. Torrey from America. The fervent desire to spread the message of conversion helped to cement Anglo-American evangelical connections. Torrey attended Yale University and after professing evangelical conversion entered Yale Divinity School. He was a Congregational minister and also began to work in wider evangelism with

Moody. Like Moody, Torrey travelled extensively in Britain as well as America, both as an evangelist and Bible teacher.[50] Other evangelistic figures were more local in their work, such as the effective Methodist preacher/evangelist Samuel Chadwick, who had a notable ministry in Leeds, Yorkshire, and was then Principal of Cliff College, Derbyshire. Chadwick's theory was that no church would languish where conversions were taking place. 'Getting people saved', Chadwick announced in 1921 in the magazine he edited, *Joyful News*, 'makes things hum'.[51] Chadwick was an example of an evangelistic minister who looked for a deep experience to characterise conversion, but the trend in the twentieth century for evangelicals to narrow conversion down to a 'decision' meant that people were often assured that if they had prayed a prayer of commitment they were definitely converted. This kind of evangelical spirituality lacked the richness to be found in earlier expressions of the tradition, which laid greater stress on the work of the Holy Spirit.

By far the best-known promoter of evangelical conversion in the twentieth century was another American evangelist who took Moody as his example, Billy Graham.[52] From a Southern Baptist background, Graham worked as an evangelist after the Second World War for the organisation Youth for Christ. In 1954, following several visits to Britain, he led a massive campaign at the Harringay Arena, London, with an aggregate attendance of over two million at all associated meetings, including 120,000 at Wembley Stadium on the closing day – the largest religious meeting up to that time in British history. Graham invited people to come forward to decide for Christ, and it is clear that many conversions took place, particularly among young people. Reflecting on Harringay in *Moody Monthly* in October 1954, Graham identified the importance of American evangelical leadership in altering Britain's spiritual state, which he described as characterised by rationalism, materialism, an irrelevant Church (with only 6–10 per cent church attendance), extreme liberalism in the pulpit, and lack of effective evangelism.[53] An Anglican, J.C.

Pollock, editor of *The Churchman*, who later became a leading writer of Christian biographies, was convinced that as a result of Graham's work the evangelistic initiative now lay with evangelicals. This was in sharp contrast to twenty years previously when evangelicals had been regarded as relics of an era long gone.[54] Throughout the rest of the twentieth century Billy Graham was the foremost international representative of evangelical Christianity, taking the message about a personal relationship with Christ across the world.

Yet evangelical spirituality, even if it has owed much to large meetings and famous speakers, has always been nurtured in local church life. Quite a number of those who profess evangelical faith have been brought up within the life of the church. Donald English, who became the leading evangelical statesman in British Methodism in the second half of the twentieth century, spoke of his first stirrings towards Christian commitment taking place as he listened to a teacher in a Bible Class connected with his local church. Later English described how when a Methodist minister gave an appeal for people to respond publicly to Christ, a good footballer who was a hero of English's, went forward. English, a sixteen-year-old, was amazed that '*he* needed to give his life to Christ! I was shaken. If *he* needed such commitment, where did *I* stand?' Following that, a meeting was held at which men who were in the Forces shared their Christian testimonies. English recalled: '"Big Bill" Stoddart, a massive 6′6″ tall, weighing twenty stones and with a voice like a fog horn, was particularly striking and someone it was difficult to ignore as he thundered "I thought I was a big man until I met Jesus!"' After the testimonies had been given the minister made a further appeal. Donald English walked forward, knelt at the Communion rail and offered his life in Christ's service.[55] It was a typical commitment made in a local setting and one that took seriously a 'meeting with Jesus'.

Conclusion

The experience of personal conversion has been a central feature of evangelicalism. Although evangelicals have been divided – at times deeply divided – over questions such as the relationship between the human and divine elements in conversion or the extent to which instantaneous rather than gradual conversions should be expected, all have agreed that there is a need for personal trust in Christ, a change of spiritual direction and a new spiritual relationship with Christ. Thus, when Charles Wesley, on 21 May 1738, came to know what he termed 'peace with God', he wrote a hymn, 'Christ the Friend of Sinners', followed later by his much more famous conversion hymn 'Wrestling Jacob'.

> Where shall my wond'ring soul begin?
> How shall I all to Heaven aspire?
> A slave redeemed from death and sin,
> A brand plucked from eternal fire.
> How shall I equal triumphs raise,
> Or sing my great Deliverer's praise?[56]

From George Whitefield to Billy Graham and beyond, there has been a strong emphasis in evangelical preaching on new birth and new life. At Graham's 1954 Harringay Crusade a leaflet which was given to those who were assigned to talk to those who came forward and to 'lead them to Christ', said: 'The actual moment of the new birth is the point at which the soul *sees* Christ crucified as his own Saviour; when the Saviour becomes *real* to him; it is a moment of vision.'[57] Towards the end of the twentieth century, however, the popularity of 'mass evangelism' and of inviting people to the front began to fade somewhat. There was less stress on the 'actual moment' of conversion. Research showed that in evangelical churches only 37 per cent of people experienced sudden conversions.[58] Churches began to seek ways to introduce people to the Christian faith which recognised the fact that people were on a journey. By far the most widely known and used of these ways has been the Alpha course, stemming from Holy Trinity Church, Brompton, London. These courses, designed for small groups of people, are held in informal settings.[59] Evangelical approaches have been changing. None the less, the aim has remained the same: to help people who have had no personal experience of Christ to have such an experience. The process through which this takes place, whether over a shorter or longer period of time, is the process of conversion.

3. 'O GIVE ME THAT BOOK!':
EVANGELICALS AND THE BIBLE

For the early eighteenth-century evangelicals, personal experience of Christ, which was of paramount importance, was nourished by Bible reading, and so evangelical leaders constantly encouraged people to read the Bible.[1] John Wesley often referred to himself as a *'homo unius libri'*, a man of one book. In the preface to his sermons, where he used this phrase, he spoke of the way of salvation as being 'written down in a book', and he continued: 'O give me that book! At any price give me the Book of God! I have it. Here is knowledge enough for me.'[2] Yet this exalted estimation of the Bible was not one that Wesley came to hold only as a result of his evangelical conversion. As early as 1729, a decade before that event, he and others in Oxford had the desire to be, as it was put, 'downright Bible-Christians'.[3] In thinking about reading the Bible, many evangelicals have urged a daily period of personal devotion, which in the twentieth century came to be termed the 'quiet time'. In addition, there has been the common evangelical practice of group Bible Study. The role of preaching in evangelical spirituality is also closely associated with the place of the Bible. Many evangelicals have seen a love for the Bible as one of the tests of whether someone has experienced the new birth. J.C. Ryle, for instance, wrote: 'Do you find it essential to your comfort to read the Bible regularly in private, and to speak to God in prayer? Or, do you find these practices irksome, and either slur over them, or neglect them altogether? ... If means of grace, whether public or private, are not as necessary to your soul as food and drink are to your body, you may well doubt whether your religion is "real".[4]

The evangelical view of the Bible

Many eighteenth-century evangelicals were influenced through a number of their significant leaders by Enlightenment ways of thinking, and as well as engaging with the Bible devotionally they tended to see it as containing a 'system of divine truth'. John Wesley used this phrase in 1754 when writing about the Bible. He continued in similar vein:

> Every part thereof is worthy of God; and all together are one entire body, wherein there is no defect, no excess. It is the fountain of heavenly wisdom, which they who are able to taste prefer to all writings of men, however wise, or learned or holy. An exact knowledge of the truth was accompanied in the inspired writers, with ... precise expression of their meaning.[5]

As David Gillett notes, this high view of biblical inspiration was not an unusual perspective among Protestants in that period, although Wesley and other evangelicals held it with particularly strong conviction and also believed in the power of the Bible's message to change lives. The Bible has been prominent in evangelicalism as the Word of God, the supreme authority to which other authorities, including experience, must submit.[6] Linda Wilson's study of the obituaries of women from Nonconformist denominations in the nineteenth century found that amongst Congregationalists, who were the largest group in her study, 47 per cent mentioned the Bible or quoted from the Bible.[7]

It is not the case, however, that evangelicals have in the past generally held to a rigid theological position on the exact nature of the inspiration of the Bible. Views about this have differed. Charles Simeon in Cambridge, a much-respected figure, wrote that in the Bible 'no error in doctrine or other important matter is allowed; yet there are inexactnesses in reference to philosophical and scientific matters, because of its popular style'. One biblical writer might, he considered, give one order of events and another might give another order. Simeon also argued that the books of the Bible reflected the differing characters of their writers. Some were poetic, while some were prosaic and plain.[8] Henry Martyn, one of the most famous evangelical missionaries of the eighteenth century, who was for a time Simeon's curate, believed that the sense of Scripture was what mattered. Both Charles Simeon and Henry Martyn placed emphasis on the inspired *meaning* of biblical discourse, rather than on the inspiration of the text extending to every individual word.[9] In 1861, at a meeting of evangelical Church of England clergy, a majority of those present believed that the Bible might have some inaccuracies on non-religious topics. It was the spiritual message of Scripture which was seen as being all-important.[10]

In America, considerable attention was given to views of the authority of the Bible by a series of theologians at Princeton Seminary, most famously the later nineteenth-century theologian B.B. Warfield. Earlier in the century the first leader of Princeton Seminary, Archibald Alexander, argued that in looking at biblical teaching it was necessary to be governed by 'the plain principles of common sense'.[11] This attitude to knowledge was developed by Charles Hodge, who tended to the view that in any generation a believer's understanding of the basic meaning of words in Scripture corresponded to that of the original writers of Scripture. Linked with this came a stress on knowing facts and reconciling apparent errors in the Bible. 'The errors in matters of fact', Hodge said, 'which skeptics search out bear no proportion to the whole. No sane men would deny that the Parthenon was built of marble, even if here and there a speck of sandstone should be detected in its structure.' For Hodge it was unreasonable to deny the inspiration of the Bible because of small differences between authors giving historical accounts.[12] There was a tendency among some evangelicals to pay less attention to a spiritual encounter with Christ through Scripture and more attention to the quest to establish a particular doctrine of biblical inerrancy. As a consequence, in some evangelical thinking the Bible itself seemed to become the dominant element in Christian experience rather than a means by which God is made known.[13]

Personal Bible reading

The typical evangelical emphasis, however, was not on mere knowledge of the content of the Bible; spirituality was about relationship with God, a relationship nurtured through personal and prayerful reading of the Scriptures. Thus many evangelicals offered advice about how to read the Bible. Henry Venn, a Church of England vicar who was a friend of John Wesley's, suggested four guidelines which he believed would help in obtaining spiritual benefit from Bible reading. These were to pray for God to show the true meaning of the passage being read, to read only a small portion at a time, to engage the conscience, will and emotions when reading, and to read the parts of Scripture most often that relate to the centralities of the Christian faith.[14] George Whitefield, in his personal reading of the Bible, spoke of 'praying over every line and word' of both the English and Greek texts.[15] Handley Moule, an influential nineteenth-century evangelical Anglican theologian in Cambridge who later became Bishop of Durham, explained in a short tract how he read the Bible. 'I keep time sacred each morning for some careful reading of the New Testament. I use a large copy and I keep a pencil in my hand to makes notes in the margin or to draw lines of connection across the page.' In the evening he read from the Old Testament. Whether studying the Old or New Testament, Moule was looking for insights into the person and work of Christ.[16] In this he was in tune with the characteristic evangelical stress on relationship with Christ and also with the thinking of Venn about a focus on the Christian centralities. Moule urged people to '[m]ake that Book your friend, and you shall surely catch the contagion of its character'.[17]

One evangelical leader whose Bible reading scheme was extensively used was the deeply devout Church of Scotland minister Robert Murray McCheyne in Dundee. He set out a method by which the whole Bible was read through in the course of a year, the Old Testament once, and the New Testament and Psalms twice. McCheyne believed that time was wasted in choosing what portions to read and he considered that his scheme resolved that question 'in a very simple manner'. It was also important for McCheyne that family worship should be more instructive for all those involved. He suggested that every member of the family could read the biblical passages set and then there could be questions and answers. Also, when those who were reading the same passages met during the day they could discuss them. McCheyne spoke of this as a way in which the 'bond of Christian love and unity will be strengthened'. It is clear that he expected the reading of Scripture to have powerful spiritual effects. He affirmed, perhaps a little idealistically: 'We shall pray over the same promises, mourn over the same confessions, praise God in the same songs, and be nourished by the same words of eternal life.' Looking at this from the perspective of his work as a pastor, McCheyne suggested that the pastor would know what was being read and consequently would be able to use this in visiting the congregation.[18]

It was because of their stress on reading the Bible that evangelicals were at the forefront of movements to encourage the distribution of the Bible and its translation into other languages. In 1804 the British and Foreign Bible Society was formed, and its work had enormous influence world-wide. A number of evangelicals who were public figures, nationally and internationally, gave their time and energy to the work of the Bible Society. As one example of the way in which the work spread, a branch of the Society, the Russian Bible Society, was formed in Russia in 1813, and the Society was supported by Alexander I, the Russian Tsar. By 1819 the complete New Testament had been translated into modern Russian and the Society was operating on a large scale, giving out portions of the Bible in Russian in response to enormous demand. For a time not only pan-European evangelicals were active in this work but the Russian Orthodox Church was also involved. In its remarkable early years, the Russian Bible Society played a vital role in enabling people to engage with the Bible for themselves.[19] In the field of Bible translation, the massive achievements of the Wycliffe Bible Translators have built upon the work of pioneer missionaries such as Henry Martyn, from Cambridge, who died in 1812 in Turkey at the age of thirty-one. He spoke of his translation of the Bible into Persian as 'making provision for future Persian saints'.[20] This expectation that the Bible would have a profound spiritual impact was always the evangelical vision.

For C.H. Spurgeon, there was a particular attitude that had to be fostered and a necessary focus that was required in reading Scripture. Like Whitefield, who was his hero, Spurgeon encouraged those reading the Bible to take time over it. 'I am afraid', he commented, 'that this is a magazine-reading age, a newspaper-reading age, a periodical-reading age, but not so much a Bible-reading age as it ought to be.' This exercise in serious reading involved meditation and prayer. Above all, Spurgeon believed that Scripture should be read in the presence of Christ. This is how he put it:

> He [Christ] leans over me, he puts his finger along the lines, I can see his pierced hand: I will read it as in his presence. I will read it, knowing that he is the substance of it – that he is the proof of this book as well as the writer of it; the sum of this Scripture as well as the author of it. That is the way for true students to become wise! You will get at the soul of Scripture when you can keep Jesus with you while you are reading.[21]

Richard Foster, in his book *Streams of Living Water*, which sets out and also helpfully analyses different traditions within Christian spirituality, speaks of the centrality of the commitment to the Bible within evangelical spirituality, and his analysis supports Spurgeon's Christocentric view of how to gain most from the Bible. For evangelicals, Foster says: 'The Christ event is the heart of Scripture. Everything in the Bible either looks forward to Christ or flows from Christ.'[22]

Group Bible study

As well as engaging in the discipline of personal Bible reading, evangelicals have nurtured their spiritual experience by group Bible study. In German pietism in the eighteenth century there was a concern to increase lay participation in church life. Stemming from a desire to achieve this goal and in particular to improve the level of spirituality in the German Lutheranism with which he was familiar, Philipp Spener proposed *collegia pietatis*, or devotional meetings, in which believers would meet to teach each other. Spener's book *Pia desideria*, published in 1675, which dealt with what he called 'Earnest desires for a reform of the true evangelical Church', had great influence across Europe. Spener included as one of his six major ideas for the renewal of the churches the 'earnest and thorough study of the Bible in private meetings'. These Bible study cells also engaged in singing hymns and in sharing Christian testimonies.[23] The communal method of prayer and study represented a significant shift away from the pulpit-centred way in which a good deal of Protestantism had been operating up to that point. Although the slogan *sola scriptura* was widely used during the Reformation period, it was pietism that developed Bible study groups which emphasised the right of private interpretation of Scripture.[24]

Count Zinzendorf picked up on this idea, and small societies for mutual spiritual edification were to be central to Moravian spirituality. Zinzendorf understood the importance of organising his followers into different types of cell groups for the purpose of corporate spiritual nurture and this concept was exported from Herrnhut to Britain and elsewhere.[25] John Wesley's Methodist societies – which met in class meetings and smaller bands each week – drew from the model of spirituality expressed by the Moravians, although Wesley placed his own distinctive mark on them, especially with his strong commitment to discipline. Wesley saw his societies as standing firm 'in the good old Bible way' and on one occasion told a group in Derbyshire to 'go straight forward, knowing nothing of various opinions, and minding nothing but to be Bible Christians'.[26] Across Europe, from the early nineteenth century, Bible study groups were to be found in various denominations. Sometimes such meetings produced new evangelical churches. In France this spiritual impetus led to the first French Baptist congregations. In 1810, to take the earliest known example of this process, a farmer in northern France found in a corner of his house a Bible. 'He read [the Bible] eagerly and lent it to his neighbours, whom he afterwards gathered together.'[27] This is a typical expression of evangelical spirituality. In Sweden many people began to meet in small groups or 'conventicles' to study the Bible, sing hymns and even celebrate the Lord's Supper.[28] English evangelicals, such as Lord Radstock, who visited Russia in the nineteenth century, promoted similar home Bible study groups. Russian high society met in each other's salons for Bible study and prayer.[29]

In the early decades of the twentieth century small Bible study groups multiplied in universities. Evangelicals in Britain were involved in the Student Christian Movement, the Inter-Varsity Fellowship of Evangelical Unions, and other movements such as the Oxford Group, led by Frank Buchman. Contributors to the history of the Inter-Varsity Fellowship (IVF) edited by Donald Coggan (later Archbishop of Canterbury), *Christ and the Colleges* (published in 1934), highlighted the crucial importance to the growth of the IVF of the way in which Christian fellowships in universities were seeking 'by the study of God's word' to achieve the mutual edification of their members'.[30] This focus was to influence large numbers of future evangelical leaders. Often the Bible study undertaken was systematic. At the meetings of the Oxford Group, by contrast, the Bible would be opened at random to receive immediate direction from God. At one meeting, however, when T.R. Glover, the Public Orator of Cambridge University, who was a supporter of the Student Christian Movement (SCM), was present, Glover questioned the method of choosing random biblical passages. To discuss thoroughly a chapter of the Bible seemed to Glover to be preferable. Buchman's reply was: 'I prefer my mixed grill'.[31] The Oxford Group later became the broader Moral Re-Armament movement, but in the 1930s it had a definite evangelical ethos. One conservative evangelical said in 1932 that he had discovered a new experience 'through the liberating Spirit of God working through the Oxford Group' and that for him the Bible was now more wonderful than ever.[32]

The place of preaching

Evangelical spirituality has given the preaching of the Word of God a central place. Those who heard the early evangelical preachers, whether brilliant orators such as George Whitefield or reasoned expositors such as Jonathan Edwards, felt that they were being brought into immediate and powerful contact with the realities of God.[33] Charles Simeon articulated the general view among British evangelicals, which was that although God was not restricted in the means he used to edify the Church, none the less 'He condescends to employ the stated ministry of His Word for the diffusion of divine knowledge'.[34] The most enduring work undertaken by Simeon is contained in a multi-volume set of *Expository Outlines on the Whole Bible*. The work was begun in 1796 with a hundred sample sermon notes for preachers and was entitled *Skeletons* because of the outline format that Simeon used. By 1801 the collection had grown to five hundred sermons and was re-designated *Helps to Composition*. Eventually twenty-one thick volumes were published by Cambridge University Press in sixteen months, with the title *Horae Homileticae*. In the preface to these volumes, Simeon wrote that the purpose of the sermon was to 'humble the sinner, to exalt the Saviour, and to promote holiness'. As with private reading of the Bible, the emphasis was on the spiritual effects of preaching and there was a clear focus on Christ. Abjuring false humility, Simeon referred to his written work as 'an expedition never known or heard of in the writings of a private man'.[35]

Drawing from his own experience as a preacher, C.H. Spurgeon spoke both to his trainee ministers at the Pastors' College and to his congregational hearers about the function of the sermon, highlighting some of the same themes as had Simeon. He warned evangelical preachers against being merely orthodox in their preaching, without conveying the experience of the love of God. For him, as he put it in one Communion sermon ('The Well-beloved'), the love of God expressed in Christ was 'a torrent which sweeps all before it when its fount breaks forth within the soul. It is a Gulf Stream in which all icebergs melt.' The instinctive response of the believer to Jesus Christ was: 'This is my Beloved and this is my Friend.'[36] Spurgeon also cautioned against turning the hearing of preaching into an exercise in which doctrinal orthodoxy was evaluated. He commented:

> I have sorrowfully observed some persons who are very orthodox, and who can repeat their creed very glibly, and yet the principal use that they make of their orthodoxy is to sit and watch the preacher with the view of framing a charge against him. He has uttered a single sentence which is judged to be half a hair's breadth below the standard! That man [they say] is not sound.[37]

Spurgeon's remedy for every kind of misuse of preaching was a spiritual one. The sermon had to have Jesus Christ at the centre. 'That sermon', he said in typically blunt language, 'which does not lead to Christ, or of which Jesus Christ is not the top and the bottom, is a sort of sermon that will make the devils in hell to laugh, but might make the angels of God to weep, if they were capable of such emotion.'[38]

In the twentieth century there was a considerable change in the way in which preaching was regarded. Horton Davies suggested in the 1960s that 'the Victorian preacher ascended a pulpit as a crown prince', and he concluded: 'The era of spell-binders is over.' Undoubtedly the age of pulpiteers passed, but for evangelicals preaching continued to be central. P.T. Forsyth, Principal from 1901 of Hackney College and the most outstanding Congregational theologian of his time, in *Positive Preaching and the Modern Mind* (1907), began with the sentence: 'It is, perhaps, an overbold beginning, but I will venture to say that with its preaching Christianity stands or falls.'[39] He also described preaching the gospel as 'a great sacramental deed'.[40] At the Keswick Convention, where thousands of evangelicals have gathered each year for one hundred and thirty years, the daily morning Bible Readings have been models of biblical exposition. Graham Scroggie, a Baptist minister who was the dominant mind at Keswick in the first half of the century, delivered the Keswick Bible Readings on twelve occasions. His conviction was that without biblical instruction the spiritual uplift gained through the Convention, with its traditional call to those present to consecrate their lives to Christ in full surrender, was transient.[41] Scroggie was awarded an honorary DD from Edinburgh University in 1927 in recognition of his ministry in Edinburgh, his place as a Keswick representative and especially his contribution to the scholarly study and teaching of the Bible.[42]

Throughout most of the twentieth century there were evangelical preachers who attracted large congregations. In North America these churches increasingly became known as megachurches. Some, notably Willow Creek, outside Chicago, geared their preaching to the unchurched.[43] In Britain the best-known twentieth-century preachers included Campbell Morgan at the Congregational Westminster Chapel, and Martyn Lloyd-Jones, who followed him at the same church. Both stressed thorough biblical exposition, and Lloyd-Jones in particular had a great influence on younger evangelical preachers. In a famous passage on preaching, which indicates his view of its spiritual impact, Lloyd-Jones said:

What is Preaching? Logic on fire! Eloquent reason! Are these contradictions? Of course they are not. Reason concerning this Truth ought to be mightily eloquent, as you see it in the case of the Apostle Paul and others. It is theology on fire. And a theology which does not take fire, I maintain, is a defective theology ... Preaching is the most amazing, and the most thrilling activity that one can ever be engaged in ...[44]

Underlying this was Lloyd-Jones' understanding of spirituality. He had been deeply influenced by the Puritans, by Jonathan Edwards, by P.T. Forsyth and by B.B. Warfield, and for Lloyd-Jones, as Gordon says, 'theological reflection by a reverent mind was a spiritually formative discipline, an exercise in passionate wisdom, a fusion of logic and prayer.'[45]

The Methodist tradition produced several preachers who were highly regarded within evangelicalism in the twentieth century. Samuel Chadwick, who was himself a powerful preacher and who trained many young preachers at Cliff College, commented regarding the training at Cliff: 'The Bible is central to the whole course...We do not ignore criticism, but our concern is with content. The Bible is accepted as the inspired, complete and infallible revelation of God, and the final authority in all matters of faith and conduct.'[46] In the mid-twentieth century, W.E. Sangster regularly attracted congregations of 3,000 at the Methodist Westminster Central Hall, London. He conducted many preaching tours within and outside Methodism. Sangster's advice to preachers regarding the message they brought was: 'Believe in it. Keep to centralities. Work at it. Make it plain. Make it practical ... Steep it in prayer.'[47] Later in the century, Methodism's most famous international preacher was Donald English, who was twice President of the Methodist Conference and was chair of the World Methodist Council. Paul Smith, another Methodist minister, wrote of Donald English that the 'clarity of his exposition left his hearers wondering why they had read that passage so often and never grasped its heart before'.[48]

The evangelical preacher aimed to reach the 'heart' of Scripture.

Within Anglicanism by far the most significant preacher of the twentieth century was John Stott, who from 1950 was Rector of All Souls' Church, Langham Place, London. Over the succeeding decades John Stott was to develop, through his teaching, his prolific writing and his many personal contacts, into a towering figure within world-wide evangelicalism. Stott, who thought deeply about the subject of preaching, looked to Charles Simeon as one of his models. He read Charles Simeon's expository sermons and followed Simeon in his commitment to Scripture as 'the Word of God to be obeyed and expounded'.[49] In the later twentieth century Stott was responsible, above anyone else in the evangelical world, for fostering a renewal of the kind of preaching which approached Scripture with reverence and devotion but also with a desire to deal with its message intelligently. Stott, writing with passion, said: 'The Church needs an instructed laity ... who are growing in their knowledge of God and of His Word, and who are thereby able to resist the subtle encroachment of modern cults. Nothing can bring about this happy state of affairs but the solid, systematic, didactic preaching of the whole Word of God.'[50] A key concept for John Stott was that the mind as well as the heart of a person mattered. 'The only worship pleasing to God', Stott declared, 'is heart-worship, and heart-worship is rational worship.'[51]

Fundamentalist approaches

The early twentieth century saw what became known as the Fundamentalist movement beginning to have an impact on evangelical theology and spirituality. A theological polarisation became evident between those who upheld more conservative approaches to the Bible and those who were open to the fruits of biblical scholarship. This polarisation had been growing within evangelicalism since the later nineteenth century, but had largely been beneath the surface and had been obscured by a common commitment on the part of all evangelicals to activism. The expansive outlook of D.L. Moody was important in this connection. But fault lines opened up. Liberals became active in attacking conservatives, as well as vice versa. A sense of Fundamentalist identity grew stronger, producing a coalition of those determined to uphold more rigid views of biblical infallibility. This approach gained a degree of support through the free distribution of *The Fundamentals*, twelve volumes published between 1910 and 1915, defending 'fundamental' doctrines. The World's Christian Fundamentals Association was formed in 1919 in the USA, with a Baptist, W.B. Riley, as its leading figure, and it was at the 1920 Northern Baptist Convention in America that the term 'fundamentalist' was coined. W.B. Riley pronounced that Baptists had entered the controversy 'knowing that it was not a battle, but a war ... and that they will never surrender'.[52] A more strident form of evangelical spirituality, involving battles for the Bible, was emerging.

In Britain the Fundamentalist movement did not have nearly the strength which it did in North America,[53] but it was promoted enthusiastically by organisations such as the Bible League, whose name indicated that a great deal of its focus was on defending the Bible. British Fundamentalism, like that in America, was characterised by both truculent protest and the 'withdrawal instinct of the sectarian'.[54] The Bible League gained the support in 1922 of 162 conservative Christian bodies in Britain for a protest against Protestant 'religious rationalism', often known as liberalism or modernism.[55] A central complaint of the Fundamentalists was that critical scholarship undermined biblical authority. James Mountain, the venerable leader of the small Baptist Bible Union, insisted – in the wake of the Bible League manifesto – that the fundamental divide was between opposing attitudes to the Bible. 'There is', he pronounced in *The Bible Call*, 'no point of contact between the Modernist and the believer.'[56] Nor, from the Fundamentalist perspective, did common spiritual experience create the possibility of contact. The

author of the aptly named *Valiant in Fight* (1937), Basil
Atkinson, a senior staff member at Cambridge University
Library and a conservative evangelical stalwart, delighted
members of the Bible League in 1925 by his outright opposition to dialogue between conservative evangelical students in
Cambridge and the more theologically mixed Student
Christian Movement. At that time the SCM embraced many
(less conservative) evangelicals, but for Atkinson it was
'apostate'.[57]

Many British and American evangelicals in the 1920s and
1930s, however, distanced themselves from what they saw as
the aggression of the Fundamentalist agenda. The spirituality
of the Keswick Convention was moderate, and was summed
up by Graham Scroggie when he expressed sympathy with
Fundamentalism's adherence to conservative views of the
Bible but deplored the bitter spirit of some Fundamentalists.
He advocated a use of the Bible which was more spiritual and
practical, highlighting the Lordship of Christ.[58] Similarly, G.T.
Manley wrote in his Inter-Varsity Fellowship Bible Study
Course in 1934 that the object of the 'Quiet Time' was to 'use
the Word to light and feed the fire of devotion'.[59] Samuel
Chadwick, shaped as he was by Wesleyan spirituality, found
the spirit of Fundamentalism unpalatable. He reminded
Fundamentalists, with their battles for orthodoxy, that there
was the danger of 'heterodoxy of temper'.[60] In his use of the
Bible Chadwick affirmed the place of biblical criticism, considering it contributed to saner conceptions of biblical
inspiration. He did not subscribe to the popular Fundamentalist idea of biblical inerrancy. His view was that 'minor errors
do not detract from the truthfulness, credibility and authority
of the Sacred Writings ... No theory of Inspiration warrants
the expectation of inerrancy and uniform authority'.[61] At the
end of his life, in 1932, Chadwick gathered his colleagues at
Cliff College together and said to them with emphasis: 'Stand
together for the Word of God', and then adding, significantly,
'not, not in any stupid sense'.[62] This terse statement summed

up the thinking of most evangelicals. Their aim was thoughtful devotion.

Later in the twentieth century there was a fresh flowering of evangelical biblical scholarship. A pioneer in this field in Britain in the 1940s was the New Testament scholar, F.F. Bruce, at Manchester University.[63] In America, Fuller Theological Seminary in California became the best-known institutional example of what was a growing movement within evangelicalism that was open to serious scholarship.[64] The rise of this new thinking, which became known as neo-evangelicalism, did not impress the Fundamentalists, and on the other hand Christians from non-evangelical traditions had apprehensions about the possible result of the advance of what they saw as a new Fundamentalism. During the time of the Billy Graham Crusades in Britain in the mid-1950s, H.K. Luce, the headmaster of Durham School, referring to the fact that Billy Graham was due to lead a Christian Union mission in Cambridge University (partly in connection with the Inter-Varsity Fellowship), expressed his anxieties. He called on religious leaders to make it plain that 'they cannot regard fundamentalism as likely to issue in anything but disillusionment and disaster for educated men and women in this twentieth-century world'. Evangelicals, of whatever hue, were being seen as Fundamentalists. John Stott, who entered the debate, was determined for his part to repudiate the fundamentalist label.[65] Fundamentalism was widely seen as rigid in its outlook, whereas the evangelical approach to the Bible which Stott sought to foster was a thoughtful one.

Conclusion

Since the Bible has been regarded by evangelicals as the Word of God, evangelical spirituality can be described as Word-centred. The heart of daily evangelical devotion has been a period of study of the Bible and of prayer. This may change somewhat in the future, since for some evangelicals the rigidity of the traditional 'quiet time' has not proved helpful.

Group Bible study, although receiving a higher profile in recent decades through home groups and cell groups within evangelical churches, has been a more consistent element of evangelical spirituality than has sometimes been thought. The place of preaching and the place of the Bible are closely connected in evangelical spirituality, since preaching has been understood as primarily an exercise in biblical exposition and application. The Keswick Convention, which moulded much evangelical spirituality in the first half of the twentieth century, was seen by preachers such as Graham Scroggie as an event offering such solid exposition and application. The Keswick Convention has continued to attract large numbers, and the model it has offered has been taken up by later evangelical gatherings such as Spring Harvest, which has become the largest annual event in Britain at which evangelicals gather. From its beginning in 1979 Spring Harvest grew substantially. It attracts at least 60,000 people each year and numbers have reached 80,000.[66] Biblical exposition is at the centre of such prominent show-cases of evangelical life. Although Fundamentalist thinking within evangelicalism has received a great deal of publicity, and some have assumed that all evangelicals are Fundamentalists, the evangelical approach to the Bible is generally more concerned about the spiritual impact of what is read or heard rather than about the attempt to make it fit an inerrantist framework. Most evangelicals would follow the thinking of J.C. Ryle in seeing the Bible as essential to a wholesome spiritual life and would affirm Spurgeon's view that Christ is the substance of the Bible.

4. 'CHRIST IN A REAL PRESENCE': THE SACRAMENTS

Whereas a stress on the Bible as the Word of God has characterised evangelical spirituality, there has often been much less emphasis on the sacraments, although P.T. Forsyth in *The Church and the Sacraments* put the classic Protestant view: 'The Sacraments are the acted Word – variants of the preached Word. They are signs, but they are more than signs. They are the Word, the Gospel itself, visible, as in preaching the Word is audible ... [This] is Christ in a real presence giving anew His redemption'.[1] There has often been a concern to distinguish evangelical beliefs about the spiritual effects of baptism and Holy Communion from the beliefs held by Roman Catholic, Orthodox or high Anglican Christians. In many Baptist churches, for example, baptism has been seen simply as a witness by the Christian who is being baptised. In evangelical Anglican churches there has been much less stress on infant baptism than in Anglo-Catholic churches. What about Communion? Again, many evangelicals have seen it solely as a sign or a memorial rather than as a means of grace. 'Evangelical spirituality', says Gillett in *Trust and Obey*, 'has most often existed with reasonably infrequent celebrations of Holy Communion – monthly or even quarterly'. The exception he notes is the Brethren movement, in which there has always been a weekly observance of the 'Breaking of Bread'.[2] While many evangelicals have been wary of sacramentalism, none the less there have been significant evangelical thinkers who have seen the sacraments as central to their spirituality.

Infant baptism

The subject of infant baptism was one to which Jonathan Edwards gave attention because it had to do with his great theme of conversion and also because of disputes in his congregation about who could be admitted to church membership. Edwards upheld the traditional practice of infant baptism within the Congregational churches, but also spoke of the baptism of adults. He wrote:

> If an adult person does sincerely and believingly give up himself to God, baptism seals salvation to him: so if the parent sincerely and believingly dedicates the infant to God, baptism seals salvation to it ... So if a parent did sincerely and with his whole heart dedicate his child to God he will afterward take thorough and effectual care in bringing up his children in the nurture and admonition of the Lord, continuing in prayer and dependence on God for them; and in that way it is sealed to them, and ordinarily they shall obtain success.[3]

The emphasis here is on the spirituality of the parents and on baptism as a 'seal'. Edwards ultimately took the position that only the children of 'visible saints' – who had given an account of personal faith and had been admitted to the Lord's Supper – were entitled to have their children baptised. The children were seen as part of God's covenant of grace. He came to oppose the 'half-way covenant' by which those who had been baptised as infants but had not made a positive profession of personal faith could have their children baptised.[4] Issues connected with the 'half-way covenant' and reception to Holy Communion finally brought Edwards' ministry at Northampton to an end in 1750.[5] Edwards' desire for authentic conversion and spiritual life was crucial to his sacramental thinking.

In England the rise of the Anglo-Catholic movement in the Church of England in the early nineteenth century led to a major controversy over baptism. Edward Pusey, one of the leaders of the Anglo-Catholic movement, made clear in 1836 his view that the regeneration of the baptised infant spoken of in *The Book of Common Prayer* was indeed a new birth, which implies 'a new nature, existence imparted; and this is actual, not metaphorical'.[6] George Gorham, who was a Fellow of Queens' College, Cambridge, and an evangelical of considerable ability, openly denied the doctrine of baptismal regeneration. Prior to Gorham's ordination in 1811, the Bishop of Ely had threatened to disqualify him on the grounds of his 'unsound' views on baptism. Gorham then went on to serve happily as a clergyman in Cornwall, but in 1847, when he sought to move to a parish just outside Exeter, Henry Philpotts, the Bishop of Exeter, subjected him to a gruelling fifty-two hours of oral and written examination over eight days, the focus being infant baptism. Gorham maintained that he upheld the position set out in the Articles of the Church of England on the sacraments: 'Where there is no worthy reception, there is no bestowment of grace.'[7] Although Gorham argued his case well, Philpotts refused to induct him, and Gorham ultimately took his case to the Privy Council, which ruled in his favour. This case made a deep impression on evangelicals, underlining the way in which their view of spiritual experience differed from High Church thinking.[8]

The evangelical paedobaptist view of what happens in baptism has not been a uniform one. Some have held that in baptism there is an admission to the privileges of membership of the visible Church. Others have taken the view that the seeds of regeneration are given to an infant at baptism. Still others have majored on the covenant promises to the children of believers. The noted evangelical Anglican Henry Venn proposed what was a common evangelical position, that the word 'regenerate' in the Church of England service was to be used 'in the highest spiritual sense, but sacramentally'.[9] In other words, infants who were baptised, although not presumed to have received 'new birth' through baptism, were the recipients of grace. The Congregational leader R.W. Dale, who from 1853 until his death in 1895 ministered at Carr's Lane

Independent Chapel, Birmingham, exercising an influential ministry, stressed the activity of God in baptism, including in infant baptism. However, he insisted that regeneration was not imparted. What was given through baptism was 'the assurance that He loves us with an infinite love, and will do His part towards saving us from sin, and bringing us to eternal glory'.[10] This assurance was initially for the parents of the infant who was baptised and was thus related to covenant theology. Later those who had been baptised could look back on the fact that this had happened to them, and draw assurance from it. William Goode, the leading evangelical Anglican theologian of the mid nineteenth century, emphasised in standard evangelical terms the necessity of faith, arguing that 'in the spiritual new birth, a living principle of faith must have been implanted to make the birth by baptism effectual to the production of being spiritually alive'.[11]

The baptism of believers

Baptists, in their theological thinking about the relationship between baptism and spiritual experience in their tradition, have not had to focus on issues raised by the practice of infant baptism, although they have sought to refute the theology behind that practice. In the eighteenth century Baptists were the only denominational body in England that baptised believers, although over time the practice of believer's baptism has become much more common within evangelicalism, especially through the spread of Pentecostalism in the twentieth century. One Baptist writer who examined the theology of baptism was Andrew Fuller, the pastor of Kettering Baptist Church, Northamptonshire, from 1782, who became the Baptist denomination's leading theologian in the later eighteenth and early nineteenth century. In this period, as in their earlier history, Baptists gave a considerable amount of attention to seeking to show that only believers, and not infants, should be baptised, and that baptism should be by total immersion.[12] But what about the spiritual significance of baptism? Andrew Fuller dealt with this issue, writing in 1802 in *The Practical Uses of Christian Baptism* about 'the influence of this ordinance, where it produces its proper effects, in promoting piety in individuals, and purity in the church'. Baptism, he argued, was also a 'solemn and practical profession of the Christian religion' and for the early Christians was an 'oath of allegiance to the King of Zion'.[13] This understanding was clearly Christ-centred.

Andrew Fuller's statement about baptism 'promoting piety' suggests a spiritual effect, although the language of an 'oath of allegiance' might point towards the aspect of human commitment. Fuller also wrote that although there was no virtue in the water of baptism it was a sign of sin cleansed away. 'Sin', he stated, 'is washed away in baptism in the same sense as Christ's flesh is eaten, and his blood drank, in the Lord's supper: the sign, when rightly used leads to the thing signified.' Forgiveness of sins, he added, takes place through 'the name' (of Jesus) in which people are baptised.[14] This appears to indicate that in Fuller's mind baptism, while not salvific, in some way confirms the individual's faith and experience. Also, on the basis of Paul's teaching about dying to sin in baptism (Romans 6:3–4) Fuller saw baptism as a commitment made by a believer to die to sin and to the world. He spoke of baptism as serving like a 'hedge' that God put in place around baptised believers, and as something that functioned as a means of preserving them from temptation. Using language about the church as a 'garden enclosed', which was a common picture in this period, Fuller warned that where the original idea of baptism was ignored, and people were 'admitted to baptism without any profession of personal religion' or else were baptised 'upon the profession of others on their behalf' (in infant baptism), then 'the church will be no longer a garden enclosed, but an open wilderness, where every beast of prey can range at large'.[15] Thus baptism, in Fuller's thinking, had a significant impact on the spiritual life of the Christian.

In 1850 C.H. Spurgeon, who was to see himself as

continuing the tradition of Andrew Fuller, was baptised in the River Lark at Isleham (bordering Cambridgeshire and Suffolk), an event which he described in this way: 'I was privileged to follow my Lord, and to be buried with Him in baptism.' The rite was, he continued, a '[s]weet emblem of my death to all the world'.[16] There was a strong emphasis in Spurgeon's teaching on the fact that baptism was a mark of Christian obedience, of following Christ. For Spurgeon, as for Fuller, baptism was also 'the mark of distinction between the Church and the world', setting out 'the death of the baptized person to the world' and his or her resurrection to a new life. Baptism was not simply a symbol: it had effects, for example an ability to testify to what had taken place in a person's life. Spurgeon described baptism as an event which 'loosed my tongue, and from that day it has never been quiet'.[17] The most immediate means by which Spurgeon's theological views, including his thinking about baptism, were promulgated, was through his preaching ministry, notably at the Metropolitan Tabernacle. His published sermons were sold across the world. At the opening of the Tabernacle, Spurgeon said that the baptistery would usually be left uncovered in order to highlight the church's Baptist beliefs.[18] Although Spurgeon often conducted baptismal services and preached on the subject of baptism, he rarely did this in a polemical way. In sermons in 1859 and 1864, however, he strongly criticised Church of England practice. His most controversial sermon on this topic was 'Baptismal Regeneration', preached on 5 June 1864.[19] In its printed form it was the best-selling sermon Spurgeon ever produced. Soon after its publication 350,000 copies had been printed, and this rose to half a million by the end of the century.[20]

Many of the growing number of evangelicals – Baptists, Pentecostals and others – who practised the baptism of believers in the twentieth century have seen it as primarily an act of witness to personal faith, and often a personal testimony is made by the baptismal candidate. However, there has been a strand of Baptist sacramentalist thinking which has explored more deeply the experience of God that baptism offers. One of the leading evangelical New Testament scholars of the twentieth century, George Beasley-Murray, the Principal of Spurgeon's College, made a massive contribution to the baptismal debate and became the foremost Baptist advocate of a sacramental approach to baptism.[21] Beasley-Murray was one of the Baptist ministers who co-operated in 1959 in the production of a book, *Christian Baptism*, which was a landmark in British Baptist theological thinking about baptism.[22] He argued that baptism was not simply a symbol but was 'an effective sign: in it Christ and faith come together'.[23] When the sacramentalism found in *Christian Baptism* was strongly criticised by other Baptists, Beasley-Murray replied that Scripture militated against the 'reduced baptism' that was being widely championed.[24] For Beasley-Murray a sacrament was 'the Word of God in action', and he compared this with preaching as the Word of God 'in free speech'. In the New Testament, he argued, baptism was inseparable from turning to God in faith, and it was through such faith that God justified a person, gave the gift of the Holy Spirit and united a person to Jesus Christ.[25] Baptism conveyed spiritual reality.

Evangelical Anglicans and Holy Communion

John Wesley's views about the benefits of Holy Communion were formulated when he was a young Church of England priest, before his later evangelical experiences, but his approach to Communion remained substantially the same throughout his life. In a sermon preached in 1788, 'The Duty of Constant Communion', Wesley urged the observance of the Lord's Supper on the grounds that it was 'a plain command of Christ'. In addition to that, there were 'great benefits' in Communion, notably 'the forgiveness of our past sins and the present strengthening and refreshing of our souls'. The Lord's Supper also, said Wesley, 'gives strength to perform our duty, and leads us on to perfection'. Clearly for him this was a meal with considerable spiritual significance. Wesley encouraged proper preparation for the Lord's Supper through meditation on Scripture and self-examination. For Wesley, frequent celebration was the ideal. He wrote:

> Let every one therefore who has either any desire to please God, or any love of his own soul, obey God and consult the good of his own soul by communicating every time he can; like the first Christians, with whom the Christian sacrifice was a constant part of the Lord's day service. And for several centuries they received it almost every day: Four times a week always, and every saint's day beside. Accordingly those that joined in the prayers of the faithful never failed to partake of the blessed sacrament.[26]

He added by way of explanation in the printed version of this sermon that it had been written over five-and-fifty years before, for the use of his pupils at Oxford. 'I have added very little', said Wesley, 'but retrenched much; as I then used more words than I do now. But I thank God I have not yet seen cause to alter my sentiments in any point which is therein delivered.'[27] In 1745 the Wesleys published *Hymns on the Lord's Supper*, which contained 166 items, among them lines like these:

> From house to house they broke the bread,
> Impregnated with life divine,
> And drank the Spirit of the head
> Transmitted in the sacred wine.

As F.C. Gill notes, these are Communion hymns which convey the depths and mystery of the Eucharist and which are intended to nourish spiritual experience.[28]

The emphasis on the Eucharist which characterised the spirituality of many Anglican evangelicals in the early nineteenth century owed a great deal to Charles Simeon. When he became a student at Cambridge the university requirement was that every student should take Holy Communion at least once a year. It was, Simeon recounted later, his worries about taking the Holy Sacrament that began some stirrings of spirituality within him. He bought a book, *The Whole Duty of Man* (the only religious book he had ever heard of), and began to read it. During this time he called to God for mercy and indeed made himself ill through doing little other than reading, fasting and praying. Then came the spiritual freedom he was seeking, and this led him to the Lord's Table to receive further spiritual benefit. He wrote, in words which emphasise the way in which his conversion had to do with an experience of Christ:

> I sought to lay my sins upon the sacred head of Jesus, and on the Wednesday began to have a hope of mercy; and on the Thursday that hope increased; and on Friday and Saturday it became more strong; and on the Sunday (Easter Day, April 4) I awoke early with those words upon my heart and lips, 'Jesus Christ is risen to-day; Hallelujah! Hallelujah!' From that hour peace flowed in rich abundance into my soul; and at the Lord's Table in our chapel I had the sweetest access to God through my blessed Saviour.[29]

It has often been thought that the trend towards frequent Communion in the Church of England in the later nineteenth century was attributable to the Anglo-Catholic Movement. Horton Davies, however, argued that it was the evangelicals of the nineteenth century who could rightly be claimed as pioneers in restoring Holy Communion to a central place in Anglican worship.[30] At a time when many Anglican churches had a quarterly Communion service, a number of Anglican evangelical leaders who were committed to reaching the working classes advocated at least a monthly celebration of Holy Communion and also introduced evening Communions. Many people in domestic service worked during the day on Sundays.[31] The Earl of Shaftesbury, a committed Anglican, and the leading nineteenth-century evangelical champion of the poor, was highly critical of the conservatism of some Anglican clergy, for example in his statement:

> Now if it were given out by a large body of the ministers of the Church that they would administer the Communion in the evening, many of the poor with whom we have to deal would be likely to attend; but if it is to be given out that the ministers of the Church of England will never consider their convenience and necessities, they will certainly stay away from the churches altogether. And how, I ask you, in such a refusal, can the Church of England call herself the 'Church of the people'?[32]

Handley Moule, writing later in the nineteenth century, upheld this emphasis. He described eucharistic communion as a 'personal interview with the Lord'.[33] Moule's *Outlines of Christian Doctrine* spoke of Holy Communion as 'an hour with God, with the Son of God'. The Christological nature of Moule's thinking is evident. He continued:

> It is a blessed hour of remembrance, of meditation; but far more. It is an hour in which He speaks to us, and as it were sensibly touches us, in the ordinance of, not our invention, but His command. The holy Bread, the holy Cup, are received as from His hand, as truly (to faith) as they were received at the first Administration.[34]

In 1895 Moule's theological interest in and contribution to this area of spiritual experience was underlined when he was awarded a DD for his scholarly edition of Bishop Ridley's volume *On the Lord's Supper*. By the time of the First World War, in *The Call of Lent*, Moule could comment: 'Far more now than in days which I can well recall it is the usage of earnest English Christians to communicate often. The holy Sacrament ... certainly suggests no reason in itself against such frequency; and to many souls the frequency brings a benefit untold.'[35]

The Supper in Nonconformity and Presbyterianism

Differing views about the Lord's Supper were expressed by evangelical Nonconformists in the eighteenth century. In *Thoughts on the Lord's Supper* (1748), Anne Dutton, a Baptist and a prolific author who corresponded with evangelical leaders such as Philip Doddridge, John Wesley, George Whitefield and Howell Harris, took a high view of Communion. She wrote in this way: 'As our Lord is spiritually present in his own ordinance, so he therein and thereby doth actually communicate, or give himself, his body broken, and his blood shed, with all the benefits of his death, to the worthy receivers.' Dutton saw the Supper as God's way of admitting believers 'into the nearest Approach to his glorious Self'.[36] By contrast, another Baptist, John Sutcliff, in *The Ordinance of the Lord's Supper Con-sidered* (1803), wrote: 'When you see the table spread and are about to partake of the bread and wine, think you hear Christ saying, "Remember me." Remember who he is ... Again: Remember what he has done'. The fact that Christ instructed believers to remember him, Sutcliff continued, clearly 'implies his absence'. As with human friends who give gifts by which they are remembered, so for John Sutcliff gazing upon the bread and wine aided the 'recollection of our absent friend'.[37] Within much of Nonconformity, the idea of the Supper as simply a memorial became common evangelical currency in the nineteenth century.[38] The 1920s and 1930s, however, saw a counter-movement among some Free Church leaders, notably Congregationalists such as Nathaniel Micklem, Principal of Mansfield College, Oxford, and J.S. Whale, President of Cheshunt College, Cambridge. This 'Genevan' movement (so termed because of a degree of indebtedness to John Calvin) encouraged a higher view of both Word and Sacrament.[39]

Within sections of the Church of Scotland and other Presbyterian bodies, considerable emphasis was placed on the extended seasons of Holy Communion, stretching over several days, which were a traditional part of Scottish

Presbyterianism. Horatius Bonar, who had a notable ministry of over fifty years in Scotland and who died in 1889 when minister of Chalmers Memorial Free Church in Edinburgh, made considerable use of these Communion seasons to foster spiritual encounter. The same was true of Bonar's friend, Robert Murray McCheyne, who increased the frequency of the celebration of Communion in St Peter's, Dundee, and who believed that ideally there should be a weekly celebration.[40] The bread and wine, they held, brought the Christian face to face with the mystery and wonder of the grace of God, to be nourished by it. This is expressed magnificently in one of Bonar's Communion hymns. In Communion the believer gazes on Christ:

> Here O my Lord, I see thee face to face;
> Here would I touch and handle things unseen,
> Here grasp with firmer hands the eternal grace,
> And all my weariness upon thee lean.
>
> Here would I feast upon the bread of God,
> Here drink with Thee the royal wine of heaven.
> Here would I lay aside each earthly load,
> Here taste afresh the calm of sin forgiven.[41]

The meetings at which people were either prepared for or took the sacrament in these Presbyterian congregations could go on for as long as four hours. Charles Simeon, on a visit to Scotland, found the length of the meetings a problem. Although at a particular point in one of the services he attended he was so moved that he was 'quite dissolved in tears', he added that those who could stay 'from beginning to end, with any profit for their souls, must be made of different materials from me'.[42]

Spurgeon often preached on the Lord's Supper. A volume of Spurgeon's Communion addresses, *Till He Come*, has a preface which notes that a number of the addresses in it were delivered to 'the little companies of Christians' who gathered around the Communion table in Spurgeon's sitting room at

Mentone, in the south of France, where he went regularly to build up his health or recuperate from illness.[43] For Spurgeon there was a real presence of Christ at the Supper, and fellowship with Christ was central. Speaking at Mentone, on the subject 'I will give you rest', Spurgeon affirmed: 'By faith, I see our Lord standing in our midst, and I hear Him say, with voice of sweetest music, first to all of us together, and then to each one individually, "I will give you rest." May the Holy Spirit bring to each of us the fulness of the rest and peace of God!'[44] But Spurgeon strongly opposed Roman Catholic eucharistic teaching, arguing on one occasion, in a sermon 'The Witness of the Lord's Supper', that 'both our reason and our spiritual nature revolt against anything so atrocious as to believe that the body of Christ – the absolute flesh and blood – can be eaten and drank ... or that it could confer any spiritual benefit upon those who could perform so cannibal and revolting an act.' In the same sermon he affirmed his belief 'in the real presence, but not in the corporeal presence'.[45] Spurgeon celebrated the Lord's Supper each Sunday, based on the custom in the early Church 'to break [bread] on the first day of the week, and I think oftener, for it seems to me that they broke bread from house to house'.[46]

A number of Keswick evangelicals, both Anglican and Free Church, also gave the Lord's Supper prominence. In 1920 Stuart Holden, an Anglican clergyman in London and later the chairman of the Keswick Convention, called for a united Communion service to take place at Keswick. He accepted that this might upset the Church of England, which did not at that time encourage inter-communion, but he urged that 'any Church that can be broken up by the plain observance of the will of God ... ought to be broken up'.[47] F.B. Meyer, another influential Keswick figure, gave the Lord's Supper a high profile, introducing a weekly observance of Holy Communion during his ministries in Baptist churches – at Melbourne Hall, Leicester, and then at the well-known Regent's Park Chapel, London.[48] His love of the natural elements led Meyer to value the tangible substances of bread and wine. He argued

that to eat the bread of the 'Sacrament' (the term he used) and
to meditate on what Christ did was to 'incorporate Him
[Christ] into our texture', just as to eat everyday bread was to
absorb the influence of heaven and earth, rain, cloud and
soil.[49] It seems that Meyer, who was deeply influenced by
Romanticism, was able to let his imagination run free when
highlighting the spiritual importance of the encounter with
Christ in the Lord's Supper.

Holy Communion and evangelical unity

When the Brethren movement emerged in the early nineteenth century, its emphasis was on believers meeting
together every week to 'break bread' without any denominational label and without the need for any clergyman to
preside. Gradually the movement began to lose this non-
denominational outlook, but it played a part in introducing
evangelicals to a simple way of observing the Lord's Supper.
The Brethren organised a Sunday morning 'breaking of bread'
service during the Keswick Convention, and in the inter-war
years this attracted up to 700 communicants.[50] Brethren
thinking affected wider Keswick practice. In 1928, when
Stuart Holden's wish to have a non-denominational convention Communion service was fulfilled, Keswick opted for a
plain celebration of Communion, in which clerical and lay
distinctions were played down, and this proved to be an
acceptable model for many conservative evangelicals. The
emphasis was on spiritual fellowship. It was noted in 1932
that the Anglican bishops on the platform served along with a
number of other ministers and lay people at Communion.[51] A
year later, 3,000 people were present at the Keswick
Communion service. *The Life of Faith*, which acted as a semi-
official mouthpiece for Keswick, commented that 'members of
the Brethren must have felt themselves in the familiar atmosphere of the breaking of the bread; the Free Churchman might
have been worshipping in his own church ... the Anglican,
accustomed to approaching the Lord's Table, must have been

thankful that on this occasion the Holy Table waited upon him'.[52]

The Evangelical Alliance also contributed to the trend among evangelicals to see taking Holy Communion together across denominational divides as something desirable. On Sunday 23 August 1854, delegates to the meetings in London at which the Evangelical Alliance was founded preached in eighty-one London churches of various denominations. This was itself an ecumenical venture, but of equal significance was the fact that Holy Communion was celebrated in St John's Chapel, Bedford Row, at 8 a.m. on that Sunday, with 150 evangelicals from a number of countries and several denominations participating. A year later, 1,200 people from fifteen nations came to Paris for an Evangelical Alliance conference which discussed various issues including religious liberty. At the close of the conference there was a united service of Holy Communion, led in seven languages – French, English, German, Dutch, Italian, Swedish and Danish.[53] As part of the Golden Jubilee Evangelical Alliance conference of 1896, two thousand people participated in a Communion service.[54] During the period in the 1960s when Gilbert Kirby was the energetic secretary of the Evangelical Alliance there were well-publicised united celebrations of the Lord's Supper. About 3,000 people gathered in the Royal Albert Hall, London, in January 1963, for example, for a united Communion service arranged by the Alliance which involved evangelicals from different traditions. This was, from the perspective of the Alliance, a visible demonstration of Christian unity.[55]

The Lord's Supper as something which united believers from different denominations was also stressed by C.H. Spurgeon. Against a nineteenth-century ecclesiastical background in which many Baptists practised closed Communion – for baptised believers only – and when the official Anglican position was that only those who had been confirmed could take Holy Communion in Anglican churches, Spurgeon argued in favour of an open Communion Table. In an address at Mentone in France, entitled 'The Well-beloved', he stated his position: 'In this room we have an example of how closely we are united in Christ ... Our union in one body as Episcopalians, Baptists, Presbyterians or Independents, is not the thing which our Lord prayed for: but our union in Himself. That union we do at this moment enjoy; and therefore do we eat of one bread, and drink of one Spirit, at His feet who is to each one of us, and so to all of us, ALTOGETHER LOVELY.'[56] The unity which Spurgeon valued was the unity of all those who had a personal experience of Christ. This 'ecumenical' spirit was expressed especially in meetings at Mentone, but preaching at the Metropolitan Tabernacle in 1877, Spurgeon affirmed: 'We are all one in Christ Jesus; we do not come to this table as Baptists, or Episcopalians, or Methodists, or Presbyterians; we come here simply as those who form one body in Christ.'[57] The widespread commitment among evangelicals to pioneering inter-communion was based on their concept of spiritual unity.

Conclusion

Although it is often thought that evangelicals have played down the sacraments, and although many evangelicals have undoubtedly stressed preaching rather than the sacraments in public worship, there have been those within evangelicalism who have placed great emphasis on baptism and the Lord's Supper. P.T. Forsyth argued in *The Church and the Sacraments* that the 'idolatry of the popular preacher needs to be balanced by more stress on the Sacraments'.[58] Both paedobaptist and Baptist evangelicals have explored how baptism can be a means of grace. Even more attention has been given by evangelicals to the spiritual benefits to be gained through the Lord's Supper. Charles Simeon, for whom the Lord's Supper was of great spiritual significance in his conversion and in his life as a Christian, suggested that virtually all 'spiritual worshippers' would agree that Christ had 'again and again, in a more abundant measure, made Himself known to them in the breaking of bread'.[59] The same high view of what is experienced at the Lord's Table was present in the preaching and practice of Spurgeon. 'The Lord's Supper', Spurgeon pronounced, 'is no funeral meal, but a festival ... It is by man called the "Eucharist", or the giving of thanks: it is not a fast, but a feast. My happiest moments are spent with the King at his table, when his banner over me is love.'[60] There could not be a clearer declaration of evangelical belief in the way spiritual experience, an experience centred in Christ, is nurtured in a sacramental setting.

5. 'SWEET SEASONS OF COMMUNION': PRAYER AND PRAISE

Evangelicals have not traditionally been known for their extensive writings on the subject of prayer. In the index of Mark Noll's book *The Rise of Evangelicalism*, 'prayer' is not an item that is included, although there is reference to 'concerts of prayer'. By contrast, the index shows the reader that 'hymnody' is a subject dealt with throughout the book. The inference that could be drawn from this is that the early evangelicals gave little attention to prayer, while focusing a great deal on the singing of hymns. It is certainly true that hymn-singing was at the heart of communal evangelical spirituality. For the early generations, as Noll puts it, hymn-singing was 'the single experience that bound them most closely to each other'.[1] Hymns have acted as corporate set prayers. Almost all significant evangelical events have involved the singing of hymns, usually hymns written by the evangelicals themselves. Yet evangelicals have also taught carefully about and practised seriously the life of prayer. John Wesley set out a scheme for prayer in 1730 and he reprinted this in 1781, showing that his thinking about the approach to prayer and the importance of this aspect of devotion had not changed significantly over these decades. His scheme encouraged both spontaneous prayer and also the use of the Anglican Collect.[2] In *Trust and Obey* David Gillett suggests that evangelicals have valued spontaneity in their spiritual experience, for example in their prayers, while having little appreciation of liturgical prayer or of the discipline of silence.[3] While this has often been true, evangelical expressions of prayer and praise have shown a considerable degree of diversity.

The life of prayer

Like other evangelical leaders and Christians of differing spiritual traditions, John Wesley inculcated through his teaching the biblical idea of 'praying without ceasing'. He explained that the Methodist believer was not always in the house of prayer,

> ... though he neglects no opportunity of being there. Neither is he always on his knees, although he often is, or on his face, before the Lord his God. Nor yet is he always crying aloud to God, or calling upon him in words: For many times 'the Spirit maketh intercession for him with groans that cannot be uttered'.[4]

Wesley continued to speak in typical fashion in this passage about prayer and the language of the heart. Prayer, for Wesley, was not only to be expressed in words, but also through silence, groans, adoration and a constant sense of God's presence.[5] Wesley was somewhat ambivalent about the use of set prayers. In giving instructions (probably in 1786) about visiting the sick, he advised that every visit should conclude with prayer. He continued: 'If you cannot yet pray without a form you may use some of those composed by Mr. Spinckes, or any other pious writer. But the sooner you break through this backwardness the better. Ask of God, and he will soon open your mouth.'[6] Nathaniel Spinckes' *A Complete Manual of Private Devotions*, which drew on prayers going back to the early Church, was the volume that was being commended by Wesley, but only as a second best. Wesley believed that in praying for someone it was important to pray in a personal way. Yet in a letter about public worship written in 1778 to Mary Bishop, Wesley commented: 'I myself find more life in the Church prayers than in the formal extemporary prayers of Dissenters'.[7] It was 'life' that was crucial.

The practice encouraged by eighteenth-century evangelicals was to rise early in the morning to pray. Selina, the Countess of Huntingdon, who was a friend of both John Wesley and

George Whitefield, established a training college, Trefecca College, at which the students were expected to rise at 5 a.m., to sing a hymn at 5.15 a.m., to engage in 'private prayer and meditation', as well as making their beds and washing themselves, until 6 a.m., and then to have a further hour of spiritual exercises.[8] William Wilberforce is an example of a hugely influential evangelical who had as his aim 'more solitude and earlier hours'. He felt that his spiritual experience was inadequate if he had 'but a hurried half hour in a morning to myself'. On one occasion he wrote in his dairy:

> Alas, with how little profit has my time passed since I came to town! ... Oh, may I be more restrained by my rules for the future; and in the trying week upon which I am entering, when I shall be so much in company, and give so many entertainments; may I labour doubly, by a greater cultivation of a religious frame, by prayer, and by all due temperance, to get it well over.[9]

It is certainly not the case that Wilberforce was a recluse. He thoroughly enjoyed company and had a very active and fulfilling life as an MP. However, he was conscious of the spiritual dangers that accompanied the hectic pace at which he lived. He remarked in 1802: 'Surely in the summer recess [from Parliament] I ought to read Scripture an hour or two every day, besides prayer, devotional reading, and meditation. God will prosper me better if I wait on Him.'[10]

Discipline in prayer continued to be a feature marking evangelical life. Hannah More, who became well known for her innovative educational work, believed that the 'hour of prayer or meditation' at the beginning of the day would consecrate the day as a whole.[11] At King's College, Cambridge, Charles Simeon was known to rise at 4 a.m. and, after lighting his fire, he would devote the first four hours of the day to prayer and study.[12] Simeon was cautious about fasting, in case he was weakened by it, but he did devote specific days to prayer coupled with fasting. John Bird Sumner, the evangelical Bishop of Chester and then, from 1848, Archbishop of

Canterbury, also rose early, lit his own fire and began the day with prayer.[13] Books were written as prayer guides. Simeon wrote *Evangelical Meditations* and Hannah More wrote *Spirit of Prayer*. For some evangelicals, morning prayer was a joyful discipline. The diaries of Robert Murray McCheyne have frequent references to its spiritual benefit. Although he frequently felt a spiritual failure, McCheyne also spoke of rising and finding Christ, described as 'Him whom my soul loveth', of 'sweet seasons of communion', of prayer as his 'most fruitful employment', and of spending 'two hours alone with God' before a busy day.[14] Simeon, however, despite his best intentions, overslept on several occasions, especially on winter mornings. He once decided he would pay a fine of half a crown to his college servant when he overslept. A few days later, lying comfortably in bed, he re-considered this plan. His next decision was that when he overslept he would throw a guinea into the river. This, apparently, he did, but only once – before deciding that he could not afford to pave the river-bed with gold.[15]

Aspects of prayer

Although early morning prayer was a constant feature of evangelical spirituality until the second half of the twentieth century, in other respects there has been variety. Some evangelicals have criticised set prayers, and evangelicals have sometimes been viewed as anti-liturgical. Bishop Ryle asserted regarding private prayer: 'As to praying out of a book, it is a habit I cannot praise. If we can tell doctors the state of our bodies without a book, we ought to be able to tell the state of our souls to God. I have no objection to a man using crutches, when he is first recovering from a broken limb ... But if I saw him all his life on crutches, I should not think it a matter for congratulation.'[16] Given that Ryle used liturgy in public worship, why did he have such worries about set prayers? He explained in *Practical Religion*: 'I believe that there are tens of thousands *whose prayers are nothing but a mere form* – a set of words repeated by rote, without a thought about their meaning ... Many, even of those who use good forms, mutter their prayers over after they have got into bed, or scramble over them while they wash or dress in the morning'. Words said without heart, he argued, were not prayer.[17] Similarly, C.H. Spurgeon, although he produced a volume of morning and evening Bible readings, with brief comments and suitable hymns, refused to include set prayers. Explaining this, he wrote: 'I have been earnestly urged to add prayers, but my conscience will not allow me to do so, although it would greatly increase the sale of the work ... To some persons the use of forms of prayer appears to be lawful; but as I cannot coincide with that opinion, it would be the height of hypocrisy for me to compose prayers for the use of others.'[18]

Other evangelicals, however, encouraged aids to personal prayer. Handley Moule suggested taking the Lord's Prayer as the guide to the great elements of prayer and their natural order. This meant, he noted, that adoration, confession and petition are included. He also spoke about the great work, as he called it, of meditation. In the process of turning thoughts into prayers, said Moule, a person's soul 'shapes its thoughts into words addressed to its eternal Friend, and so the thought is both defined and hallowed in a wonderful way'.[19] Here we have the characteristic evangelical stress on personal relationship with Christ. P.T. Forsyth spoke of the need for 'serious, thinking, private prayer ... prayer with the historic sense, church-nurtured and Bible-fed'.[20] Spontaneity could, said Forsyth, be 'gruesome', as when a young man began his prayer (in Forsyth's hearing) with the words 'O God, we have come to have a chat with thee.' Prayer and theology, Forsyth argued, must interpenetrate to keep each other 'great, and wide, and mighty'.[21] For him prayer was 'an art to be learned', rather than something entirely natural. 'Associate much', Forsyth advised, 'with the great masters ... especially with the Bible; and chiefly with Christ. Cultivate His Holy Spirit. He is the grand master of God's art and mystery in communing with man.'[22] Samuel Chadwick, a powerful figure within the

Methodist holiness constituency, used Catholic devotional manuals and the Anglican Prayer Book, especially during Lent. He had a particular interest in the spirituality of the mystics and considered that 'such praying may need to be learned at the feet of instructors'.[23]

Evangelicals have encouraged meditation on Scripture, but have been less inclined to think of silent contemplation in prayer as a helpful exercise. However, George Whitefield, an inveterate activist, saw meditation as 'a kind of silent prayer, whereby the soul is frequently as it were carried out of itself to God'.[24] Silence during times of prayer was also commended by Handley Moule. Noting that this discipline had been used in all ages, and especially by the Quakers, Moule commented that it had 'come into recognition and use in a new degree latterly among ourselves, and from many sides testimony is given to its spiritual value'. He continued: 'To let the articulate activities of the mind, as much as may be, lie still, while the consciousness in a profound quiet simply recollects the Lord and hearkens before Him, not least when this is done in company together, is a method of devotion assuredly fitted to foster in the inner world both light and peace.'[25] Writing in the *Baptist Times* in 1935, F.C. Spurr, a Baptist evangelist and pastor, argued that although the word 'Retreat' had a 'Catholic' sound for many Baptists (and was therefore regarded with suspicion), the idea was in fact in line with the words of Christ, 'Come ye yourselves apart and rest awhile' (Mark 6:31). Spurr had experimented in the use of retreats, with groups of people going away for three or four days to spend time in silence, thought and prayer. He commended retreats as a way to obtain 'a new accession of spiritual power'.[26] In wider Christian traditions silent prayer and retreat are seen as components of a life of contemplation. Martyn Lloyd-Jones spoke emphatically about the importance of this aspect of prayer. 'Contemplation of God, adoration and worship are', he affirmed, 'the highest expression of our love to God.'[27]

A common emphasis in prayer as practised among

evangelicals has been on prayer for God's blessing, either on the person praying or on others – both friends and enemies. This kind of prayer may have as its focus particular needs. The hymn 'What a Friend we have in Jesus' expresses these sentiments well, sentiments that reflect the author's own struggles, in its third verse:

> Are we weak and heavy-laden,
> Cumbered with a load of care?
> Precious Saviour, still our refuge:
> Take it to the Lord in prayer.
> Do thy friends despise, forsake thee?
> Take it to the Lord in prayer;
> In His arms He'll take and shield thee,
> Thou wilt find a solace there.[28]

John Fletcher, Vicar of Madeley, Shropshire, who at one time John Wesley hoped would be his successor, made a habit of praying quietly for each person present when he was in a group, and it was noted that this produced 'life and energy' which enriched everyone.[29] C.H. Spurgeon, preaching on the prayer of Jabez for God's blessing (1 Chronicles 4:10), encouraged Sunday-school teachers, tract distributors, local preachers, 'whatever you may be, dear brother or sister, whatever your form of service', to pray this particular prayer.[30] Asking others to engage in prayer for one's personal needs has also been important for evangelicals. When Spurgeon was suffering from one of his periodic bouts of illness, he wrote: 'Perhaps if the church met for prayer, I should be speedily restored.' The prayer took place, and Spurgeon reported: 'As soon as the church had resolved to meet for special prayer for me, I began rapidly to recover.'[31] It is not that evangelicals have generally considered such prayer to have the power to alter God's sovereign purposes. Rather, God has usually been seen as having chosen to work through prayer. As F.B. Meyer rather dramatically put it: 'Believing prayer supplies the Almighty with the fulcrum on which He rests the lever of His omnipotence.'[32]

Praying together

Individual prayer has always been closely linked, in evangelical spirituality, with believers praying together. In the early evangelical movement family prayers were encouraged. According to G.W.E. Russell, a journalist and politician who wrote a history of the evangelical movement, the use of *Family Prayers*, a book compiled by Henry Thornton, was a distinctive sign of nineteenth-century evangelicalism. Thornton was a banker, an MP, and a member of the campaigning group of evangelicals in Clapham (sometimes known as the Clapham Sect) of which William Wilberforce became the best-known member.[33] Russell recalled that in his own family there were daily family prayers and that his father read prayers from books by Thornton, by Wilberforce, or by Ashton Oxenden, Bishop of Montreal.[34] Another widely-used book, also entitled *Family Prayers*, was by Edward Bickersteth, a prime mover in the formation of the Evangelical Alliance in 1846. His book of prayers, published in 1842, contained a complete course for eight weeks, and also forms of prayers for special occasions like moving house or choosing a school, and for saints' days.[35] In 1862 Joseph Wigram, the evangelical Bishop of Rochester, wrote *The Cottager's Family Prayers*, based on biblical themes. He spoke about all the members of households kneeling together, and suggested that 'one of them should read a proper form of prayer, and all the others follow him'. They should repeat the Lord's Prayer and close with the blessing.[36] Guided family devotion was a common experience in evangelical homes in that period.

Communal prayer outside the home has also been at the heart of evangelical spirituality. John Wesley's *Journal* for 1 January 1739 records that he was with about sixty friends, including his brother Charles, George Whitefield and other prominent leaders in the Methodist Awakening, for a 'love feast' in Fetter Lane, London, and that they experienced God's power in their communal prayer. He wrote:

About three in the morning, as we were continuing instant in prayer, the Power of God came mightily upon us, insomuch that many cried out for exceeding joy, and many fell to the ground. As soon as we were recovered a little from that awe and amazement at the presence of his Majesty, we broke out with one voice, 'We praise thee, O God; we acknowledge thee to be the Lord.'[37]

Although such powerful events have probably not been common, regular prayer meetings have marked evangelical congregations from the eighteenth century onwards. John Newton described prayer meetings as 'the most profitable exercises (excepting public preaching) in which Christians can engage'. He believed that they tended to 'kill a worldly, trifling spirit, to draw down a divine blessing upon all our concerns, compose differences, and enkindle (or at least to maintain) the flame of divine love amongst brethren'.[38]

Often those who meet to pray have an expectation that God will answer their requests in specific ways. Thus C.H. Spurgeon said to his congregation on one occasion in 1866: 'Dear friends, we are a huge church, and should be doing more for the Lord in this great city. I want us, tonight, to ask him to send us *some new work*; and if we need money to carry it on, let us pray that *the means may also be sent*.' Spurgeon asked a number of people to come up on the platform to pray about this matter, and during the prayer it seemed that Spurgeon 'knew that the answer had come'. A few days later Mrs Anne Hillyard, a widow, wrote to Spurgeon offering him the enormous sum of £20,000 to found an orphanage. Mrs Hillyard was not a member of Spurgeon's congregation and indeed at that point was an Anglican. Thirty years later, one of those who had prayed on the platform that evening, and who was then a student at Spurgeon's Pastors' College, commented: 'Surely the Orphanage was born of prayer.'[39] Nineteenth-century Brethren figures, notably George Muller and J. Hudson Taylor, emphasised 'prayer and faith' as the means by which their work was sustained. Muller's orphanage in Bristol and Hudson Taylor's China Inland Mission promoted the practice of praying for their needs, but not advertising them. This became known as the principle of 'living by faith', and commitment to this principle underlay the 'faith missions', which were to see enormous growth. The key was a relationship with God in prayer.[40]

United prayer by evangelicals ranged well beyond the local church or even a particular mission group. In 1748 Jonathan Edwards published a call to prayer with the remarkable title *An Humble Attempt to Promote an Explicit Agreement and Visible Union of God's people through the world, in Extraordinary Prayer, for the Revival of Religion, and the Advancement of Christ's Kingdom on Earth, pursuant to Scripture Promises and Prophecies concerning the Last Time.* This call, which had echoes of the continuous prayer being practised by the Moravian community in Herrnhut – a practice which was seen as crucial to effective world mission – was taken up in Britain. A number of ministers in Scotland sent over to America an account of a 'concert for prayer', as they termed it, which they hoped would find acceptance among 'Christian brethren everywhere', and in 1784 a Prayer Call was issued to the Northamptonshire Baptist Association by John Sutcliffe, in Olney, who had recently read Edwards' *Humble Attempt*. The 'call' was for prayer on the first Monday evening of each month. There was a focus on prayer for the spread of the gospel 'to the distant parts of the habitable globe', and it is significant that William Carey, who was to pioneer Baptist mission overseas, was a member of Sutcliffe's congregation. In 1789 Sutcliffe reprinted the *Humble Attempt*. He set out his own vision of 'thousands upon thousands' of people, of different denominations, 'divided into small bands in their respective cities, towns, villages and neighbourhood ... offering up their united prayers'.[41] What united these groups was their experience of Christ.

The place of hymn-singing

Evangelicals were united, too, by the hymns that they sang. These vividly expressed the heart of evangelical spirituality. An outstanding example is Charles Wesley's 'And can it be?', with its expression of heart-felt praise and wonder at what Christ has done:

> 'Tis mystery all! Th' Immortal dies:
> Who can explore His strange design?
> In vain the first-born seraph tries,
> To sound the depths of love divine.
> 'Tis mercy all! Let earth adore!
> Let angel minds inquire no more.

This is followed by a typical evangelical expression of assurance:

> No condemnation now I dread;
> Jesus, and all in Him, is mine!
> Alive in Him, my living Head,
> And clothed in righteousness divine,
> Bold I approach the eternal throne,
> And claim the crown, through Christ my own.

Charles Wesley is estimated to have written over 8,000 hymns – on average more than one each week. In introducing the *Collection of Hymns for the Use of the People of God Called Methodists* (1780), John Wesley spoke of the book as expressing 'experimental and practical divinity'. John Wesley, who liked bold songs of assurance, encouraged his brother in his work (although he once described some of his brother's hymns as 'namby-pambical'), and in fact it was through the hymns written by Charles, marked as they were by vibrant theology and splendid poetry, as much as through Methodist preaching, that the evangelical message spread. The hymns were also a means of prayer. A section of the *Collection of Hymns* was devoted to intercession for the world, with God described several times as the 'universal Friend'.[42]

Evangelical hymn-writers multiplied in all denominations. John Newton and the poet William Cowper, at Olney, the Baptist minister, John Rippon, with his own 'Collection', and women hymn-writers such as Ann Steele, another Baptist, all contributed to an expanding hymn-singing culture among evangelicals in the later eighteenth and early nineteenth centuries.[43] William Cowper suffered with deep depression and some of his hymns tended to reflect his personal struggles. John Newton, however, was in the mainstream of assured evangelical spirituality. He echoed Augustus Toplady's theme, in his famous hymn 'Rock of Ages', with his 'Glorious things of Thee are spoken':

> On the Rock of Ages founded,
> What can shake Thy sure repose?
> With salvation's walls surrounded,
> Thou may'st smile at all Thy foes.

Building on the many hymns of the Evangelical Revival, the nineteenth century saw a further flowering of evangelical hymnody. Edward Bickersteth produced *Christian Psalmody* in 1833, and his son, Edward Henry Bickersteth, edited a replacement entitled *Hymn Companion to the Book of Common Prayer*. In the later nineteenth century this was the most used hymnbook in evangelical Anglican parishes in England. *Hymns Ancient and Modern* was the book that appealed to High Church parishes.[44] New kinds of hymns emerged. As Ian Bradley traces in *Abide with Me*, gospel hymns such as those by the American Fanny Crosby, 'Blessed assurance' and 'To God be the glory', became hugely popular on both sides of the Atlantic.[45] Crosby, who was blind, anticipated that in heaven she would see 'the face of the One who died for me'. Her enormous output of hymns, over 8,000, conveyed the classic evangelical themes in new ways. One of her most famous hymns had an assured relationship with Jesus at its heart:

> Blessed assurance, Jesus is mine!
> Oh, what a foretaste of glory divine!

Heir of salvation, purchase of God.
Born of His Spirit, washed in His blood.
refrain:
This is my story, this is my song,
Praising my Saviour all the day long.

At the Keswick Convention meetings, held from 1875, the hymns of a British hymn-writer, Frances Ridley Havergal, the daughter of a Church of England clergyman, such as 'Take my life and let it be, consecrated Lord to Thee', were of crucial significance.[46] D.L. Moody and his co-evangelist/singer, Ira D. Sankey, introduced many new hymns, in a style that resembled music hall ballads. These were collected together as *Sankey's Sacred Songs and Solos* and were used widely in evangelical churches until at least the 1960s. Despite the changes in style, the use of hymns remained central to the corporate spirituality of many evangelicals.

Developments in prayer and worship

Significant developments took place over the course of the twentieth century within evangelicalism which affected thinking about prayer and praise. In the first half of the century the fact that evangelical life in Western countries such as Britain was not buoyant meant that there was a survival mentality in which rules about precisely how to survive were more readily accepted. These rules included methods of prayer, specifically details about the conduct of a daily quiet time. However, the growth of evangelicalism in the post-war years, coupled with moves in the wider culture towards freer ways of living, meant that from the 1960s the daily quiet time was less and less a form of devotion carried out according to hard and fast rules. In 1972 John Stott commented:

It [the quiet time] has certainly stood the test of time and brought untold benefit to many generations of Christians. I myself am old-fashioned enough to retain confidence in it as an extremely valuable discipline. But it is still only

a tradition; it has not been laid down in Scripture ... Nor
was such a practice possible before the invention of print-
ing and the availability of cheap Bibles for all.[47]

A major contribution to changing evangelical approaches to
prayer was made by Richard Foster. In 1978 he published
Celebration of Discipline, a volume which introduced many
evangelicals to a wide range of spiritual exercises from different Christian traditions. In Britain this book was commended
by the best-known leader of the time within the charismatic
renewal movement, David Watson, and it was partly through
the influence of renewal that evangelicals embraced what
were for them new possibilities in prayer.[48]

Major changes have taken place in recent decades in the
area of communal prayer. Family prayers have declined in
importance with the advent of more individualistic ways of
living within many families in the Western world. There have
also been changes in attitudes to church prayer meetings in
evangelical congregations. At the beginning of the twentieth
century R.A. Torrey could say: 'The prayer meeting is the most
important meeting in the church. If your church has no prayer
meeting, use your influence to have one.'[49] But since the 1960s
many evangelical churches have replaced the mid-week
church prayer meeting with home groups. David Gillett
suggests that these small groups, which have emphasised
mutual sharing and prayer, have lost something of the earlier
evangelical vision for intercessory prayer.[50] There have, however, been those evangelicals who have continued to give
attention to corporate intercession, especially for revival. In
the earlier twentieth century the Pentecostal League of
Prayer, founded by a barrister, Richard Reader Harris, set up
groups that prayed for revival,[51] and a focus on revival was an
enduring element in evangelical spirituality in the whole of
the century. The Evangelical Alliance has had its world-wide
Weeks of Prayer, held during the first week of each new year,
and these helped to inspire the denominations to pray for
'Christian unity'. As another example of united prayer, in

1987 a number of evangelicals in Britain launched the idea of prayer walks, under the title 'March for Jesus'.[52]

In the area of communal worship the twentieth century saw a continued interest in the balance between liturgy and spontaneity in congregational prayer and praise. Horton Davies, in *Worship and Theology in England*, delineates what he calls the 'School of Spontaneity' in the Free Churches in the early twentieth century, a school which took the view that 'to retain a liturgy is to remain in the adolescent stage of the spiritual life'.[53] F.B. Meyer, a Baptist, is seen by Davies as one of the 'rebels' against this 'school of spontaneity'; Meyer incorporated in public worship both liturgical forms and free expressions of praise.[54] A similar approach to that of Meyer was taken by P.T. Forsyth. In his *Soul of Prayer*, in 1916, he wrote: 'Public prayer, therefore, should be in the main liturgical, with room for free prayer.' He argued for the use of 'those great forms which arose out of the deep soul of the Church before it spread into sectional boughs or individual twigs'.[55] In the mid twentieth century a leading Christian and Missionary Alliance figure, A.W. Tozer, who had a powerful ministry in the city of Chicago, and then became even more famous as a pastor in Toronto, Canada, trenchantly attacked what he called 'hillbilly' styles of worship. He had a widespread impact in the English-speaking world through his call for authentic worship, 'the missing crown jewel in evangelical Christianity', to be properly restored.[56]

Finally, prayer and worship were affected in the twentieth century by the rise of Pentecostalism and of the charismatic movement. An early Pentecostal emphasis was on praying in tongues. There has also been a stress on exuberant praise. Donald Gee, the first British Pentecostal to write about the history of the movement, compared the joyless 'bondage of custom' found in traditional denominations with Pentecostal 'glory' in worship. Others spoke of the movement's remarkable note of praise.[57] This emphasis was taken up from the 1960s in the charismatic renewal movement within the major denominations. Graham Kendrick became the most influential writer of new material for worship, with such fine hymns as 'The Servant King', and hymns by Kendrick and other new writers were spread in Britain through events such as Spring Harvest.[58] It is sometimes thought that the concerns expressed within the liturgical renewal and also by people like Tozer for a reformation in worship were at odds with the calls for freedom heard within the charismatic movement. Yet there were shared interests and on occasions parallel developments. In 1960 Dennis Bennett, an Episcopalian clergyman in the liturgical tradition, announced to his parish in Van Nuys, California, that he had spoken in tongues.[59] In the same year two English Baptists, Ernest Payne and Stephen Winward, published a liturgical guide, *Orders and Prayers*, and under the heading 'Pentecostal Worship' they spoke about the Spirit endowing believers with 'gifts' to enable them to 'participate in the worship of the assembly'.[60] Over recent decades evangelicals from different backgrounds have sought to express what Robert Webber has called an 'Ancient-Future Faith'.[61]

Conclusion

The evangelical tradition has taken prayer with great seriousness. Personal prayer has been strongly emphasised, but to a greater extent than has usually been the case in other Christian traditions the members of local congregations have been encouraged to participate together in prayer meetings. This has been seen not primarily as an exercise in liturgical prayer, although there have been evangelicals who have valued liturgy, but as something more spontaneous. Prayer meetings have been a means of encountering God and an opportunity to pray for his kingdom to be extended. Robert Murray McCheyne gave a classic exhortation in 1840 about prayer meetings:

> Meet weekly, at a convenient hour. Be regular in attendance. Let nothing keep you away from your meet-

ing. Pray in secret before going. Let your prayers in the meeting be formed as much as possible on what you have read in the Bible ... Pray that you may pray to God, and not for the ears of man. Feel his presence more than man's. Pray for the outpouring of the Spirit on the Church of Christ and for the world ... Pray for the conversion of your friends, of your neighbours, of the whole town. Pray for the sending of the gospel to the Jews, and to the Gentile nations.[62]

All the ingredients of the prayer life within the evangelical tradition are here: discipline, private prayer, study of Scripture, an experience of God, a desire for the Church to be revived, and a concern for others to be converted. A century later much of this was still in place, but since then evangelical approaches to prayer have become more varied. Evangelicals still pray, however, for the 'outpouring of the Spirit on the Church of Christ and for the world'.

6. 'O LAMB OF GOD, I COME': EVANGELICALS AND THE CROSS

In evangelical thinking, the life of the Christian following conversion is to be a life of fellowship with Christ shaped by the Word and the sacraments and by prayer and praise. Living in the light of the cross of Christ has also been seen as a crucial element in evangelical spirituality. The response to the cross was expressed by many evangelicals in the words written by Isaac Watts, 'When I survey the wondrous cross'. David Gillett, noting that this is perhaps the most famous and well-loved of all hymns about the cross, highlights its 'combination of meditation on the story of the crucifixion with a powerful response from the worshipper'.[1]

> When I survey the wondrous cross
> On which the Prince of glory died,
> My richest gain I count but loss,
> And pour contempt on all my pride.

The commitment required in the spiritual life has been seen by evangelicals as costly – what was gain is counted as loss. Yet this is not a legalistic obedience. It stems from devotion. In 1831, Charles Simeon, then aged seventy-one, had been at Holy Trinity Church, Cambridge, for forty-nine years. He was asked how he had surmounted the persecutions of the early years of his ministry and his reply took him to the suffering of Christ on the cross. Simeon commented that 'we must not mind a little suffering for Christ's sake ... Let us rejoice in the remembrance that our holy Head has surmounted all His suffering and triumphed over death. Let us follow Him patiently; we shall soon be partakers of His victory.'[2] In the twentieth-century persecution of evangelical Christians world-wide intensified, for example under Communist regimes in Eastern Europe and China. The spirituality of the cross expressed by Simeon has remained relevant.

The theology of the cross

The doctrine of Christ's death on the cross as a substitution for sin has been central to evangelical spirituality, although different understandings have been offered regarding some of the details of the doctrine. David Gillett, writing about this aspect, comments that nothing 'is as vital to evangelicals as the objective truth of the cross and a person's conscious acceptance of all that it offers as God's gracious provision of forgiveness, reconciliation, and eternal life'. He continues:

> An exposition of substitutionary atonement allows the whole mystery of the cross to be communicated in a manageable compass: the hearer is given a step-by-step explanation of the relationship between the eternal God, the historical event at Calvary, and his or her present spiritual state. The need for response can be clearly shown and the way opened for the individual to enter here and now into the benefits of what Christ did two thousand years ago.[3]

These benefits have to do not only with entering into an initial relationship with God, but also with the outworking of that relationship in a life of obedience. John Wesley spoke of what Christ did on the cross 'for us', but also what God does 'in us', as Christians experience the life of Christ by the Holy Spirit.[4] Here is the note of personal fellowship.

Wesley himself took the view that the redemption of Christ on the cross was for all humankind. This was in contrast to the theological position of some of the other streams of Protestantism. Puritans such as John Owen argued that the death of Christ was for the elect, not for the whole world.[5] John Wesley, preaching in 1740 in Bristol, on the theme of

'Free Grace', referred to the text in Romans (10:12) concerning the Lord being 'rich in mercy to all that call upon him'. Wesley addressed the objection: 'But you say, "No; he is such only to those for whom Christ died. And those are not all, but only a few, whom God hath chosen out of the world; for he died not for all".' In response, Wesley quoted a number of biblical texts speaking of Christ taking away the sins of the world and being the saviour of all.[6] George Whitefield, from the Calvinistic standpoint, replied to Wesley's sermon in a letter in which he looked forward to the time when he and Wesley would be 'closely united in principle and judgment as well as heart and affection'. In similar vein, Wesley hoped that in the future 'God will do what man cannot, namely, make us both of one mind. Then persecution will flame out, and it will be seen whether we count our lives dear unto ourselves, so that we may finish our course with joy.'[7] The significant note struck was the unity in 'heart and affection' of those who had known the power of the cross in their personal experience, despite theological differences over the extent of the atonement.

The view of the cross as redemptive and also as that which shapes Christian living has continued to be central to evangelical theology. Spurgeon, who was deeply concerned that the passion of Christ should be seen as substitutionary, none the less emphasised that in the cross there was an encounter with Jesus himself, not simply a reliance on what he had done. 'As for me', said Spurgeon in 1886, 'God forbid that I should glory save in the cross of our Lord Jesus Christ, since to me that cross is identical with Jesus himself. I know no Jesus but he who died the just for the unjust.'[8] In another sermon preached two months later he spoke about the 'great mystery' of the cross.[9] For Handley Moule the cross was the means of redemption, to be received by faith, but was also a place of surrender. 'Faith', he wrote, 'meets and embraces its twin sister, the soul's Surrender'. This he perceived as issuing in holy living.[10] Among the evangelical theologians who expounded the theology of the cross in the early twentieth century were James Denny, in *The Death of Christ* (1902), and P.T. Forsyth, in his powerful volumes on the person and work of Christ. In a chapter in *The Work of Christ*, entitled 'The Great Confessional', Forsyth dealt with spiritual experience lived out in the light of the cross:

> It is not enough to have in the Cross a great demonstration of God's love, a forgiveness of the past which leaves us to fend for ourselves in the future. Is my moral power so great after all, then, that, supposing I believe past things were settled in Christ's Cross, I may now feel I can run in my own strength? ... Nay, we must depend daily upon the continued energy of the crucified and risen One. We must depend daily upon the action of that same Christ whose action culminated there but did not end there. His death is as organic with His heavenly life as it was with His earthly ... It is by His work from heaven that we appropriate His work upon earth. He guarantees our perfection as well as our redemption.[11]

For Forsyth, Christian spirituality was the continual out-working of redemption. The Christian life was one of dependence on what Christ did on the cross. 'The essence of Christianity is not just to be spiritual', Forsyth averred, 'it is to answer God's manner of spirituality which you find in Jesus Christ and Him crucified.'[12]

Within the Keswick movement, F.B. Meyer explored the cross in a way that linked the theological issues with experience. In the 1890s Meyer wrote in standard evangelical terms of the need to 'satisfy the claims of a broken law' through the cross. Jesus was substitute and representative, delivering people from the penalty and power of sin.[13] Meyer never deviated from his belief in the substitutionary atonement of Christ, arguing that to make the atonement merely an example of self-sacrifice was to remove 'the peace-giving conception of God in Christ bearing the curse and shame',[14] but he saw increasingly the death of Christ as being 'a tidal wave out of the heart of God', rather than something which 'pacified and mollified the Father's anger'.[15] Writing in *The Baptist*

Times, he explicitly repudiated the thought of Jesus 'averting the vindictive wrath of God', and he argued that God's love, in Jesus, 'assumed to itself, in some mysterious manner, the guilt and demerit of a world's sin'.[16] Meditating in 1928, almost at the end of his life, on the subject of the Trinity, Meyer reflected that in his early years the cross was presented as though God needed to be propitiated before he could 'open the sluice gates of his love'. In fact, Meyer stated, the self-giving of Jesus was an act of God, and without this Christological perspective he believed the atonement was obscured.[17] Ultimately, for Meyer, the cross was 'not simply a dogma or doctrine, but an experience'.[18] A theory of the atonement or a rational basis for it was not necessary, so long – as Meyer put it in 1909 – as the fact was 'consistent with universal experience, and with my own'.[19]

The cross and evangelical devotion

Despite the differences between the strands of the eighteenth-century evangelical revival over Calvinistic doctrine (which Charles Wesley referred to in one hymn as 'hellish doctrine'), the best-known hymns from both Calvinists and Arminians articulated the same evangelical sentiments regarding the cross. In 1776 a hymn appeared which became one of the most popular among evangelicals on both sides of the Atlantic. It was written by Augustus Toplady, who was a virulent anti-Arminian:

> Rock of Ages, cleft for me,
> Let me hide myself in Thee!
> Let the Water and the Blood,
> From Thy riven Side which flow'd,
> Be of Sin the double Cure,
> Cleanse me from its Guilt and Pow'r.[20]

There is little or no difference between the experience of cleansing articulated by Toplady and that described by Charles Wesley in his hymn 'O for a thousand tongues to sing', which was the first hymn in the later Wesley hymnbooks and was intended 'for the anniversary day of one's conversion'. After the initial verses expressing general praise and prayer, there is a focus on Christ's redemption:[21]

> O for a thousand tongues to sing
> My great Redeemer's praise,
> The glories of my God and King,
> The triumphs of his grace!
>
> He breaks the power of cancelled sin,
> He sets the prisoner free;
> His blood can make the foulest clean;
> His blood availed for me.

None the less, there were tensions in the early evangelical movement over the cross as a focus of devotion. The Moravians were distinctive for the stress they placed on the way in which the cross of Christ not only achieved forgiveness but also had a powerful ongoing impact on spiritual experience. An emphasis on the wounds of Christ produced intense devotion among Moravian believers.[22] In 1734, as Count Zinzendorf was burning a pile of papers he saw one flutter to the ground, and when he picked it up he read these words: 'Oh, let us in Thy nail-prints see, Our pardon and election free.' He regarded this as a direct message from God, and began to focus on the suffering Christ on the cross and in particular on the title 'Lamb of God'. This became the famous 'Blood and Wounds Theology' of the Moravians. One of John Wesley's leading associates, John Cennick, became a Moravian. Cennick was attracted by the power of the 'Blood and Wounds Theology', and when he read a 'Litany of the Wounds' composed by Zinzendorf he shed tears of joy. Over time, however, rather than concentrating on the moral and spiritual value of the cross, increased attention began to be paid by the Moravians to the physical details of crucifixion. By 1743 Zinzendorf was stating: 'We will look for nothing else in the Bible but the Lamb and His Wounds.' This intense form of spirituality did not impress John Wesley.[23]

The emphasis on the cross in devotion was, however, to continue to be a feature of evangelicalism in the nineteenth
century. The explicit Moravian influence on wider evangelical
spirituality has not been pronounced, but the focus on the
blood of Christ and the Christian's ongoing response to
Christ's self-giving has been a notable theme. William
Cowper's hymn 'Praise for the Fountain Opened' has been, as
James Gordon notes, both loved and hated. Its reference to a
'fountain filled with blood', in which sinners are plunged,
seems to many people to be tasteless.[24] However, to others it
evokes the picture of a stream of healing love, particularly
through the following verse:

> E'er since by faith I saw the stream,
> Thy flowing wounds supply,
> Redeeming love has been my theme,
> And shall be till I die.

For Cowper himself, whose struggles with depression continued to the end of his life, there was comfort to be found in
the 'redeeming love' of the cross. It was this love which elicited
a response from the believer. John Newton, who produced
with Cowper the 'Olney Hymns', wrote about this experience,
with specific reference to Christ: 'We are His by tie and right;
He made us, He redeemed us, He reclaimed us and we are His
by our own voluntary surrender of ourselves.'[25] Fellowship
with Christ was deeply personal.

Victory in the cross

The work of Christ on the cross as a victory over the powers
of evil has also been a theme in evangelical spirituality. The
Christ who died was victorious, and rose from death.
Spurgeon put it in this way:

> The cross was a battlefield to him, wherein he triumphed
> gloriously. He was fighting with darkness: with the
> powers of darkness of which Satan is the head; with the

darkness of human ignorance, depravity, and falsehood ... He bore their onset, endured the tremendous shock of their assault, and in the end, with a shout of victory, he led captivity captive.[26]

The way in which this was worked out in evangelical spirituality was through taking up the cross, as disciples of Christ, and through spiritual conflict. Those who respond to the crucified Christ find themselves in a spiritual battle in which the way of victory is through what Christ has done. J.C. Ryle wrote that if the Christian believer had the nature of an angel, then warfare would not be so essential. 'But with a corrupt heart, a busy devil and an ensnaring world, he must either "fight" or be lost.'[27] One area in which the corruption of the heart was seen was in sexual sin. F.B. Meyer wrote a widely used booklet, *A Holy Temple* (1901). In this book, which he said was 'For Men Only', he argued that sexual continence produced 'vivacity, muscular strength, manliness and daring'. Meyer discerned a spiritual link between moral and physical fitness and commended sport, exercise and a hard bed.[28] There were also the temptations of the 'world'. Hannah More was a member of a select group of literary women in London, and among her friends were Samuel Johnson, Sir Joshua Reynolds, the portrait painter, and David Garrick, the actor, who produced Hannah More's plays at the Drury Lane theatre. But More's evangelical faith led her to be suspicious of 'the agitation of the world', although even in her times of withdrawal from worldly affairs she did not achieve the spiritual improvement she craved.[29] Victory was not easy.

Behind the temptations of the 'flesh' and the 'world' was the activity of the devil. Jonathan Edwards argued in *The Distinguishing Marks of a Work of the Spirit of God* that 'many delusions of Satan' could appear at the same time as 'a great religious concern prevails'. His perspective was that even in 'real saints' it was the case that 'the kingdom of God and the kingdom of the Devil remain for a while together in the same heart'.[30] Whereas Edwards saw the activity of the devil as being 'for a while', some later evangelicals gave warfare against Satan a more central place. In 1912 Jessie Penn-Lewis, who was for a time a prominent Keswick figure, co-wrote with Evan Roberts *War on the Saints*, on the subject of deliverance, through the cross of Christ, from 'deceiving spirits among the children of God'.[31] As the twentieth century progressed, there was increasing emphasis on 'spiritual warfare' in prayer. Rees Howells, who set up the Bible College of Wales in 1924, emphasised prayer for international affairs. The College community gave itself to intercession throughout the Second World War. There was a call 'to fight the battles of the Kingdom, as really as if called to fight on the Western Front'.[32] With the rise of the charismatic movement came a concern to see people 'delivered' who were believed to be under demonic oppression. In 1981 David Watson, by then the best-known Anglican charismatic leader in Britain, in his widely read *Discipleship*, referred to Edwards and Penn-Lewis, and outlined a range of ways in which he believed Satan was at work and in which there could be victory through, significantly, 'the power of the cross'.[33]

In the light of the perceived world of spiritual warfare, there have been many exhortations to evangelicals to be courageous disciples. The evangelical story has included many examples of suffering for the sake of Christ. C.H. Spurgeon, preaching in 1875 on the theme of obedience to the call of God, quoted one of the simplest of evangelical choruses, drawn from the Old Testament example of Daniel:

> Dare to be a Daniel,
> Dare to stand alone;
> Dare to have a purpose true,
> Dare to make it known.[34]

This did not mean that the way to victory was simply by being splendidly bold in following Christ. For Spurgeon, God's people were not simply activists; they were, as he put it in one sermon, 'a thoughtful people', who should do 'a great deal of remembering and considering'. This idea was closely aligned to Spurgeon's constant stress on the importance of believers remembering what Christ had done on the cross, supremely through their participation in the Lord's Supper. In a typical affirmation of Puritan spirituality, Spurgeon continued: 'Our noble forefathers of the Puritanic sort were ... independent and self-contained men, who could hold their own in the day of conflict; and the reason was because they took time to meditate, time to keep a diary of their daily experiences, time to commune with God in secret.'[35]

While the stress on spiritual struggle has been important, the influence of Keswick teaching on evangelical spirituality meant that increasingly the victory of the cross was connected not with human effort, even divinely aided effort, but with full surrender to Christ. The sentiment was expressed in the verses of the hymn 'Trust and Obey', published in 1887 by an American Presbyterian minister, John Sammis, who heard about a testimony – 'I am going to trust, and I am going to obey' – given by a young man during one of D.L. Moody's meetings.[36] Handley Moule, in his *Thoughts on Christian Sanctity*, insisted that Christ must be the focus of Christian living. He quoted the maxim of the Puritan Richard Baxter that a Christian should take ten looks at Christ for one at self.[37] Following Christ was linked by Moule to a personal relationship with Christ as Friend. For Moule, friendship with Christ had a central place. He suggested that the more that someone discovered this friendship, the deeper would be their spiritual commitment. The more that I see myself, said Moule, as 'my Master's friend', then 'the more I own myself, first and always, His property and His slave'. He quoted the following lines by John Newton about the love of Christ expressed in his self-giving on the cross, and also about assurance of the friendship of Christ:

> One there is, above all others,
> Well deserves the name of friend;
> His is love beyond a brother's,
> Costly, free, and knows no end:

They who once His kindness prove
Find it everlasting love.[38]

Receiving and giving 'Calvary love'

A classic description of receiving the love of God in Christ is
found in the hymn 'Just as I am', written in 1835 by Charlotte
Elliott and reckoned to be one of the finest hymns in the
English language.[39] The sentiments were drawn from the
words of a Swiss evangelist and hymn-writer, Cesar Malan,
who had been instrumental in Elliott's evangelical conversion.
Although this hymn has often been used in evangelistic
settings, for example by Billy Graham, Elliott wrote it when
she was – as a Christian – suffering from depression and
doubt. Her motto was the text: 'If any man will come after me,
let him deny himself, take up his cross daily, and follow me'
(Mark 8:34). She decided to write a hymn which focused not
on the contribution of human effort to spirituality, but on
divine acceptance through the cross. These are the first two
verses:

Just as I am, without one plea,
But that Thy blood was shed for me,
And that Thou bid'st me come to Thee,
O Lamb of God, I come, I come.

Just as I am, and waiting not
To rid my soul of one dark blot,
To Thee whose blood can cleanse each spot,
O Lamb of God, I come, I come.[40]

This view of how a believer relates to the crucified Christ is
rather individualistic, but there has also been an awareness
by evangelicals that the life of Christian discipleship is lived
out in community. Amy Wilson Carmichael, who was the first
missionary to go out from Keswick with funding channelled
through the Keswick Mission Committee, became famous
within world-wide evangelicalism through her Donahvur

Fellowship in India and through such devotional classics as
His Thoughts Said ... His Father Said and *If*.[41] She went to
Donahvur in 1895 and for over half a century thereafter the
Donhavur community cared for homeless children, especially
those who had been child prostitutes. Amy Carmichael wrote
nearly forty books and had an enormous influence on evangelical spirituality. In *If*, written in 1938, she wrote powerfully
about what she called 'Calvary Love'. Here are examples of
her sixty-four sayings:

> If I belittle those whom I am called to serve, talk of their
> weak points in contrast perhaps with what I think of as
> my strong points; if I adopt a superior attitude, forgetting
> 'Who made thee to differ? And what hast thou that thou
> hast not received?' then I know nothing of Calvary love.

> If I cannot in honest happiness take the second place (or
> the twentieth); if I cannot take the first without making a
> fuss about my unworthiness, then I know nothing of
> Calvary love.

> If the praise of others elates me and their blame
> depresses me; if I cannot rest under misunderstanding
> without defending myself; if I love to be loved more than
> to love, to be served more than to serve, then I know
> nothing of Calvary love.[42]

The remedy for the lack of 'Calvary love' in the life of an evangelical believer was always to come back to the cross of Christ
('Just as I am') to receive forgiveness for sin and new spiritual
power.

David Gillett places such evangelical devotion to Jesus as
the Lamb of God, together with the daily awareness of sin and
forgiveness, alongside Roman Catholic devotion to the Sacred
Heart of Jesus.[43] Certainly there has been a willingness on the
part of some evangelicals to draw from Catholic devotion. In a
talk to an Evangelical Alliance audience in 1901, F.B. Meyer
acknowledged his indebtedness to 'saintly mystics'.[44] These

included Francis of Assisi, Brother Lawrence and Madame
Guyon.[45] Meyer's description of the cross as 'fresh today', with
the nails 'not rusted or blunted', has overtones of mystical
meditation on Christ's sufferings, and he could deduce from
the mystery of the indwelling Christ that every Christian was
a mystic.[46] In the same period Alexander Whyte, minister of
Free St George's, Edinburgh, in his book *Thirteen Appre-
ciations*, commended Jakob Boehme, a German Lutheran
theologian of the seventeenth century who was known for his
mystical writings, and Lancelot Andrewes, the high Anglican
bishop. Whyte commended and had correspondence with John
Henry Newman, and also corresponded with Father John, a
Russian Orthodox spiritual director.[47] Writing later in the
twentieth century, A.W. Tozer's list of thirty-five recommended
books, for those who (as he put it) would know 'the deep things
of God', included medieval and sixteenth-century Catholic
mystics such as Julian of Norwich, Meister Eckhart and John
of the Cross. A minority of the books recommended by Tozer
were by Protestant authors.[48] Evangelicals were prepared to
mine the wealth of wider devotional writing, especially in
thinking about the relationship of the believer to the crucified
Christ.

The emergence in the early twentieth century of broader
forms of evangelicalism, expressed within Anglicanism by the
Anglican Evangelical Group Movement (AEGM) and within
Methodism by the Fellowship of the Kingdom, meant that
there was a fresh evaluation of traditional evangelical thinking about a number of questions, including the atonement.
The spirituality of the AEGM was expressed in the Cromer
Convention, which began in 1928 as an alternative to
Keswick.[49] The message of the cross of Christ was an evangelical distinctive that was defended by those on the liberally
inclined wing of evangelicalism at a time when there was a
considerable stress within the High Church tradition on the
incarnation. Writing in 1918, Vernon Storr, a Canon of
Westminster Abbey and the AEGM's creative leader,
suggested that 'the Atonement coupled with the doctrine of

the Spirit, whose work it is to make the death of Christ effective in our lives, is the most real and blessed of truths'.[50] Yet Storr rejected Anselm's concept of 'satisfaction' as a mechanical theory, saw the substitutionary model of the atonement as inadequate, and was unconvinced by the idea of Christ as representative. For Storr, the moral influence theory of the atonement alone had the support of Christian experience.[51] His view, reflecting the tendency in English theology in the 1920s to question the traditional doctrine of divine impassibility, was that it was the suffering love of God expressed in the pain of the cross that drew human response.[52]

The cross and the life of obedience

For evangelicals, therefore, the cross of Christ is both the way by which salvation is received and the means through which the life of obedient discipleship is sustained. It is also the pattern for the Christian life. Charles Simeon once reflected on his own name 'Simeon', which is the same as Simon, the one who was compelled to bear the cross for Jesus. For him this connection was one that had spiritual significance. Charles Simeon commented in a way that illuminates the evangelical understanding of taking up the cross:

> What a word of instruction was here – what a blessed hint of encouragement! To have the Cross laid upon me, that I might bear it after Jesus – what a privilege! it was enough. Now I could leap and sing for joy as one whom Jesus was honouring with a participation in his sufferings.[53]

Later in the century, in his thinking about the demands of Christian discipleship, Handley Moule commended disciplines often associated with Roman Catholic spirituality, such as fasting and confession. 'I shall not be suspected of any lack of loyalty to my most dear Mother Church, Catholic and Reformed', said Moule, referring to the Anglican Church, 'if I say here that the Roman Catholic Church has some important lessons to teach us.' Moule noted that evangelicals of an earlier generation had 'practised [fasting] resolutely and severely'.[54] The way of the cross was one that required spiritual attentiveness.

One of the important evangelical figures in the early twentieth century who was engaged in a profound exploration of the implications of the life of discipleship was Oswald Chambers, who became famous through his popular book of daily devotional readings, *My Utmost for his Highest*. In his comments on being 'partakers of Christ's sufferings' (1 Peter 4:13), Chambers wrote:

> In the history of the Christian Church the tendency has been to evade being identified with the sufferings of Jesus Christ; men have sought to procure the carrying out of God's order by a short cut way of their own. God's way is always the way of suffering, the way of the 'long, long trail'.[55]

Chambers also stressed that discipleship involved the hard work of understanding the faith. In his thinking about the cross he was indebted to the writings of P.T. Forsyth, and in turn Forsyth spoke of Chambers as combining in an unusual way 'moral incision and spiritual power'.[56] As a leading figure within the international Wesleyan holiness network, Chambers warned those in that particular constituency – with its stress on experience – to avoid 'intellectual sloth'.[57] From 1911 to 1915, as Principal of a Bible Training College in London, Chambers dedicated himself to stimulating broader thinking about spirituality. As an amateur psychologist, an artist and a poet, he found it easy to think of the whole of the cosmos as God's sphere of operation, and he argued for a broader vision of the work of Christ.[58] Chambers was prepared to speak publicly against theological liberalism, but his concern for the reality of Christ in human experience meant that he appreciated the popular book, *The Jesus of History*, by the liberal evangelical T.R. Glover.[59] The impact of Chambers was cut short, however, by his death from peritonitis in 1917 at the age of forty-three.

What about the place of women as disciples of Christ? Catherine Booth's advocacy of female ministry had considerable impact from the 1860s onwards. The holiness tradition to which Catherine Booth and the Salvation Army belonged stressed the Spirit's coming at Pentecost as the secret of power. The Spirit fell upon women and men. If women could prophesy through the Spirit, then they could also communicate the gospel. These points were taken up by Jessie Penn-Lewis in *The "Magna Carta" of Woman "According to the Scriptures"*, which first appeared in 1919, at the point when the first British women had gained the vote. Penn-Lewis argued that it was the cross of Christ – which was central to her theological thinking – that had removed the distinction between men and women in the service of God. Both men and women followed Christ as disciples who identified with the crucified Christ. Penn-Lewis drew from Katharine Bushnell, an American doctor whose *God's Word to Women* developed material used from 1906 in her Woman's Bible Correspondence Class. These studies included consideration of biblical texts which seemed to restrict female ministry. In her own book, Penn-Lewis observed that in revivals women often prophesied. A church silencing women, for Penn-Lewis, would 'silence the Holy Ghost'.[60] Despite writings of this kind, the restriction of public ministry so as to exclude women, and insistence on the submission of women to men, has persisted in some sections of evangelicalism.

Probably the finest treatment of the cross from within later twentieth-century evangelicalism is John Stott's *The Cross of Christ* (1986). As well as carefully expounding the theology of the atonement, Stott dealt with themes like the conquest of evil and the 'community of celebration' that lives 'under the cross'. Stott used the Moravians of the eighteenth century as an example of a community of men and women 'comprehensively stimulated by the cross'. He drew attention to their seal, bearing the inscription in Latin 'Our Lamb has conquered; let us follow him'. The focus of the worship at Herrnhut, Stott emphasised, was 'Christ crucified'. At the same time they were also called 'the Easter people', because it was the risen Lamb whom they adored. This gave a strong sense of assurance. Stott noted that Zinzendorf described the Moravians as God's 'happy people'.[61] For Stott it was important that worship of Christ should be biblical and rational. Yet this did not mean that the emotions were not involved in a person's relationship with God in Christ. Stott spoke, in his study of the work of the Holy Spirit, in very personal terms of experiences of the Spirit in which there was 'a quickening of our spiritual pulse, a leaping of our heart, a kindling of our love for God and man'. This could and did happen, he observed, 'in the dignified reverence of public worship, or in the spontaneous fellowship of a home meeting, or at the Lord's Table, or in private prayer'. In the response of Christian obedience, a response to the crucified and risen Christ, there is an acknowledgement of who is the Lord. 'We become still and *know* that God is God.'[62]

Conclusion

The words of Isaac Watts have summed up for many evangelicals throughout the centuries their understanding of the cross as a reality in their spiritual experience:

> Forbid it, Lord, that I should boast,
> Save in the death of Christ my God!
> All the vain things that charm me most,
> I sacrifice them to His blood.
> Were the whole realm of nature mine,
> That were a present far too small;
> Love so amazing, so divine,
> Demands my soul, my life, my all.

The cross demands a response. Yet as Jonathan Edwards insisted, this obedience is not to be understood as a legal requirement, but as a response of love to the love of God.[63] At the same time, it is a costly response to what was a supremely costly sacrifice by Christ. For P.T. Forsyth, if there was no cross there was no Christ: 'When pain ends gain ends too.'[64] In the twentieth century, evangelical cross-centred spirituality has been maintained within and often in contrast to a broader theological context, at least in English Anglicanism, of an incarnation-centred theology.[65] Yet there were commonalities across theological boundary lines. B.L. Manning, Senior Tutor of Jesus College, Cambridge, wrote in 1942: 'So in piety, do extremes agree: Catholic and Evangelical meet, and kiss one another at the Cross'.[66]

7. 'THE HIGHEST BEAUTY': THE HOLY SPIRIT AND HOLINESS

The evangelical focus on the cross should be seen alongside an appreciation of the risen Christ who is present with believers by the Holy Spirit. A recurring theme in evangelical spirituality has been the reality of the power of the Holy Spirit to enable the Christian to live a life that is holy and is also effective in terms of mission. The way in which this reality is understood has been far from uniform. By the later nineteenth century there were three distinct 'holiness' streams within evangelicalism – the Calvinist, Wesleyan and Keswick traditions.[1] Of these, Keswick became the most influential among British evangelicals. In the twentieth century Pentecostal and charismatic movements added their own dimensions of experience of the Holy Spirit. Despite these differences, evangelicals were united in believing that holiness was a fruit of conversion, was focused on the cross, was nurtured by the Bible and was expressed in vigorous activity. As one American Methodist holiness preacher typically put it: 'Activity for God is a consequence of a healthy soul.'[2] But none of the strands of evangelicalism believed that good works were the way by which a person achieved favour with God. Knowledge of God was a gift. The advice that George Whitefield gave to a young convert would have been widely accepted across the spectrum of evangelical spirituality from the eighteenth century onwards: 'We have nothing to do; but to lay hold on him [Christ] by faith, and to depend on him for wisdom, righteousness, sanctification and redemption.' Whitefield went on to urge that a true faith in Christ 'will not suffer us to be idle ... it fills the heart, so that it cannot be easy, till it is doing something for JESUS CHRIST'.[3]

Holiness in the Calvinist tradition

At times the radical holiness streams of spirituality have been marginalised in telling the story of evangelicalism, with Reformed or Calvinist perspectives dominating.[4] It is also the case, however, that evangelical interest in Pentecostal spirituality has meant that the holiness movements, which helped to produce Pentecostalism, have been given greater attention in recent writing. Perhaps it has not been sufficiently recognised that evangelicals in the Calvinist tradition have themselves developed a rich understanding of holiness. Jonathan Edwards grounded his view of holiness in a theology of the Trinity and the concepts of beauty and harmony. For Edwards the ultimate expression of holiness, which he described as 'the highest beauty', is found in the inner life of the Trinity.[5] Edwards wrote that holiness brought 'sweet calmness' and 'calm ecstasies' to the individual Christian's experience. In a remarkable picture, he spoke of how holiness could produce self-acceptance (could make the soul 'love itself'), of the way in which God loved and delighted in the holy person, and of the response of the whole of the natural world, since 'even the sun, the fields and trees love a humble holiness'. The picture he painted of harmony in the natural world was then used by Edwards to illustrate vividly the quality of the harmony existing in the relationship between the human being whose life was holy – a person who was 'like a garden planted by God' – and the divine Trinity, 'where the sun is Jesus Christ, and the blessed beams and calm breeze, the Holy Spirit'.[6]

Neither Edwards nor any of his successors in the Calvinist tradition, however, underestimated the malevolent power of sin, a power that had to be overcome if the beauty of holiness was to be exhibited. Indeed concentration on the difficulties of living the holy life and on the problem of the continuing presence of inner sin became something of a hallmark of much Reformed spirituality. Augustus Toplady, the evangelical Anglican clergyman who launched some of the strongest attacks on John Wesley, once compared the sinner's 'debt of sin' with England's 'national debt'. He calculated that at the rate of one sin each second every person who reached the age of eighty was by that time guilty of 2,522,880,000 sins. Since no one could pay off such a debt, he concluded, reliance must certainly be on Christ alone for redemption. Then, having established this position, there followed the caption 'A living and dying prayer for the holiest believer in the world', introducing Toplady's hymn 'Rock of Ages'. The allusion by Toplady to the 'holiest believer' may be a sarcastic reference to John Wesley and his doctrine of Christian perfection. Despite the context of theological warfare, and despite Toplady's rather bizarre calculation of human sin, 'Rock of Ages' vividly expressed for many the need for cleansing from the guilt and power of sin.[7]

In the later nineteenth century, J.C. Ryle wrote what became a classic work on this subject of living a holy life. Written from a robustly Reformed perspective, it was simply entitled *Holiness*. In an extended definition of holiness and of the holy person, Bishop Ryle suggested that holiness included 'the habit of being of one mind with God, according as we find His mind described in Scripture'. He argued that a holy person would shun every known sin, and keep every known commandment; would strive to be like Christ; would cultivate all the virtues found in Scripture; would follow after purity of heart; would live in the fear of God (by which, he explained, he did not mean the fear of a slave but the fear of a child, who wishes to live as if he was always before his father's face, because he loves him); and would seek humility, faithfulness and spiritual-mindedness.[8] In another of his books, *Practical Religion*, Ryle asked how much his readers knew of practical Christian holiness. He insisted that holiness was not absolute perfection and freedom from all faults. Ryle, in line with

Christian tradition, stressed the spiritual battle that characterised the Christian life:

> The wild words of some who talk of enjoying 'unbroken communion with God' for many months, are greatly to be deprecated, because they raise unscriptural expectations in the minds of young believers, and so do harm. Absolute perfection is for heaven, and not for earth, where we have a weak body, a wicked world, and a busy devil continually near our souls. Nor is real Christian holiness ever attained, or maintained, without a constant fight and struggle. The great Apostle, who said 'I fight, I labour, I keep under my body and bring it into subjection' (1 Corinthians 9:26, 27), would have been amazed to hear of *sanctification without personal exertion*, and to be told that believers only need to sit still, and everything will be done for them![9]

James Packer, Professor of Theology at Regent College, Vancouver, Canada, eloquently advocated Reformed thinking on holiness in his book *Passion for Holiness*. Earlier, in a preface to Ryle's *Holiness*, Packer gave testimony to the way in which reading this volume had helped him to see that his attempts in his early life to 'repeatedly reconsecrate himself', which he sought to do in order to find spiritual power, were based on 'overheated holiness teaching'.[10] Certainly *Passion for Holiness* draws deeply from J.C. Ryle, but Packer also shows the breadth and creativity to be found within the Reformed tradition at the end of the twentieth century. For him holiness has to do with humanness. 'Christians', says Packer, 'are meant to become human as Jesus was human.' Packer commends books by Richard Foster and others, volumes which include some spiritual disciplines that draw from Catholic spirituality. Also, he makes positive comments about Pentecostalism and the charismatic movement in a chapter entitled 'Growing Strong: The Empowered Christian Life'. Packer argues that 'a Christianity that is prepared to go on cheerfully without any signs of God's supernatural transforming power in people's lives shows a very unbiblical spirit'.[11] This is a view which commands wide support in evangelicalism.

Wesleyan holiness

Some have regarded John Wesley's conception of Christian perfection or of 'perfect love' as the most original of his doctrinal contributions. Wesley regarded the doctrine of 'full sanctification' or Christian perfection as the 'grand *depositum* which God has lodged with the people called Methodists'.[12] In this area, however, he was out of line with much common Protestant thinking of his time. Sanctification was understood by Wesley as the developing work of God in the human soul from the time of conversion. There was also, for him, a definite stage and consequent condition that he called full or entire sanctification. This blessing was attainable, but once attained could be lost. At the heart of Wesley's thinking about the fully sanctified life were the concepts of an undivided desire to please and serve God and a 'perfect love' for God which excluded sin. In his famous 'Brief Thoughts on Christian Perfection', Wesley said that by perfection he meant 'the humble, gentle, patient love of God, and our neighbour, ruling our tempers, words and actions'. This was 'always wrought in the soul by a simple act of faith' and therefore happened 'in an instant'. Where this experience of sanctification did take place it was usually 'many years after justification'.[13]

This was not a doctrine of 'sinlessness'. There was, according to Wesley, no absolute perfection before heaven, and indeed Wesley maintained that the term 'perfection' had been thrust on him. The way in which Wesley described his position is carefully nuanced, although he is perhaps not always consistent. Crucially, human failures that were not intentional were not seen by him as sins. What Wesley was looking for, above all, was growth in grace. It was not the case, as Wesley saw it, that the whole of salvation was given at once. He wrote:

Neither dare we affirm, as some have done, that all this salvation is given at once. There is indeed an instantaneous, as well as a gradual, work of God in His children; and there wants not, we know, a cloud of witnesses who have received, in one moment, either a clear sense of the forgiveness of their sins, or the abiding witness of the Holy Spirit. But we do not know a single instance, in any place, of a person's receiving, in one remission of sins, the abiding witness of the Spirit, and a new, a clean heart.[14]

Although Wesley had been influenced by writers in the field of spirituality such as William Law and Jeremy Taylor, he had not found in them the spiritual assurance he was seeking. It was the discovery of this assurance that led him to look for a life of constant communion with God, of purity of heart. These themes of assurance and purity of heart were summed up by Charles Wesley in one of his finest hymns, 'Love divine, all loves excelling' with its words:

Jesu, Thou art all compassion,
Pure, unbounded Love Thou art ...

Finish then Thy new creation,
Pure and spotless let us be ...[15]

This experience meant being changed 'from glory into glory' and as a consequence the Christian had greater enjoyment of God, with a resultant increase in happiness. The evangelical tradition, influenced by such optimism, became known as one that valued 'happiness and holiness'.[16] These both flowed from relationship to Christ.

What part did the Holy Spirit play in this experience of perfect love? Wesley was wary of those, as he put it, who had 'imagined themselves to be endued with a power of working miracles, of healing the sick by a word or a touch, of restoring sight to the blind; yea, even of raising the dead', and he referred to a recent 'notorious instance' that he and others knew of false claims being made.[17] Wesley was, none the less, committed to the crucial role of the Holy Spirit. Unlike John Fletcher of Madeley, however, Wesley did not see the experience of entire sanctification in terms of a baptism of the Spirit similar to that experienced by the disciples on the Day of Pentecost. It was in the nineteenth century that Pentecostal terminology as a way of explaining sanctification became common. Wesley wrote many pastoral letters, and in 1749 he said this to a Roman Catholic:

> I believe the infinite and eternal Spirit of God, equal with the Father and the Son, to be not only perfectly holy in Himself, but the immediate cause of all holiness in us; enlightening our understandings, rectifying our wills and affections, renewing our natures, uniting our persons to Christ, assuring us of the adoption of sons, leading us in our actions, purifying and sanctifying our souls and bodies, to a full and eternal enjoyment of God.[18]

Inward renewal through the Holy Spirit produced a full-orbed holiness which had outward effects.

In the mid nineteenth century, holiness teaching in North America was revitalised. James Caughey, an American revivalist who also preached in England, emphasised the possibility of instant sanctification. Methodist 'camp meetings' (so called because families camped during these gatherings), at which the messages of salvation and sanctification were proclaimed, became highly popular in America. In New York, 'Tuesday' meetings, as they came to be known, were addressed by a Methodist, Phoebe Palmer. This Wesleyan holiness theology as expounded by Palmer was taken up by William and Catherine Booth and the Salvation Army. Phoebe Palmer's introduction of 'altar terminology' – a 'shorter way' to holiness through laying one's all on the altar, often signified by kneeling at the communion rail – affected British and American revivalism.[19] It marked a new direction in thinking about spiritual power. For many Salvationists in Britain and America the most uncompromising promoter of Wesleyan spirituality was Samuel Logan Brengle. As a

Methodist theological student in Boston, Massachusetts, Brengle had been led in 1885 into the experience of entire sanctification by Daniel Steele, Professor of Theology at the University of Boston. When William Booth later came to Boston, Brengle was captivated. 'Here, certainly', he decided, 'is God's greatest servant upon earth today'.[20] Within three years Brengle was in London, successfully applying to William Booth to join the Army. Two months after his entry as a cadet, Brengle wrote to Elizabeth, his wife, indicating that he felt his work was to promote holiness.[21] His appointment as the Army's 'International Spiritual Special' gave Brengle freedom to propagate holiness teaching that served as the basis of much of the Army's spirituality in the early twentieth century.[22]

In the later nineteenth and early twentieth century era, 'full salvation' (as Christian perfection was by then often termed) was widely claimed by people within the various Wesleyan movements. Compared with John Wesley himself, holiness teachers of this period made more of instantaneous experience and less of love perfected.[23] None the less, they often appealed to Wesley and Fletcher as their authorities, although the final appeal was always to the Bible. In 1871 some younger Methodist ministers came together in York for a conference aimed at the promotion of 'scriptural holiness'.[24] The Methodist Southport Convention was started in 1885 in order to 'make more vital the traditional faith of Methodism'.[25] Hugh Price Hughes, who came to epitomise the Wesleyan Forward Movement and who combined progressive evangelistic and social concern with revivalist spirituality, hoped that Southport would be 'the Pentecost of modern Methodism'.[26] Thomas Cook, an outstanding Methodist Connexional evangelist, was the convener. Southport and later Cliff College promoted Wesleyan holiness in Britain.[27] The holy life was often defined in rather narrow terms. It was claimed that Cliff College stood, in the early 1920s, for full salvation, aggressive evangelism and smashing the drink traffic.[28] This more rigid stance contrasted with the moderation of another holiness stream – the Keswick Convention.

Keswick spirituality

The huge revival of interest in the subject of the life of holiness in the 1870s produced a variant of holiness teaching that would find its focus in the annual Keswick Convention, held in the English Lake District. Influences came from America and England. Teaching about sanctification promoted by the leading American evangelist Charles Finney and by Asa Mahan, President of Oberlin College, Ohio, was important.[29] Conferences 'for the promotion of spiritual life' were held at Mildmay Park, North London, under an influential evangelical Anglican clergyman, William Pennefather.[30] Prominent evangelical laymen such as Stevenson Arthur Blackwood, the chief executive of the Post Office, Lord Radstock, and Sir Thomas Beauchamp played a leading part in encouraging spiritual advance. A significant event was the Broadlands Conference of 1874, when about one hundred invited people – which included, for instance, the author George MacDonald – met for six days in July 1874 at Broadlands, near Romsey, in Hampshire, the home of William and Georgina Cowper-Temple (later Lord and Lady Mount-Temple).[31] The main speakers at Broadlands were Robert and Hannah Pearsall Smith from North America, who had a Quaker background.[32] Concepts such as the 'higher Christian life', which was the title of a book by an American Presbyterian, W.E. Boardman, 'the rest of faith' and 'full surrender' were discussed. Hannah Pearsall Smith wrote the highly influential book *The Christian's Secret of a Happy Life* (1875). One Anglican clergyman who was powerfully affected in this period was Evan Hopkins, the energetic Vicar of Holy Trinity, Richmond, through whom the theology of Keswick was to a large extent to be fashioned.[33]

About 1,000 people attended meetings in Oxford in 1874, arranged by Alfred Christopher, Rector of St Aldate's, Oxford, at which one speaker put the issue starkly: 'Which will you have – sanctification by works or sanctification by faith?'[34] A much larger holiness convention was held at Brighton from 29 May to 7 June 1875. Here the crowds from across Europe, which filled the Dome, the Pavilion, the Corn Exchange and the Town Hall, were estimated at between 7,000 and 8,000.[35] The speakers included the Pearsall Smiths, Asa Mahan, Evan Hopkins, H.W. Webb-Peploe, Vicar of St Paul's, Onslow Square, London, and Theodore Monod from Paris.[36] The American evangelist D.L. Moody sent a message of support. At one meeting Hannah Pearsall Smith, who was the most sought-after speaker, took up the theme of 'the Overcoming Life'. She said that she would not call it 'the higher Christian life', but simply *the* life of the believer.[37] For T.D. Harford-Battersby, of St John's Church, Keswick, the Oxford Convention was decisive. He spoke years later of how he had received 'a revelation of Christ to my soul' that was 'extra-ordinary, glorious and precious' and had continued to illuminate his life.[38] At Brighton Harford-Battersby announced that 'Union Meetings for the Promotion of Practical Holiness' would be held from 29 June 1875 in a tent in Keswick. The term 'higher life' would be replaced by more acceptable phrases such as 'practical holiness'. Given the Romanticism of the period, Keswick was an attractive venue: the Romantic setting was in tune with the experience.[39] A new holiness perspective, with a particular focus on a life of trust in Christ, would remould older thinking.

As Evan Hopkins saw it, there were three views of sanctification within evangelicalism. There was, firstly, the Calvinist tradition that holiness was achieved by earnest effort. Secondly, there were concepts, popularised within Wesleyan thought, of the 'clean heart', with sin eradicated. But for Hopkins the correct view, which became the accepted Keswick position, was that there was the possibility of perpetual 'counteraction' of sin, although never the destruction of the sinful nature. Hopkins was keen to show Calvinists that by contrast with some Wesleyan holiness thinking this new teaching was moderate. He emphatically denied that holiness consisted in 'the eradication of sin'.[40] Hopkins set out his understanding of holiness in *The Law of Liberty in the Spiritual Life*.[41] At Keswick, Hopkins would be available during after-meetings to help individuals with questions about the life of faith. He would encourage 'a definite transaction' with God. Often people would stand up as a sign that they had yielded to the Holy Spirit. Hopkins placed emphasis on 'a decisive act of the will'.[42] J.C. Ryle delivered a paper to the Islington Clerical Meeting (the main gathering of evangelical Anglican clergy) on 'Instability among Modern Christians', and he sought to refute Keswick ideas, but Webb-Peploe used Islington and other such gatherings as means of spreading Keswick teaching. At one celebrated meeting Webb-Peploe's message was followed by a peroration from the chairman who began: 'Heresy! Heresy!! Damnable Heresy!' Against a background of persistent allegations by Anglican figures that sinless perfection was taught at Keswick, Webb-Peploe insisted that Keswick was 'most carefully guarded by an insistence on the fact that sin remains in us to the last'.[43] Keswick teaching about deeper consecration to Christ would gradually find acceptance among evangelical leaders.

A crucial element in the growing power of Keswick from 1875 to the early twentieth century was its strength within the Anglican constituency.[44] But the numbers of non-Anglicans gradually increased. Church of Scotland and other Presbyterian ministers began to appear at Keswick in the 1880s, the most notable being Elder Cumming, whom the American evangelist D.L. Moody had previously observed to be a particularly cantankerous individual. Cumming was dramatically affected by his attendance at Keswick in 1882, when he was minister of Sandyford Church of Scotland, Glasgow. Cumming's influence was felt by other Scottish ministers.[45] The greater challenge for Keswick, however, with its motto 'All One in Christ Jesus', was to attract the large English Nonconformist constituency. Many Free Church ministers were concerned that Keswick embodied escapism

from the world. One influential advocate of an evangelical
social gospel, R.W. Dale, in Birmingham, gave tentative
support to holiness teaching,[46] and another Congregationalist,
G. Campbell Morgan, minister of Westminster Chapel,
London, spoke at Keswick several times from 1900.[47] But the
Free Church figure who bridged in an outstanding way the
divide between an inner-directed piety and outward-directed
social concern was F.B. Meyer, who became Keswick's leading
international speaker. He came to an experience of consecration through the impact of C.T. Studd and Stanley Smith, two
of the famous 'Cambridge Seven' missionaries who went to
China in 1885 with the China Inland Mission.[48] Keswick's
influence often spread through personal contacts and these
reached across denominations.

Keswick's continuing influence

The large numbers of evangelicals who attended Keswick in
the twentieth century – normally over 5,000 and sometimes
up to 10,000, with many more at mini-Keswicks across
Britain – meant that the Keswick style of spirituality had
great influence. It was marked by traditional evangelical
biblicism. From the 1880s Keswick's expository Bible
Readings, held each morning of the Convention, were introduced. These were a focus and an attraction. There was
always a concern in these expositions to be Christ-centred.
H.W. Webb-Peploe addressed Keswick more often than any
speaker. His style was commanding and uncompromising, and
his biblical exegesis – he gave detailed scriptural expositions
at the Bible Readings without the use of notes – was invari-
ably an inspiration to Keswick-goers. Another crucial shaper
of the Keswick tradition was Handley Moule, Principal of
Ridley Hall, Cambridge, before becoming Bishop of Durham,
who was a Keswick speaker and apologist for thirty years
from the 1880s. After embracing the Keswick message,
through Evan Hopkins, Moule spoke of how he had been
aware of 'discreditable failures in patience, and charity, and

humbleness' in his own ministry.[49] Through his speaking and
writing, Moule gave Keswick ecclesiastical and theological
respectability which assisted its further growth.

The tradition of biblical exposition and application was
continued by Keswick leaders such as the Baptist minister
Graham Scroggie, George Duncan, who had ministries in the
Scottish Episcopal Church and the Church of Scotland, and
Alan Redpath, who became minister of Moody Memorial
Church, Chicago. The most influential thinker was Scroggie,
whose stress was on the Christian submitting to Jesus as
Lord. This represented a new way of formulating the Keswick
message of consecration and was to become standard thinking
in evangelicalism.[50] At times the working out of this could be
rather legalistic. Another change was that there was less
expectation of a crisis experience at the Convention. This
change was highlighted by the only Methodist to take a leading role at Keswick in its early decades, Charles Inwood, a
forthright preacher from Ireland, who spoke at twenty-one
Keswicks and travelled widely throughout the world on behalf
of the convention movement. In the early twentieth century
Inwood commented on the way in which the 'process' rather
than the 'crisis' of sanctification had assumed more prominence in Keswick thinking.[51] The speakers at Keswick,
although they spoke of 'full salvation', as did Inwood's
colleagues in the holiness movements in Methodism, did not
make common cause with the Methodist advocates of a
specifically Wesleyan doctrine of holiness found at the
Southport Convention or Cliff College. Keswick spirituality
retained its broader evangelical appeal.

Keswick helped to foster a sense of pan-national as well
as pan-evangelical spirituality. Holiness conventions were
convened across Europe, across the English-speaking world
and in many other countries where missionaries were serving.
In 1891 Meyer made his first trip to North America, invited by
D.L. Moody to speak at the annual conference which Moody
hosted at Northfield, Massachusetts, a conference which
stressed evangelical unity. Meyer was followed by others such

as Webb-Peploe, who made a deep impression in 1895 on the influential American missionary statesman A.T. Pierson.[52] There were apparently some protests because of fears about forms of perfectionism. But A.J. Gordon, who was a respected Baptist minister in Boston, New England, had already been preaching a similar message at Northfield. Keswick could also act as a conduit for spirituality from elsewhere. In 1937 Keswick was challenged by a fresh spiritual movement when a missionary in Ruanda (now Rwanda), Stanley Smith, related how open confession of sins, which had begun among Africans, had subsequently spread to missionaries. The 'deep spirituality' of African church leaders was recognised, and this would be channelled into British evangelicalism through speakers such as Roy Hession and his book *The Calvary Road*. J.E. Church, a medical missionary with the Church Missionary Society, reported to Keswick on 'Times of refreshing in Ruanda'.[53] Festo Kivengere, a child of the East African Revival who became a bishop in Uganda, spoke at Keswick in the 1970s.[54]

The baptism of the Spirit

There was, however, a resistance at Keswick to Pentecostal spirituality, with its teaching that Christians should seek the baptism of the Spirit and spiritual gifts such as speaking in tongues. It became increasingly common in the holiness movements in the nineteenth century to talk about a 'Pentecostal' experience, but this experience had to do with power over sin rather than power to exercise spiritual gifts. One rather provocative holiness leader, Richard Reader Harris, who was committed to Wesleyan holiness spirituality, offered £100 to anyone who could prove from Scripture that sin must necessarily remain in the believer. It was in 1901, following one of Reader Harris' Pentecostal League of Prayer events in Perth, Scotland, that Oswald Chambers was (as he put it himself) 'baptised with the Holy Ghost'.[55] Andrew Murray from South Africa, a minister of the Dutch Reformed Church, made a huge impact speaking at Keswick in 1895 on the baptism and filling of the Spirit. Murray had written a devotional classic *Abide in Christ*, but later he explained, 'I became much exercised about the baptism of the Holy Spirit, and I gave myself to God as perfectly as I could to receive this baptism of the Spirit'.[56] Yet none of these figures were sympathetic to the claims made about supernatural gifts by the Pentecostal movement.

The strongest link between Keswick spirituality and Pentecostalism was the Welsh Revival of 1904–5. As with the previous revivals of the eighteenth and nineteenth centuries, there was a stress both on the Church being spiritually revived and society being affected. In 1903 a Keswick-type convention was held for the first time in Wales, at Llandrindod Wells. When F.B. Meyer, who was one of the speakers at that Convention, gave an opportunity at the final Convention meeting for expressions of surrender and dedication it seemed, according to the *Life of Faith*, as if everyone wanted to receive 'the fullness of blessing'.[57] This event was one of several factors that helped to stimulate the Revival of the following year, in which the most notable revival leader was the young Evan Roberts, a former coal miner.[58] There was, however, some tension between the moderation of Keswick spirituality and the uninhibited fervour of the experiences in Wales. J.B. Figgis, a respected Keswick figure, commented that, when 300 people from Wales came to Keswick in 1905, 'the torrent from the Welsh hills meeting the sluggish stream of English propriety threatened tumult'.[59] Keswick's largely Anglican leadership embodied the sense of 'propriety'.

In the meantime, the heightened spirituality of the Revival was spreading. F.B. Meyer, who took a great interest in the Welsh Revival, was one of those who carried the news of what was happening in Wales to wider audiences. In April 1905 he spoke for eight days to large audiences in Los Angeles, stressing what he had experienced of the Revival. One of those present on 8 April 1905 was Frank Bartleman, who was to be central in Pentecostal growth. He spoke of being stirred as

Meyer 'described the great revival going on in Wales, which he had just visited'.[60] These and other holiness influences led to a number of ministers in Los Angeles seeking the baptism of the Spirit with speaking in tongues. Most notable among these was William J. Seymour, a black holiness preacher with Baptist roots who studied at Charles Parham's Bible school in Houston, Texas, where tongues speaking took place in 1901. Seymour himself began to speak in tongues, and from 14 April 1906 led the Azusa Street Mission, Los Angeles, which was key to the spread of Pentecostalism.[61] Four years prior to this, in 1902, Meyer had been fascinated when he discovered, during a visit to Estonia, that the gift of tongues was being used in Estonian Baptist churches.[62] An Anglican evangelical clergyman in the Sunderland area, Alexander Boddy, was one British Keswick evangelical who embraced the new movement emanating from Azusa Street, and he wrote *Pentecost for England* in an unsuccessful attempt to persuade Keswick to embrace Pentecostal pneumatology.[63] Keswick's caution was to be a continuing factor in evangelical attitudes to Pentecostal spirituality.

None the less, the world-wide spread of Keswick had created international evangelical networks which were carriers of the news of the Welsh Revival and which then, at least in some cases, served to foster Pentecostal spirituality. An example in India was the 'Mukti' (meaning salvation) community, founded and led by an outstanding Indian Christian leader, Pandita Ramabai, from a distinguished Hindu family. Mukti was home to many young widows and orphans. The Keswick missionary meeting in 1898 heard a memorable address from Ramabai, who was a remarkable scholar of Sanskrit, a Bible translator and social reformer. She stated that she had learned from Keswick about receiving the Holy Spirit's power. Her vision was for 1,000 Spirit-filled Indian women to empower other Indian women.[64] In December 1904, after receiving news from Wales, Ramabai 'started prayer circles of ten girls each, urging them to pray for the salvation of all nominal Christians in India and across the world'. In June 1905 it was reported that the Holy Spirit fell upon a large group of girls at Mukti, with weeping, confession of sin and prayers for power in evidence. A Brethren preacher, G. H. Lang, after spending time at Mukti, wrote that girls 'were lost for hours in the transport of loving Jesus and praising Him'. Long periods were devoted to intercessory prayer. Lang spoke of a thousand voices all praying aloud together. Speaking in tongues was also in evidence.[65] Pentecostalism and then the charismatic movement of the 1960s and beyond were to embody new forms of spirituality.

Conclusion

Evangelical understandings of the power of the Holy Spirit and holy living have been varied – Calvinist, Wesleyan, Keswick and charismatic. The Calvinist tradition has been, and continues to be influential. J.C. Ryle typically wrote: 'Sanctification, again, is a thing which does not prevent a man having a great deal of inward spiritual conflict ... In saying this, I do not forget that I am contradicting the views of some well-meaning Christians, who hold the doctrine called "sinless perfection". I cannot help that.'[66] Yet the experience recounted by the Keswick leader T.D. Harford-Battersby resonates with evangelicals: 'Christ was revealed to me so powerfully and sweetly as the present Saviour in His all-sufficiency.' Harford-Battersby came to trust in Christ more deeply.[67] David Bebbington suggests that the evangelical world is likely to be increasingly polarised between Calvinist and charismatic views. He considers that traditional Wesleyan and Keswick emphases have faded to a large extent within wider evangelicalism. What remains most prominent is the holiness tradition that has the longest pedigree (Calvinism), which generally attracts the more conservative, and the most recent spiritual movement (charismatic renewal), which has attracted the more progressive.[68] This may not be the full picture, since Wesleyan holiness is still propagated through denominations such as the Church of the Nazarene, and there is renewed interest in the Keswick tradition, perhaps in part because its teaching about the 'rest of faith' has resonance for those evangelicals exploring contemplative spirituality. Also, many contemporary evangelicals would not want to see their spirituality as restricted to any one of these sub-sets of evangelicalism. Despite the differences outlined above and even the polarisation that has taken place at times, all evangelicals would agree with Jonathan Edwards that holiness is 'the highest beauty'.

8. 'THAT MYSTICAL BODY':
THE FELLOWSHIP OF BELIEVERS

Evangelical spirituality has never been rigidly individualistic. There has always been a corporate dimension to evangelical experience. Evangelicals have generally stressed the centrality of the ministry of the Word, the place of the sacraments (although in this area the Salvation Army is an exception), and the importance of the fellowship of believers. Many evangelicals have been committed quite explicitly to models of spirituality shaped by their denominational traditions, whether Calvinist, Wesleyan or Baptist. However, there has always been a strong strain of pan-denominationalism in evangelicalism. At the first Keswick Convention, in 1875, the text 'All One in Christ Jesus' (a quotation from Galatians 3:28) was hung above the platform.[1] This motto, which was chosen by a Quaker, Robert Wilson, was taken up by conventions across the world that drew their inspiration from Keswick and the emphasis on spiritual unity has characterised many other evangelical gatherings such as Spring Harvest. Derek Tidball comments that '[t]he oneness they [evangelicals] espouse at such gatherings is based on the consciousness of what they share together. They are conscious of having been converted to Christ and desiring to live for him.' It is this shared experience of fellowship, rather than allegiance to ecclesiastical institutions, that is of greatest importance to them.[2] What part, then, does the traditional belief in the one holy catholic and apostolic Church have within an evangelical spirituality that emphasises the spiritual unity of believers?

The unity of the Church

Bruce Hindmarsh, writing in *Evangelical Ecclesiology*, asks:
'Is Evangelical Ecclesiology an Oxymoron?' From an examination of early evangelicalism he concludes that there was no
distinctively evangelical doctrine of church order, that evangelicals discerned the mystical Church among the divided
visible churches, and that while celebrating the spiritual
union of all the regenerate the movement was marked by
separatism. As examples of the schisms, Hindmarsh notes
that John Wesley and George Whitefield divided from each
other in the 'free grace' (Calvinist-Arminian) controversy of
1739, that Wesley, Whitefield and the Moravians split a year
later over the question of quietist spirituality, and that the
Countess of Huntingdon went through evangelical chaplains
like serial lovers.[3] Yet Whitefield, for example, was adamant
that a spiritual fellowship existed between believers. He
wrote to a Presbyterian minister:

> What a divine sympathy and attraction is there between
> all those who by one spirit are made members of that
> mystical body, whereof JESUS CHRIST is the head! ...
> Blessed be GOD that his love is so far shed abroad in our
> hearts, as to cause us to love one another, though we dif-
> fer as to externals: For my part, I hate to mention them.
> My one sole question is, Are you a christian?[4]

This expresses the classic evangelical position. Church order
is secondary to spiritual reality. Roger Olsen, writing in
Evangelical Ecclesiology, suggests that there is a unique
compatibility between Free Church life, with its emphasis on
personal conversion as constitutive of the local 'gathered
church' community, and evangelical spirituality.[5] Evangelicals
tend to emphasise the fellowship of believers as lying at the
heart of what it is to be the Church of Christ.

Does this mean, therefore, that evangelical spirituality has
little interest in the visible unity of the Church? This has
quite often been the case. Indeed there have been evangelicals

who have seen it as their duty to separate from the wider Church. The spirituality of the evangelical movements that have taken this position has frequently been shaped by convictions about the importance of principled separation from what was doctrinally, ecclesiologically and spiritually 'unclean'. The biblical text 'Come out from among them' has often been employed.[6] A fiercely separatist outlook was to be found in the nineteenth century among Brethren and Strict Baptists, groups that owed much to clergy who had left the Church of England in the 1830s. Thus the views of the Brethren, who were to have a considerable influence on evangelical thinking about church life, owed a great deal to the teaching of J.N. Darby, a curate in Ireland who came to the conviction that existing ecclesiastical life was apostate and withdrawal was mandatory. Brethren commitment was to simple church life in which believers met for the Lord's Supper (breaking of bread) without clerical leadership.[7] This approach, which sought for a purer Church, was to surface again through new voices in the twentieth century, for example in the 'Little Flock' movement in China, led by Watchman Nee.[8]

In the 1960s there were severe tensions in British evangelicalism over unity. In 1966, at the National Assembly of Evangelicals arranged by the Evangelical Alliance, Martyn Lloyd-Jones, as a keynote speaker, encouraged evangelicals to stop being an evangelical wing in what he believed would be a 'comprehensive, total, national, territorial church', and instead to 'start afresh'. Lloyd-Jones issued a call for a fellowship of local evangelical churches which would be free from what he saw as the theological compromises entailed in ecumenical or wider denominational involvement.[9] John Stott, who was chairing the meeting, brought the evening to a sensational end. Both history and Scripture, asserted Stott, were against what Lloyd-Jones had said. 'Scripture', Stott continued, 'is against him; the remnant was within the church not outside it.'[10] Although relatively few evangelicals left their denominations at that time, new charismatic churches later

emerged in Britain which rejected the existing denominations. The idea of a 'denominational ceiling', beyond which
further spiritual development was impossible for those in
historic denominations, was a favourite concept in these
Restorationist (restoring the New Testament church) groups.[11]
Terry Virgo, one of the Restorationist leaders, or 'apostles',
considered that denominational leaders defended the status
quo whereas present-day apostles produced spiritually
mature churches.[12]

The history of evangelicalism suggests, however, that separation from the existing denominations has not been the
policy generally advocated by evangelical leaders. John
Wesley's reading of the Bible, coupled with the Enlightenment
thinking of his time, meant that he valued Christian unity. At
the Methodist Conference of 1757 his hope that there might
be 'a national union of evangelical clergy' was set out. He saw
this union as drawing together Methodist societies and the
evangelicals in the Church of England. Evangelicals within
these different streams, although they were aware of their
denominational distinctives, recognised their common convictions and common experience of Christ. Thus Samuel Walker
of Truro, as a result of his own evangelical experience, urged
that 'all friends of the Gospel', although differing denomina-
tionally, should 'unite in heart for the support of the common
cause'.[13] This was a call for spiritual, not organisational union.
But there was little support. Even the clergymen who spoke of
a common evangelical cause were wary of any moves that
would undermine the Established Church. Wesley later
returned to the theme, arguing for a union based on evangelical beliefs and characterised by holiness of life on the part
of those involved, rather than a union in opinions, expressions
or outward order. By 1769, however, Wesley had come to the
view that his efforts to achieve wider unity had been fruitless.
The evangelicals whom he had hoped to draw together he now
saw as a 'rope of sand'.[14]

The evangelical instinct for wider spiritual fellowship came
into play again, however, in the late eighteenth and early

nineteenth centuries. In 1795 a Congregational minister, David Bogue, preached a memorable sermon at the formation of the London Missionary Society (LMS), a society which initially drew together Anglicans and Nonconformists. This inaugural event, for Bogue, marked 'the funeral of *bigotry*'.[15] Although Bogue was over-optimistic, evangelical co-operation was to increase. The British and Foreign Bible Society, formed in 1804, was a mark of the desire for united evangelical endeavour.[16] Ministers from different denominations, such as the Church of England evangelical leader Edward Bickersteth, began to encourage united prayer. Spiritual renewal was central. A German leader, Dean Kniewel of Danzig, made a tour through England, France, Belgium, Switzerland and Germany in 1842 to forge closer spiritual links between leaders in different denominations.[17] In the same year, John Angell James, the Congregational minister who preceded R.W. Dale in Birmingham, proposed a union among Dissenting churches to combat infidelity and also 'Popery, Puseyism and Plymouth Brethrenism'.[18] At a conference in Liverpool in 1845 on evangelical unity, James was more positive, stating: 'In every chorus of human voices, the harmony depends on the "key-note" being rightly struck: that note I am now appointed to give and it is LOVE.'[19] John Angell James was in fact sounding a typically evangelical note.

The holiness of the Church

For evangelicals the expressions of spiritual reality in the life of the Church normally have priority over formal ecclesiastical structures. Douglas Brown, the best-known Baptist evangelist in England in the 1920s, wrote in trenchant fashion: 'There is a painful lack of driving force in our church life. We seem to be living in days of much programme and little power, many schemes and little sanctity, multitudinous activity and small progress'.[20] Local church fellowship has traditionally nourished evangelicals and there has, therefore, been considerable stress on the ways in which the various aspects of local church life can be made most effective. Structures have been seen as necessary, but as flexible.[21] An early evangelical example of this process is the way in which John Wesley established his societies. These were not congregations, but they highlight the importance of communal spirituality. The account of this development was first published in 1743 as preface to *The Nature, Design, and General Rules of the United Societies, in London, Bristol, Kingswood, and Newcastle-upon-Tyne*:

> In the latter part of the year 1739 eight or ten persons, who appeared to be deeply convinced of sin and earnestly groaning for redemption, came to Mr. Wesley in London. They desired, as did two or three more the next day, that he would spend some time with them in prayer and advise them how to flee from the wrath to come, which they saw continually hanging over their heads.

Wesley organised a weekly meeting in London, on a Thursday evening, at which he gave the group spiritual advice and at which communal prayer was made.[22] Methodist society or class meetings, with class leaders, then spread. In a sermon on 'Obedience to Pastors', Wesley argued that Methodists did not need to regard the parish priest as their pastor. He envisaged people finding a 'spiritual pastor' or 'spiritual guide'.[23] Local class leaders often functioned in this way.

Among Baptists, the conversionism of the Evangelical Revival led to renewal. Dan Taylor, who founded the New Connexion of General Baptists in 1770, was a notable Baptist leader and church planter who modelled himself on Wesley. Robert Robinson, converted under George Whitefield in 1752, told Whitefield that he attended the Tabernacle, where Whitefield preached, 'pitying the poor deluded Methodists, but came away envying their happiness'. Robinson kept the date, 24 May 1752, the same date as Wesley's Aldersgate experience fourteen years earlier, as his spiritual birthday.[24] The impact of this spiritual experience is clear. In 1761 Robinson commenced ministry at what became St Andrew's Street Baptist

Church, Cambridge. This church, formed in 1721, had declined to thirty members, but under Robinson a new building was erected and congregations grew to 600. Robinson saw a local congregation as 'a voluntary society of Christians', agreed in faith and worship, and committed to the Lord and one another. A church 'covenant' among the members elaborated on this commitment. Among other things, members agreed 'mutually to love and pray for each other; to walk in faithfulness, forbearance, and tenderness to each other; to discharge to the best of our powers all those duties which we owe to one another, according to the light of nature, or the directions of scripture'.[25] This presented a typical Baptist or believers' church vision of corporate spirituality, in which the emphasis was on inter-personal relationships as a key element in spiritual growth. Within this tradition, C.H. Spurgeon suggested that younger Christians could learn from 'more experienced and more instructed Christians'.[26] Holy living was the aim.

The increasing individualism of the Victorian era militated against the idea of a covenanted community, and in the twentieth century new questions were raised for evangelicals, mainly Congregationalists and Baptists, in this 'gathered church' tradition. B.L. Manning, who was a leading Congregational layman, argued in the 1930s for a higher view of the church as a divine agency. 'The Church', he maintained, 'is the creation ... of the Good News.'[27] Others who formed part of the 'Genevan' movement in Congregationalism took the same view. Nathaniel Micklem, of Mansfield College, Oxford, saw a true congregation as a spiritual body. Congregational churches were comprised of 'visible saints', separated from the world, meeting in fellowship, free to judge and fit to be present.[28] But in practice a Congregational church of 200 to 250 members might find that only twenty people came together to seek to discern God's will through the church members' meeting,[29] which vitiated the ideal. The sense of responsibility that had in an earlier period marked membership in Baptist churches had also weakened, as Ernest Payne,

the Baptist Union General Secretary, noted in 1952.[30] There
was increasing dissatisfaction among Baptists from the 1960s
onwards over the quality of church members' meetings. From
the 1980s Nigel Wright, later Principal of Spurgeon's College,
London, contributed to new thinking about Free Church
ecclesiology. He wrote a widely read book, *Challenge to
Change*, suggesting ways to achieve the spiritual renewal of
church members' meetings, for example by moving away from
voting procedures and placing more reliance on members
prayerfully seeking to reach consensus.[31]

Evangelical Anglicans in the nineteenth and twentieth
centuries came to issues of church life from a different
ecclesiological standpoint. In the mid nineteenth century two
Anglican evangelical thinkers, Hugh McNeile and Edward
Arthur Litton, expounded their position on ecclesiology. For
McNeile the 'One Holy, Catholic and Apostolic Church' was
the 'invisible Church' consisting of all true believers. The
visible Church embraced true believers and 'false professors'.
Similarly, Litton spoke of seeking to find the members of
Christ's body in the visible Churches of Christ. For him the
spiritual energy which animated each Christian flowed
directly from the head of the body, Christ, to each member of
the body. These were typical statements, illustrating that
evangelicals valued the visible Church, but their primary
loyalty was to the invisible Church and to local congregational
life.[32] This set Anglican evangelicals apart from the Anglo-
Catholic Movement, which equated the visible Church –
provided it was under Episcopal oversight and could claim
apostolic succession – with Christ's mystical body. To a great
extent evangelical Anglican parishes have created their own
life and have often drawn relatively little from wider
Anglicanism. An example in the nineteenth century of how
effectively this could work was in Cheltenham. Through the
ministry in Cheltenham of Francis Close, evangelical spirituality flourished to such an extent from the 1820s that
Charles Simeon commented: 'Here at Cheltenham I have
almost heaven on earth.'[33]

By the mid twentieth century Anglican evangelical thinking was moving in new directions. The National Evangelical Anglican Congress (NEAC) held at Keele University in April 1967, which David Bebbington has described as the chief landmark in the post-war evangelical renaissance,[34] represented a shift away from the policy of seeking to develop evangelical life in relative isolation from the wider Church. NEAC, which was chaired by John Stott, declared that the initial task for divided Christians was 'dialogue at all levels and across all barriers'. The evangelical leadership within Anglicanism signalled its desire to enter this dialogue. Whereas many evangelicals were wary of the World Council of Churches (WCC), at Keele there was an acceptance that all those who confessed the Lord Jesus Christ as God and Saviour according to the Scriptures, and sought to fulfil together their calling to the glory of the one God, Father, Son and Holy Spirit (the WCC basis), had a right to be treated as Christians, and it was accepted that on this basis wider engagement would take place.[35] The older view held by many evangelicals, that questions about ecclesiology were 'secondary', and that spiritual fellowship could take place without reference to such questions, was being disputed.[36] In 1970 the publication of *Growing into Union*, part-authored by J.I. Packer and Colin Buchanan, two leading Anglican evangelicals, which espoused evangelical-Anglo-Catholic cooperation, illustrated that some evangelicals were viewing spiritual life in more ecclesial, catholic terms.[37]

The Church Catholic

There has, in fact, been a long tradition of evangelical commitment to catholicity. John Wesley produced a *Christian Library* which drew from the classics of the Western Church and also some Eastern Church authors, from a number of high Anglicans and supremely from the English Puritans. His use of such varied material was an expression of his 'catholic spirit'. The preface to the *Christian Library* says:

I have endeavoured to extract such a collection of *English Divinity,* as (I believe) is all true, all agreeable to the oracles of God: as is all practical, unmixed with controversy of any kind; and all intelligible to plain men: such as is not superficial, but going down to the depth, and describing the height of Christianity. And yet not mystical, not obscure to any of those who are experienced in the ways of God. I have also particularly endeavoured to preserve a consistency throughout, that no part might contradict any other; but all conspire together, 'to make the man of God perfect, thoroughly furnished unto every good word and work'.[38]

The expression 'not mystical' in this context probably means that Wesley wanted the kind of writing that was clearly expressed, although in a broader sense the practical Wesley had doubts about the value of the writings of the mystics. He also felt free to excise Calvinistic statements in the Puritan authors he used. His aim in the *Christian Library* was not to stimulate theological dispute but to produce 'a complete body of Practical Divinity'.[39] Catholicity had deeper spirituality as its goal.

Evangelical leaders have also sought to promote catholicity by seeking to encourage universal expressions of church fellowship. At the conference in London in 1846 which launched the Evangelical Alliance, Ralph Wardlaw, a Congregational minister from Glasgow who had earlier written a paper entitled 'A Catholic Spirit', emphasised that the conference was being held primarily to 'confess' Christian union. There were representatives from more than twenty Protestant denominations present in London to wrestle with the difficult issues confronting them regarding unity, but in Wardlaw's mind a spiritual union already existed. What was important was that it should be demonstrated. Wardlaw himself presented this resolution to the conference:

That this Conference, composed of professing Christians of many different Denominations, all exercising the right of private judgment, and, through common infirmity, differing in the views they severally entertain on some points, both of Christian doctrine and ecclesiastical Polity, and gathered together from many and remote parts of the World, for the purpose of promoting Christian Union, rejoice in making their unanimous avowal of the glorious truth, that the Church of the living God, while it admits of growth, is one Church, never having lost, and being incapable of losing its essential unity. Not, therefore, to create that unity, but to confess it, is the design of their assembling together. One in reality, they desire also, as far as they may be able to attain it, to be visibly one; and thus, both to realize in themselves, and to exhibit to others, that a living and everlasting union binds all true believers together in the fellowship of the Church of Christ.[40]

The nature of corporate evangelical spirituality is clearly expressed: it is a 'living ... union' of 'true believers'. Other Evangelical Alliance leaders, such as Sir Culling Eardley Smith, had a strong sense of the universality of Christian witness. At Evangelical Alliance meetings in Geneva in 1861 he described the privilege he felt at being 'in the midst of the Universal Church, in the midst of an assembly from which no one believing in a God of salvation is excluded'.[41] Fellowship with Christ was the basis of unity.

A key figure in the renewed international evangelical impetus which the Evangelical Alliance promoted from the later 1860s onwards was a Swiss-American, Philip Schaff. The roots of Schaff's spirituality were in German pietism. He was a theologian and historian of the American German Reformed Church, and became a professor at Union Theological Seminary, New York, in 1869. Schaff was initially critical of the Evangelical Alliance, but after his experience of Alliance meetings in Berlin in 1857 he became a strong supporter. From the 1860s until his death in 1893 he was a central personality in the growth of the international Alliance movement. Schaff's broad ecumenical vision derived from his Lutheran and Reformed connections and he envisaged the possibility of the ultimate coming together of the Roman Catholic, Protestant and Orthodox Churches in one body.[42] The Alliance was making an impact in a number of countries in this period and its emphasis on catholicity mirrored its sense of representing the Church across the world. Evangelical Alliance work in France in 1878 was seen as a testimony to 'true catholic unity', while at an Alliance conference in 1881 J.C. Ryle spoke of the Alliance's testimony to the essential unity of 'the whole Catholic Church', and in 1884 there was a call from Philip Schaff, which was taken up by others, for expressions of 'genuine catholicity'.[43] This kind of thinking contributed to the emergence of the Ecumenical movement in the twentieth century.

The Evangelical Alliance's promotion of catholicity, however, which stressed spiritual union, was challenged as a result of the formation in 1948 of the WCC.[44] In 1946 the British Alliance stated that it had nothing but goodwill for the existing British Council of Churches (formed in 1942) and the proposed WCC, describing them as potentially 'great and representative bodies'. It stressed its own distinctively evangelical witness.[45] A year later the Alliance published an 'Evangelical Charter', which stated:

> As the World's Evangelical Alliance is an alliance not of churches, nor of church societies, but of individual Christians, its relationship with the World Council of Churches is clear. The World Council of Churches may (as some believe) have come into existence partly as a result of the prayers and witness of the World's Evangelical Alliance, but its objective is entirely different. The Alliance advocates the close unity of Protestantism and works for a more real fellowship between all evangelicals. It believes that here in real spiritual unity (a unity which already exists) and not in an outward uniformity (a uniformity which would have to be imposed against

insuperable difficulties) lies the hope of revival and Christian victory.[46]

There is a supposed contrast here between spiritual unity and outward uniformity. In fact, the WCC never stated that it was in favour of uniformity, and the early leadership of the WCC was certainly committed to spiritual as well as organisational oneness. In subsequent decades there would be a measure of convergence between the evangelical understanding of 'real spiritual unity' and the wider ecclesiastical world. In the 1970s Cardinal Suenens, the Roman Catholic primate of Belgium who encouraged charismatic renewal, seemed to be as much at home among evangelicals as Catholics.[47] Often the common ground was shared spiritual experiences.

The Apostolic tradition

The catholic view of the Church, which gives a central place to episcopally ordained ministry and Apostolic tradition, may seem to be in direct opposition to the emphasis within the believers' church position on the personal spiritual relationship with God known by members of local church fellowships. Wesley, however, seemed to find both of these ecclesial views appropriate. As Frank Baker suggests, Wesley can be found supporting 'a historical institution of bishops and inherited customs', with ministers expounding the Bible and administering the sacraments 'in such a way as to preserve the ancient tradition on behalf of all those who were made members by baptism'. Yet Wesley also embraced the idea of societies or fellowship groups in which believers share 'the apostolic experience of God's living presence and also a desire to bring others into this same personal experience'.[48] Ultimately, Wesley's thinking, as is evident in his correspondence with those who wished to stress ecclesiastical distinctives, was evangelistic, activist and pragmatic. He asked: 'What is the end of all ecclesiastical order? Is it not to bring souls from the power of Satan to God, and to build them

up in His fear and love?' Given the priority for him of conversion and spiritual growth, Wesley concluded: 'Order, then, is so
far valuable as it answers these ends; and if it answers them
not, it is worth nothing.'[49]

This pragmatic approach to unity was taken up and
developed among evangelicals in Britain and in North
America. Samuel Simon Schmucker, a central figure in the
founding of the first ecumenical American Lutheran body and
also a respected Professor of Theology at the Lutheran seminary in Gettysburg, Pennsylvania, published a *Fraternal
Appeal to the American Churches* (1838), advocating full
recognition of membership and ministries between different
denominations. He wished, as his book's sub-title put it, for
'Catholic Union on Apostolic Principles'. A year later the
Society for the Promotion of Christian Union was created in
America.[50] Schmucker's influence was felt within the
Evangelical Alliance. He urged that world conferences on
unity should be held, and an appeal to this effect was
published in 1873. By this time there were increasing
hopes among many evangelicals for increased international
co-operation. From the 1880s, the conferences at Northfield,
Massachusetts, which were organised by D.L. Moody, inspired
a new generation of evangelicals such as John R. Mott, who
was a key figure at the historic World Missionary Conference
in Edinburgh in 1910.[51] Moody was committed not only to
unity but also to the vision for world mission in the later nineteenth century that was channelled through the massive
international Student Volunteer Movement.[52]

A few evangelicals in the Church of England in the 1870s
and 1880s, influenced by High Church thinking and practice,
promoted what they called 'Evangelical Catholic' principles.
The most prominent was George Howard Wilkinson, who was
appointed Bishop of Truro in 1883, and was later Primus of
the Scottish Episcopal Church. In 1877 E.W. Benson, who was
to become Archbishop of Canterbury, encouraged Wilkinson to
pass on 'what you understand and express by "Evangelical-
Catholic" teaching'.[53] From the 1870s, St Peter's, Eaton

Square, London, where Wilkinson was then Vicar, became known as perhaps the leading parish church in England.[54] Wilkinson introduced a daily eucharist and also prayer meetings on mid-week evenings, creating 'a novel kind of Church life'.[55] Another catholic evangelical was Arthur James Mason, the Church of England's first Canon Missioner and the Lady Margaret Professor of Divinity in Cambridge. Arthur James Mason wrote *The Ministry of Conversion*, in which he recommended John Wesley, George Whitefield and Charles Finney as exemplars in the field of evangelism. In one passage in the book he spoke about how 'a truly contrite soul which has found her way to the Living Saviour, and has felt the touch of His hand ... and is walking in His way within the unity of the Church, has the right to believe herself absolved and justified from her past sins and set right with God forthwith.'[56] Along with the message of a personal relationship with the risen Christ, the importance of being 'within the unity of the church' was being emphasised.

For most evangelicals, however, to be apostolic was not about ecclesiastical tradition. Rather it concerned the proclamation of apostolic doctrine and having the same experience of Christ as was recorded in the New Testament. It was this that connected evangelicals with each other. In the later 1950s and early 1960s, as General Secretary of the Evangelical Alliance in Britain, Gilbert Kirby was a strong advocate of the view that the Holy Spirit was pointing Christian people with new urgency towards deeper spiritual unity. A World Evangelical Fellowship was active from the early 1950s and over seventy societies and Bible colleges were linked together in the Evangelical Missionary Alliance.[57] In 1983, following some years of considerable tension within British evangelicalism over ecumenical issues, Clive Calver became General Secretary of the Evangelical Alliance. For Calver, awareness of evangelical tradition was an important element in thinking about contemporary evangelical experience. He spoke of discovering 'exactly what the heartbeat of the Evangelical Alliance was', and his conclusions were to have considerable significance for evangelicalism. Calver began to champion two causes: the first was the dream espoused by the Alliance's founding fathers, a dream of effective evangelical co-operation, and the second was the recovery of the commitment of Victorian evangelicals such as Lord Shaftesbury and William Booth to bringing about changes in society.[58] Evangelicals continued to press for spiritual unity and to promote their activist spiritual tradition.

Conclusion

It is not the case that evangelicals have seen their spiritual experiences as detached from ecclesial matters. Early evangelicals sought to understand their new spiritual awareness in relation to both local church life and the wider Church. Wesley insisted that he 'dare not exclude from the Church catholic all those congregations in which any unscriptural doctrines, which cannot be affirmed to be the "pure word of God", are sometimes ... preached'. He was prepared to argue, against some strands of Protestant thought, for Roman Catholics as being 'within the pale of the catholic Church'. For Wesley what mattered was that people should hold to 'one Spirit, one hope, one Lord, one faith and one God and Father of all', and if that was the case, he could cope with wrong opinions and mistaken modes of worship.[59] There have been evangelicals who have strongly opposed links with those who are not evangelicals, but evangelicals have over the centuries been active in the field of Christian unity. For them this has been primarily a unity built around spiritual experience – the experience of Christ. This experience is nurtured in the local setting and evangelical theologians such as Stanley Grenz have continued to explore this dynamic.[60] The ecumenical exchanges of the past century, however, as James Packer has argued, have brought a greater awareness among many evangelicals of 'churchly' issues. 'Churchliness', Packer suggests, means recognising the centrality of the Church and the primacy of the corporate life of Christian people in the purposes of God. Locally, he suggests, it means mutual involvement, openness and ministry within the congregation; ecumenically, it means realising brotherhood with all Christians.[61] Although the focus for evangelicals has often been primarily the fellowship of believers in the local congregation, there have been evangelicals who have had a vision of a Church that is united, holy, catholic and apostolic.

9. 'EXPECT GREAT THINGS, ATTEMPT GREAT THINGS': A MISSIONARY SPIRITUALITY

Preaching on 'The Church', and in particular on 'One Lord, one faith, one baptism', John Wesley explained that believers had 'one Lord', and that he was the one 'who has now dominion over them, who has set up his kingdom in their hearts, and reigns over all those that are partakers of this hope'. To obey Christ, Wesley continued, 'to run the way of his commandments, is their glory and joy.' Believers do this, he emphasised, 'with a willing mind'.[1] In his publication *A Collection of Forms of Prayers for Every Day in the Week*, Wesley prayed for 'a lively, zealous, active and cheerful spirit, that I may vigorously perform whatever Thou commandest'.[2] This is a classic evangelical desire. At its heart has been an understanding of Christ as Lord. A particular emphasis has been on obeying the 'great commission' of Christ to go into all the world and make disciples (Matthew 28:19, 20). Evangelicalism has been and is a movement in which priority has been given to reaching others with the gospel. From the eighteenth century onwards, evangelical faith has spread in a variety of ways. Sometimes outward-directed evangelical activity has had individual conversions as its sole aim, but often evangelical mission has also included addressing wider needs. For many evangelicals social action has been an integral part of spiritual life. The most striking exception to this was in the first half of the twentieth century, when many evangelicals retreated from society. This change of direction has been seen as a 'great reversal'.[3] The historic evangelical approach, however, has been broader, based on an understanding that Jesus is Lord of all.

Transatlantic revivals

The activist spirituality of the early evangelical movement, especially in relation to evangelism, was exemplified by the pioneering leaders such as George Whitefield and John Wesley. Their approach to the communication of the message was also a pragmatic one. In 1737, as Whitefield initiated the public revival that was to spread across England, he described in his personal journal (which was later published) his own ministry. His account of what Mark Noll describes as his 'frenetic pace', was written without any false modesty:

> The congregations continually increased, and generally, on a Lord's Day, I used to preach four or five times to very large and very affected auditories, besides reading prayers twice or thrice, and walking, perhaps, twelve miles in going backwards and forwards from one church to the other. But God made my feet like hind's feet, and filled me with joy unspeakable at the end of my day's work. This made me look upon my friends' kind advice which they gave me, to spare myself, as a temptation.[4]

When Whitefield and William Seward, his travelling companion, visited Bristol in February 1739, however, the clergy would not open their pulpits to preachers whom they saw as marked by 'enthusiasm' – what today would be called 'fanaticism'. Whitefield therefore spoke in Bristol's Newgate prison and to the miners of Kingswood colliery. His move to open-air preaching was shocking. It is, however, an example of the evangelical instinct to use all possible means to communicate the message. Reflecting on his first experience of preaching in the open fields, Whitefield vividly expressed his own spiritual experience: 'Blessed be God! I have now broken the ice! I believe I was never more acceptable to my Master than when I was standing to teach these hearers in the open fields.'[5]

Evangelical approaches to evangelism have often been innovative and at times controversial. The early evangelical espousal of new methods of communicating generated a fear of public disorder, and Whitefield was officially warned that he could be suspended from Church of England ministry and then excommunicated.[6] He carried on his work undeterred, however, speaking to crowds of up to 12,000 people. Some climbed trees to hear him and others listened on horses or in carriages. Whitefield's sermon style, which was compelling and dramatic, and well suited to the open air, was indebted to some extent to the developing world of drama. One insightful study of Whitefield's approach, by H.S. Stout, is entitled *The Divine Dramatist*.[7] Whitefield's ebullient personality had great appeal in North America. The powerful events of the Great Awakening in New England meant that his ministry had particular impact in that region.[8] The story of the evangelical vision for evangelism is bound up with transatlantic spiritual influences, and Whitefield was the pioneer in this respect. Almost half of Whitefield's later ministry was in North America. He was also highly effective in Scotland, for instance at revival meetings in Cambuslang, near Glasgow, when he was reckoned to have had at least 20,000 hearers. The reports of these meetings were modelled on the *Narrative of Surprising Conversions* by Jonathan Edwards. One minister, James Robe, wrote a *Faithful Narrative of the Extraordinary Work of the Spirit of God at Kilsyth*.[9] New spiritual influences crossed and re-crossed the Atlantic.

The spiritual commitments of John and Charles Wesley as evangelists were similar to those of Whitefield, despite their differences in theology. Charles Wesley made a point of speaking about Christ to fellow-passengers when travelling by coach. On one occasion a lady was so offended she threatened to beat him, but on another occasion Charles so impressed a passenger that the coach stopped for a time of prayer. Charles recorded: 'We sang and shouted all the way to Oxford.'[10] John Wesley repeatedly noted in his *Journal*, 'I offered them Christ'. Many Methodist societies flourished. In Norwich, for example, in late 1751, Methodist preaching led to a huge revival. Over 2,000 people joined the Methodist society, despite considerable violence against the Methodists.[11] By the time of his death John Wesley had travelled about 300,000 miles and preached about 45,000 sermons. He established a Methodist Connexion which had about 1,500 lay preachers. Part of his achievement was to encourage women to take leadership.[12] The example of John Wesley also had a profound impact on William and Catherine Booth and the Salvation Army. In 1882 George Scott Railton, the son of a Methodist minister and one of William Booth's earliest helpers, wrote *The Saved Clergyman or the Story of John Wesley*, a book which consisted of descriptions of early Methodist evangelism and especially the courage shown by John Wesley and the Methodists in the face of persecution. Railton concluded: 'Whoever wishes well to the Church or the nation, let him follow John Wesley's example.'[13]

Evangelical growth, at times dramatic growth, was a feature of North American Christianity in the nineteenth century. Baptist and Methodist growth far outstripped population growth in the early decades of the century. Francis Asbury, the first Methodist bishop in the United States, was closely associated with the 'camp meetings' which contributed to the remarkable advance that took place. In these revivals it was common for people attending meetings to drop down 'as if shot dead'. They could remain on the ground for an hour or more. One respected minister, James Finley, said: 'The falling down of multitudes, and their crying out (which happened under the singing of Watts' hymns, more frequently than under the preaching of the Word) was to us so new a scene, that we thought it prudent not to be over hasty in forming any opinion of it.'[14] The period 1857–9 saw a widespread revival which had effects in America and Britain. The focus initially was on business people, with Chicago an important centre. Edwin Orr, in his studies of revivals, sees this movement as a 'second Evangelical awakening', although he does not distinguish between local spontaneous awakenings and carefully organised evangelistic meetings.[15] The American evangelist James Caughey attracted large crowds to his preaching at Surrey Gardens, London, in this period.[16] D.L. Moody, who was active in the YMCA in Chicago, emerged as the most effective transatlantic evangelist of the later nineteenth century. His preaching was acceptable to evangelicals from varied backgrounds, a notable example being his hugely successful 1873–5 campaign around Britain.[17] American evangelicalism was becoming increasingly influential.

The spirituality of the transatlantic revival that marked the late 1850s was strongly orientated towards prayer. The Evangelical Alliance played a significant role through its extensive co-ordination of united prayer. There were also spontaneous outpourings of spiritual fervour, often associated with intercessory prayer, in certain areas in Northern Ireland, Wales and Scotland – particularly close-knit communities, for example the Scottish fishing communities between Aberdeen and Inverness.[18] Existing congregations belonging to established denominations were revived and new groups, such as the Brethren, grew significantly.[19] This revival was also characterised not only by spiritual power but by unusual physical phenomena. Some, including evangelicals, criticised what they saw as unhealthy and unbiblical emotionalism.[20] James McCosh, who had studied under Thomas Chalmers at Edinburgh University, and then became Professor of Logic and Metaphysics at Queen's College, Belfast, wrote on 'The Ulster Revival and Its Physiological Accidents'.[21] He argued that the prostrations, trembling and other phenomena associated with the revival could function as legitimate marks of the Holy Spirit's work, although they required authentication in the changed moral and spiritual character of those who experienced them. In taking this view, McCosh echoed the earlier analysis of revival by Jonathan Edwards.[22] These issues were to recur during the twentieth century as evangelical identity was increasingly influenced by Pentecostalism and charismatic spirituality.

Societies for world mission

The eighteenth-century evangelical awakenings led directly to missionary endeavours by Protestants. By the end of the eighteenth century Christian churches were to be found in many countries in the world, mainly because of mission by the Roman Catholic and Orthodox Churches, but Christianity was by no means a world-wide movement. General changes in the eighteenth century, such as travel by steamship, facilitated the growth of world mission, and the spread of British colonial rule was a factor that provided new opportunities for specifically Protestant missionary activity.[23] There had been some wider mission by Protestants before this: the Society for Promoting Christian Knowledge (1699) had a concern for overseas mission and David Brainerd worked among the North American Indians through the Scottish Society for the Propagation of Christian Knowledge (1710). In 1732 the Moravians, at Herrnhut, committed themselves to what proved to be a remarkable missionary work, reaching places such as Greenland and Lapland. But it was the working through of the spiritual effects of the transatlantic evangelical revival that made the most marked difference in Protestant thinking about world mission. Thomas Coke, a Methodist, placed missionaries in the West Indies, and the London Missionary Society, formed in 1785, which initially attempted to unite Anglicans and Dissenters, became the missionary society of the Congregationalists. Jonathan Edwards' *An Humble Attempt*, with its vision of 'the Advancement of Christ's Kingdom on Earth', was crucial in the story of evangelical missionary developments. The 'Prayer Call' in 1784 by the Northamptonshire Association of Baptist Churches flowed from this, and a further consequence was the formation in October 1792 of the Particular Baptist Society for Propagating the Gospel Among the Heathen, later known as the Baptist Missionary Society (BMS).[24]

The prime mover behind the formation of this Society was a young Baptist minister in Leicester, William Carey. His spiritual vision was set out in a book and a sermon. The book, published in 1792, was *An Enquiry into the Obligation of Christians, to Use Means for the Conversion of the Heathen*. The sermon, delivered on 30 May 1792 to the Northamptonshire Baptist Association, was entitled 'Expect great things, attempt great things'. On the following day the business of the Association continued, but Carey was insistent, asking: 'Is nothing to be done?' It was decided, despite reluctance on the part of some, that a plan be prepared for forming a Baptist Society for mission. In the area of spirituality, the significance of the BMS was that Carey challenged the influential high Calvinism found in the Baptist denomination. John Gill, the chief promoter of this brand of Calvinism, which denied that the gospel should be offered to unbelievers, was probably the most widely read Baptist writer of the period. In 1779 Robert Hall Snr, a Baptist minister in Leicestershire, preached against high Calvinism and this address was published in 1781 as *Helps to Zion's Travellers*. Carey said: 'I do not remember to have read any book with such raptures.' New spiritual energy was being generated. In 1785 Andrew Fuller, of Kettering, wrote *The Gospel Worthy of all Acceptation*, which argued for the free offer of the gospel and became the most powerful critique of high Calvinism. Fuller became BMS Secretary and Carey went as a missionary to India.[25]

Evangelical involvement in world mission grew rapidly in the nineteenth century. Evangelical Anglicans, stimulated by Charles Simeon from Cambridge, and John Venn, Rector of Clapham, formed their own society in 1799 – the 'Society for Missions to Africa and the East' – which from 1812 was known as the Church Missionary Society. The Wesleyan Methodists followed in 1813. Denominational societies were then joined by interdenominational missionary organisations. The most famous promoter of this form of missionary enterprise was James Hudson Taylor, who went to China in 1853 with the Chinese Evangelisation Society. In 1865 Hudson Taylor formed the China Inland Mission (CIM) which became the largest Protestant mission in the world. Among the main principles were interdenominationalism, no educational requirements for missionary candidates, the stipulation that missionaries would wear Chinese dress and identify with the local people, the principle of work being directed on the spot rather than from Britain, an emphasis on evangelism, and the conviction that all funds were to be raised 'by faith' rather than through appeals for money. This last element had obvious affinities with Keswick spirituality. In the same way that a faith mission repudiated dependence on human support in the area of finance, so a Christian who had entered into the rest of faith refused to rely on human effort for holiness. Clearly there could also be tensions between rest and activism. But Taylor, who said that he had entered into the experience of holiness by faith before it was taught at Keswick, was an outstanding example of the way spiritual consecration led to pioneering mission.[26]

By 1887 the Keswick Convention was a major recruiting ground for the CIM and other overseas missionary agencies. Although the Convention stated that its message was not primarily about evangelism or foreign mission, it was customary for large numbers of young people to respond – at a meeting held at the end of the Convention week – to calls for dedication to overseas mission. Keswick's view of mission was that it should be distinctly conversionist in intent. Brian Stanley, in *The Bible and the Flag*, outlined two parallel British missionary traditions, one understanding mission as embracing a broader humanitarianism, and the other, arising especially from the holiness movements, that was more inclined to limit the Christian message to one of individual salvation.[27] Although Keswick was not so closely linked with the broader understanding of mission, its connections were wider than the faith missions, especially because of the transatlantic evangelical network. The Student Volunteer Missionary Union started at D.L. Moody's Northfield conference in 1886 when over 6,000 Volunteers signed a card saying that they were willing to go overseas. The watchword used was 'the evangelisation of the world in this generation', and A.T. Pierson, the American minister and missionary thinker, who spoke at British and American conventions, including Keswick, was associated with the origins of this watchword.[28] A broad range of mission enterprises owed their initiation to evangelical spirituality.

One woman who typified the missionary spirituality of this period was Lilias Trotter. Born in 1853, Lilias was taken by her mother to Broadlands where she heard Robert and Hannah Pearsall Smith. It is probable that she was one of the youngest people present. She then attended the Oxford and Brighton conferences and was also active in the Moody and Sankey campaigns. In 1876 she met the painter, writer and social reformer John Ruskin, an archetypal Romantic figure, while touring with her family in Switzerland. Ruskin believed that Lilias Trotter's gifts meant she could have a brilliant future as an artist and he invited her to stay at his home beside Lake Coniston in the Lake District. The friendship continued, with Ruskin suggesting that Lilias was the only person likely to help him in his difficulties about faith. He wrote to her as 'Darling St Lilias'. Ruskin was on the edge of the Broadlands network through his friendship with Georgina Cowper-Temple. The influence of Ruskin on Trotter's painting, as on the style of other young artists of the period, was considerable, and there was huge pressure on Trotter to become a full part of Ruskin's artistic circle. She was, however, feeling a strong call to engage in missionary service, and from 1888 until her death in 1928 most of her life was spent in sacrificial mission work in Algeria and elsewhere in North Africa. She continued to paint, but instead of the wider acclaim she might have gained as an artist, she became known to missionary-minded evangelicals as the enterprising founder and leader of the Algiers Mission Band. Spirituality and mission were intertwined.[29]

'Action is the life of virtue'

Mission also included action for social change. In 1797 William Wilberforce published his very influential *A Practical view of the prevailing Religious System of Professed Christians in the Higher and Middle Classes in this country contrasted with Real Christianity*. This sold over 7,000 copies in six months. Wilberforce spoke about the social context: the increase in prosperity for some, the growth of towns and cities, and the growing social problems. He argued for a sense of responsibility brought about by a turn from nominal Christianity to real Christianity on the part of the rich.[30] Together with other members of the Clapham group of evangelicals, Wilberforce gave priority in his socio-political activity to campaigning against slavery, although other campaigns were launched, for example the promotion of Sunday observance. John Wesley published his *Thoughts on Slavery* in 1774 and his last letter was to Wilberforce urging action against the 'execrable villany' of the slave trade. For Wesley the campaign was a spiritual one in which Wilberforce needed divine help, otherwise he would be 'worn out by the opposition of men and devils'.[31] From 1789 Wilberforce frequently introduced measures in the House of Commons against the slave trade and had an influence on his friend William Pitt, the Prime Minister. Wilberforce introduced a new style of campaigning – pressure politics – and used propaganda to influence public opinion. Also he was probably the greatest orator of his age. But the campaigners were opposed by huge vested interests since British trade was thought to be dependent on slaves. With eventual formal abolition of the British slave trade in 1807, Wilberforce pressed for slavery to be illegal, and this took place in 1833. This campaign was a paradigm for all subsequent efforts by evangelicals to achieve spiritual change in society.[32]

Other efforts were made in fields such as education. Robert Raikes began his Sunday Schools in 1780 and this developed into a massive movement. Hannah More established schools from 1789. William Wilberforce, visiting More in 1787, discussed what could be done about local poverty and the lack of spiritual help for people in the Mendips. In a parish of 2,000 people, almost all very poor, More found that only one family had a Bible, and that was used to prop up a flower-pot. Hannah and her sister Martha attempted to make school classes entertaining as well as educational. Evangelicals have given considerable attention to the nurture of children. Hannah More was not only a social activist but also a prolific writer, her complete *Works* amounting to eleven volumes. She summed up evangelical attitudes to social problems when she wrote: 'Action is the life of virtue, and the world is the theatre of action'.[33] Evangelical efforts in the field of education increased levels of literacy, and those who learned to read were encouraged to read the Bible. Active supporters of the British and Foreign Bible Society included Wilberforce, Lord Teignmouth, who became the first President of the Society (and thought of the post as more important than any other office he held, including being Governor General of India and a Privy Councillor), Lord Bexley and the Earl of Shaftesbury, both of whom became Society Presidents.[34] Nonconformists such as R.W. Dale, in Birmingham, and Spurgeon and Campbell Morgan in London, spoke out on social and also political issues that affected ordinary people. Dale was especially interested in education and made connections between this issue and the challenge of dealing with the fundamental causes of poverty and crime.[35] Education was a central evangelical theme.

Evangelical action on a whole range of social issues grew in importance throughout the nineteenth century. It is estimated by Kathleen Heasman that by the second half of the nineteenth century perhaps three-quarters of the charitable organisations in Britain could be regarded as evangelical in character and control.[36] The Earl of Shaftesbury, to take perhaps the best-known example of an evangelical social reformer of this period, worked tirelessly for better conditions for working people. Shaftesbury's biographer, Edwin Hodder, writing in 1884, noted that Shaftesbury, who spoke of himself as an 'Evangelical of the Evangelicals', considered it was from evangelicals that most of the great philanthropic movements of the nineteenth century had sprung.[37] Many missions were started, such as the London City Mission.[38] Thomas Barnardo established a centre in East London (which had been a gin palace) and this grew to become a huge organisation caring for children in need. By the end of the century the famous survey by Charles Booth, *Life and Labour of the People in London*, recorded that there was a mission in almost every street in the poorer areas of London. The variety was enormous and included temperance missions, work for prisoners, help for the blind and deaf, and the orphanages set up by C.H. Spurgeon and George Muller.[39] Thomas Chalmers, the leader of the evangelicals in the Church of Scotland, addressed social needs he encountered in his ministry in Glasgow.[40]

Spiritual renewal and social-evangelistic endeavour often went hand in hand, for example in the work of William Pennefather, at St Jude's, Mildmay. As well as holding large devotional conferences, the Pennefathers began the Mildmay Mission, which was hugely influential. Deaconesses were trained for social and evangelistic ministries, a concept taken up by others including the Baptist denomination. For these activists social wrongs were sins. William Booth, a holiness advocate and social activist, wrote: 'Our campaign is against Sin!'[41] Josephine Butler, who campaigned successfully in the 1880s for the repeal of the Contagious Diseases Acts, under which prostitutes were given health inspections while no action was taken regarding their clients, spoke of those who supported her by prayer when debates were taking place in the House of Commons. Butler pressed for the age of consent for lawful sexual intercourse to be raised from twelve to sixteen (her research in Liverpool showed that of 9,000 prostitutes, 1,500 were under fifteen) and this goal was achieved in 1885. She believed her campaigns advanced when they were 'openly baptised, so to speak, in the name of Christ', and she thought she had observed in the 'sceptical and worldly atmosphere of Parliament' something new – 'signs of a consciousness of a spiritual strife going on'.[42] F.B. Meyer became well known for his contribution to the rehabilitation of offenders. During his ministry in Leicester in the 1880s he discovered that men coming out of prison were quickly drawn back into crime. With the co-operation of the governor, he visited the prison daily, taking discharged prisoners to a coffee house for a plate of ham. Meyer also found ex-prisoners employment. A minority, Meyer admitted, 'turned out very badly', but he claimed that many were converted and the prison population was reduced.[43] Social improvement was undergirded and shaped by spiritual experience.

The same processes were taking place in America, and transatlantic links were evident. In 1881 A.B. Simpson resigned from his pastorate at the wealthy Thirteenth Street Presbyterian Church in New York. As he saw it, his church wanted to have within its ranks respectable Christians, but Simpson, who would go on to found the Christian and Missionary Alliance, wanted 'a multitude of publicans and sinners'. Simpson had seen Spurgeon's church in London and said that his own 'plan and idea' of a church was like Spurgeon's. The rich and poor were side by side. This meant that the church was a mission and the mission was a church. He wrote:

> We believe the ideal mission is the ideal Church, not a down town chapel where the masses are to be worked upon but a loving brotherhood of Christian equality and fellowship where the rich and poorest are at the same communion table and the lives rescued from the lowest ranks are put to work in equal fellowship with their more cultured brethren.[44]

Both America and Britain saw the emergence of the 'social gospel', as it was termed. Walter Rauschenbusch, a Baptist minister in New York City, has been rightly viewed as the founder of the social gospel.[45] The term began to be used increasingly in England in the late 1880s and 1890s by

Baptist leaders such as John Clifford, probably the best-known national advocate of what was called the 'Nonconformist Conscience'.[46] For evangelicals like Clifford, Meyer and the Wesleyan leader, Hugh Price Hughes, the social gospel was not at odds with a spiritual message: it was, rather, the application of the belief in Christ's Lordship to society as a whole.

Church and world – the twentieth century

The Welsh Revival of 1904–5 is an example from the twentieth century of how spiritual renewal can affect Church and society. Evan Roberts, the best-known figure in the revival, who had been a coal-miner for twelve years, was at a conference in September 1904 for the deepening of spiritual life and was deeply moved by a prayer by a well-known evangelist, Seth Joshua, which included the words 'bend us'. Roberts was led to pray in anguish, 'Bend me'. Out of this experience a mission team of young people emerged.[47] As the team conducted meetings many miners were dramatically changed: one striking story is about the pit ponies not being able to understand the 'swear-free' language of the converted miners. The work ethos in the coal mines was transformed: it was reported that management and workers seemed to get on better, although there was some concern at an early stage that enthusiastic prayer meetings might take up work time. There was also reconciliation between different groups of miners. People who had been careless about paying bills, paid what they owed, and longstanding feuds in local communities were settled.[48] The Welsh Revival also, as has been seen, played a crucial part in the birth of Pentecostalism. Although at least 100,000 people were added to the churches in Wales, in some cases people affected by the Revival left the mainline denominations for mission halls and new Pentecostal churches.[49]

A significant twentieth-century evangelistic movement with a strong contemporary thrust was the Oxford Group, led by Frank Buchman. In 1901, as a Lutheran theological

student, Frank Buchman attended the Northfield Conference.
The visit 'completely changed' his life and he dedicated himself to winning people for Christ.[50] Buchman, who was also
deeply affected by Oswald Chambers and Jessie Penn-Lewis,
sought to engage with people outside the churches. By 1933
(as reported in the London *Evening Standard*) a meeting convened by the Group in the House of Commons attracted so
many MPs that it 'emptied smoking rooms and the floor of the
House alike'. The Group's main speaker was Carl Johan
Hambro, President of the Norwegian Parliament and of the
League of Nations Assembly.[51] The Group's magazine, *Rising
Tide*, was being translated into nine languages in the 1930s,
with over one and a half million copies being sold, mainly in
Europe and America. A campaign in Denmark filled the
biggest hall in Copenhagen every night for a week. At
Hamlet's Castle at Elinsore, 10,000 people crowded into the
castle courtyard.[52] In typical evangelical terms, Buchman
urged people to see Jesus Christ as the answer to human need
and to seek 'a mighty awakening of the living Spirit of God'.[53]
When 1,600 people attended a Group meeting in the Town
Hall in Bournemouth, in 1936, comparisons were made with
Wesley and Whitefield. It is significant that Group meetings
made personal testimonies, not preaching, central.[54]
Experience of Christ was a priority.

Other ways of reaching people were evident. In 1925
Samuel Chadwick announced his determination to enlist
Methodist Friars to evangelise England, and from 1926 these
uniformed 'Cliff Trekkers' went out in bands each year to
attempt the task. Chadwick conceived of his Friars as an
Order, raised up as were Francis of Assisi, the Wesleys and
William and Catherine Booth.[55] Rodney ('Gipsy') Smith also
worked within and beyond Methodism as an evangelist. From
the 1940s this kind of approach to evangelism was adopted by
the interdenominational London Bible College (LBC). As with
the Cliff College trekkers, teams of LBC students travelled
widely. Their vision was 'not for crowded meetings, but for
finding out needy, difficult places'.[56] Also in the 1940s, Youth

for Christ (YFC), which originated in America, began to have a significant impact in Britain. Edwin Orr, a chronicler of revivals, suggested that the huge impact of Youth for Christ could be attributed to the utilisation of modern techniques. Although Orr could pinpoint few differences between the methodology of YFC and Tom Rees, who was perhaps the best-known post-war British evangelist, the YFC organisation seemed to him to convey a more vibrant atmosphere.[57] The palpable power of the best-known YFC preacher, Billy Graham, captivated British audiences and prepared the way for the later, large-scale Graham campaigns. YFC comments on youth rallies in the 1940s were uncompromisingly triumphant: in 1947 Birmingham was 'in the grip of a revival'. In Pontypridd memories of the Welsh Revival were evoked.[58]

Evangelical thinking about social involvement changed during the century. Although many of those who developed the social gospel were evangelicals, in the early twentieth century it became conventional wisdom among many evangelicals that the social gospel was a product of theological liberalism. In 1924 E.L. Langston, Vicar of Emmanual Church, Wimbledon, who was a Keswick speaker, expressed his fear that 'the Social Gospel will take the place in many pulpits of the Gospel of the Grace of God'.[59] In 1949 Basil Atkinson, a leading statesman behind the Cambridge University Christian Union, said that the only work given to the Church was evangelisation. Social ministry, as an end in itself, was rejected by Atkinson.[60] The National Evangelical Anglican Congress at Keele University in 1967, however, made the statement that evangelism and compassionate service belonged together in the mission of God.[61] A recovery of an older vision was evident. Others writers in the post-war decades who encouraged social involvement included the American evangelical theologian Carl Henry,[62] and radicals such as Ronald Sider, in particular through his book *Rich Christians in an Age of Hunger* (1977), and Jim Wallis, of the Sojourners Community in Washington, DC, with his book *The Call to Conversion* (1981). The sixteenth-century Anabaptists have been a source of inspiration in the thinking that has taken place about radical discipleship.[63] In 1968 the Evangelical Alliance created the relief agency TEAR Fund. Evangelicals were also galvanised into action by legislation which they did not like, for example on abortion or Sunday trading. The Festival of Light of 1971 evolved into the socially active CARE Trust. A key aim has been to recover the social message of the Bible.[64]

Finally, evangelical mission in the twentieth century became more global. Ease of travel meant that there was much more emphasis on people, especially young people, undertaking mission in other countries for shorter periods of time. A pioneer in this area in the 1960s was an American, George Verwer, who called for a 'spiritual revolution' among evangelicals.[65] Verwer, who moved to Britain, founded Operation Mobilisation, which became a large-scale inter-denominational and international missionary enterprise. Other organisations, such as Youth With A Mission, developed in similar ways. A crucial milestone in evangelical thinking about world mission was the International Congress on World Evangelization, held in July 1974 at Lausanne, Switzerland. There were nearly 2,700 participants and over 1,000 observers. From Lausanne came a more comprehensive understanding of evangelical experience as global, rather than Western, and a more holistic view of the gospel. Two Latin Americans, Rene Padilla and Samuel Escobar, argued for social, political, economic and environmental issues to be seen within the scope of mission. Rene Padilla spoke scathingly about an evangelical sub-culture playing down discipleship. Gilbert Kirby, Principal of London Bible College, was Congress chairman when the final statement – the Lausanne Covenant – was presented. It included an affirmation of evangelical socio-political involvement.[66] In the 1990s many evangelicals in a number of countries took up the issue of the way debt was crushing countries in the two-thirds world. In 1998, under the auspices of the Jubilee 2000 campaign, 70,000 people, many from churches, formed a human chain in Birmingham to highlight the issue to world leaders at an economic summit. The British government later called for a review of debt relief.[67]

Conclusion

From the beginning of the evangelical movement, active engagement in evangelism and social action was central. 'The Christian spirit', stated Thomas Chalmers, 'must live by working'.[68] Social and political endeavour, as well as evangelism, was seen by most evangelicals in the eighteenth and nineteenth centuries as an outworking of spiritual experience. The call was to expect and to attempt 'great things'. Prior to the 1880 general election C.H. Spurgeon wrote and distributed leaflets in the boroughs of Lambeth and Southwark urging voters not to elect a Conservative, as had happened at the last election, but to support the Liberal candidates. He wrote:

> Are we to have another six years of Tory rule? This is just now the question. Are we to go on invading and slaughtering, in order to obtain a scientific frontier and feeble neighbours? How many wars may we reckon upon between now and 1886? What quantity of killing will be done in that time, and how many of our weaker neighbours will have their houses burned and their fields ravaged by this Christian (?) nation? Let those who rejoice in War vote for the Tories; but we hope they will not find a majority in Southwark.[69]

This robust perspective was lost to some extent in the early twentieth century and the focus came to be on individual conversion rather than social change. However, the earlier holistic spiritual vision was largely recovered during the second half of the twentieth century. Lausanne, in 1974, represented both an opportunity for evangelicals to unite for world mission and an opportunity to map out a new direction for evangelicals which would again include social action. Here was a spirituality which was not confined to the Church but which saw Jesus as Lord of the whole earth. In 1987, at a huge annual InterVarsity Christian Fellowship convention in Illinois, USA (The 'Urbana' convention), George Verwer of Operation Mobilisation concluded a keynote address with a challenge which sums up the evangelical understanding of a mission spirituality: 'Let us mobilize and let us go forth making Jesus Christ absolute Lord every day of our life until we are with him'.[70]

10. 'THE LORD COMETH': EVANGELICALS AND THE LAST TIMES

Evangelical thinking about the future has shown considerable variety.[1] Very often there has been the feeling of living in or near to the last times, which some evangelicals have seen as being times of revival but which others have believed will be times of apostasy. There has been much focus on Revelation chapter 20, with its references to a period of 1,000 years in which Satan is bound. Earlier evangelicals were often post-millennial. Those in this theological tradition, which drew from the thinking of the Puritans of the seventeenth century,[2] believed that the world would be gradually Christianised and that Christ's return would follow a golden age (perhaps not literally of 1,000 years, but certainly a lengthy period of time) in the history of the Church. They were optimistic in their spirituality. But in the nineteenth century the premillennial understanding of the Last Things, which taught that Christ would return to overthrow the Antichrist and to inaugurate a reign of 1,000 years, grew in popularity among evangelicals. Coupled with this the idea became prominent within evangelicalism that the world was a 'wrecked vessel' and that the main task was to rescue people out of it. There was much greater stress on the spread of evil than on the spread of the gospel. This did not mean that evangelicals became inward-looking or apathetic. The object of Christian activity was to save as many people as could be saved and great energy was devoted to that purpose. A third view to be found among evangelicals, amillennialism, takes biblical references to the millennium as being figurative and as applying to the whole period between Christ's first and second advents. Despite these differences, evangelicals have generally been united in believing that at the time of the end there will be a final judgement.

The postmillennial view

Postmillennialism, which was probably dominant among evangelicals until the second half of the nineteenth century, generated great hopes of the Christianisation of the world. The spread of the gospel was seen by many as having the potential to transform whole social structures and to bring about an age of peace and prosperity, with great advances in education, the arts, sciences and medicine.[3] The most influential postmillennial theologian of the eighteenth century was Jonathan Edwards. In his book, *A History of Redemption*, Edwards proposed the view that the gospel would spread in the future in ways that would supersede anything that had been seen up to that point. Edwards wrote:

> There is a kind of veil now cast over the greater part of the world, that keeps them in darkness, but then this veil shall be destroyed, Isa. 25:7, 'And he will destroy in this mountain the face of the covering cast over all people, and the veil that is spread over all nations'. And then all countries and nations, even those that are now most ignorant, shall be full of light and knowledge. Great knowledge shall prevail everywhere. It may be hoped that then many of the Negroes and Indians will be divines, and that excellent books will be published in Africa, in Ethiopia, in Turkey – and not only very learned men, but others that are more ordinary men, shall then be very knowing in religion, Isa. 32:3–4, 'The eyes of them that see shall not be dim; and the ears of them that hear shall hearken. The heart also of the rash shall understand knowledge'.[4]

This represented, at the time, a hugely optimistic outlook. The prophetic views of Edwards inspired William Carey and other English-speaking Protestant missionaries. Carey and his

Baptist Missionary Society colleagues, in their *Form of Agreement* at Serampore, India, spoke of the certainty in their minds that the conversion to Christ of the people of India would take place in the 'not very distant period'.[5]

The Wesleyan, German Pietist and Moravian streams of revival and renewal in the eighteenth century had a similar outlook. Although Wesley never used the words premillennial or postmillennial in his *Works*, his expectation seems to have been of the gradual spread of the gospel.[6] Samuel Pearce, a Baptist minister, felt for the first time 'a passion for missions' when he heard Thomas Coke, the eighteenth-century Methodist missionary statesman, preaching in a Methodist chapel on 'Ethiopia shall soon stretch out her hands unto God' (Psalm 68:31).[7] The use of the word 'passion' is significant as an indicator of the way in which the hope of the conversion of the world operated in the realm of evangelical spiritual experience. Within the Pietist tradition, John Albert Bengal, a disciple of the Pietist leader Philipp Spener, argued in 1740 that there should be missions by Protestants to Jews and Gentiles. He was looking for a time when there would be a full conversion of Jews to Christ and he believed that this would lead to the wider blessing of the world.[8] The Moravians were deeply influenced by Pietism and, in turn, the Moravian vision for world mission had a profound influence in England. The Moravian missionary enterprise was viewed by other evangelicals as an example of the way in which world mission could be a force for civilisation.[9] This was a typical postmillennial outlook.

In the early nineteenth century evangelical leaders such as Charles Simeon showed little interest in debates about an imminent and visible return of Christ. The received belief among evangelicals regarding the future was still a postmillennial one. Simeon's curate, Henry Martyn, who went on to engage in missionary work in India and Persia, looked for the spread of the Christian faith in Islamic countries.[10] In Scotland Thomas Chalmers similarly wrote about 'that universal reign of truth and of righteousness which is coming'.[11]

Samuel Waldegrave, soon before he became Bishop of Carlisle, devoted his Bampton Lectures, published in 1866, to arguing for postmillennialism. He looked for the coming of a future, spiritual kingdom of Christ, as envisaged in Revelation chapter 20. The personal return of Christ would follow the thousand-year period of blessing.[12] By this time, however, evangelical views were changing. In part this was due to political factors, such as the Napoleonic Wars, which sapped British national confidence. The belief that the future would be marked by continuous progress was shaken. The optimism of the Enlightenment was also faltering. As a mark of this change of thinking, Edward Bickersteth, the best-known and the most colourful evangelical in the Church of England after Simeon, decided in the 1830s to write a book on the second advent and in the course of writing it he changed his position and adopted premillennialism. Bickersteth would go on to reiterate his premillennial beliefs at the founding conference in 1854 of the Evangelical Alliance.[13] 'Expectations', as David Bebbington puts it, 'that the gospel would usher in a superior world order were dismissed by the new school as a sinister deception.'[14] The hopeful spirituality of postmillennialism was giving way to a new mood.

The rise of premillennial thought

The new mood was epitomised by Edward Irving, a young and flamboyant Scottish Presbyterian minister. Irving, who had assisted Thomas Chalmers in Glasgow before moving to a ministry in London, enjoyed considerable fame in the 1820s as the minister of the Church of Scotland's congregation in Hatton Garden, London. Several of London's aristocrats and political and literary figures came to hear his dramatic preaching. But Irving succeeded in alienating many evangelical leaders. In 1824, in a highly controversial sermon preached before the London Missionary Society, Edward Irving argued that missionaries should not go abroad supported – in financial and other ways – by missionary societies. Rather they should renounce all human support. Later his espousal of speaking in tongues meant that he found even more of the evangelical establishment ranged against him. In turn he condemned the 'love of order, moderation, piety and prudence' that characterised many evangelicals.[15] Irving was later put out of Church of Scotland ministry on account of his Christological views and he set up the Catholic Apostolic Church, which combined charismatic and liturgical elements. The radical thinking and Romantic sensibilities that characterised Irving meant that he was attracted to the apocalypticism of the premillennial view. He was prominent at conferences on this topic at Albury Park, Surrey, hosted by Henry Drummond, a wealthy banker, and attended by a number of younger evangelical leaders.[16] The spiritual outlook was changing.

Another key figure in the upsurge of interest among many evangelicals in the subject of Christ's second advent was John Nelson Darby, a young Anglican curate from County Wicklow, Ireland (and a godson of Lord Nelson). Darby left the Church of England and became the most formative thinker within the developing Brethren movement of the 1830s and 1840s. He had a significant impact beyond the Brethren through his preaching, his writing and his personal conversations. For Darby, the present 'dispensation' – the era of the Church – was destined to end in spiritual apostasy and he argued that complete withdrawal from existing ecclesiastical structures was demanded.[17] A number of evangelical Anglicans in Oxford who showed a considerable interest in the subjects of prophecy and ecclesiology seceded from the Church of England, among them the early Brethren leader B.W. Newton and a future Strict Baptist leader, J.C. Philpot, a Fellow of Worcester College, Oxford.[18] Much attention was given to study of the book of Revelation. A book by S.R. Maitland on Daniel and Revelation, published in 1826, inspired the 'futurist' view, which was that Revelation referred to events that were still in the future.[19] Futurist premillennial interpreters were themselves divided, with J.N. Darby (whose *shema* was to be popularised in the Scofield Reference Bible of 1909) suggesting that there would be a 'secret rapture' of the Church at the return of Christ, which could take place 'at any moment', and that Christ would subsequently come back *with* his saints in a public appearance to reign for a thousand years. Others, such as B.W. Newton, although in the futurist camp, rejected Darby's scheme and expected a period of severe judgement, 'the great tribulation', before Christ's visible return.[20] All of this generated much spiritual anticipation.

At the other end of the spectrum from the futurists were those interpreters of Revelation (sometimes described as preterists) who asserted that the whole of the book had already been fulfilled – that the first three or four centuries of the Christian Church had witnessed its entire accomplishment. Still others, known as historicists, believed that the books of Daniel and Revelation were intended to give insights into the unfolding of world events throughout the centuries up to the end, and they were therefore greatly interested in interpreting 'signs of the times'. Two books by a Presbyterian minister, John Cumming, written in 1848 and 1854, *Apocalyptic Sketches* and *Signs of the Times*, represented an attempt to popularise a four-volume scholarly work advocating the historicist approach, *Horae Apocalypticae* (1844), by E.B. Elliott, a Fellow of Trinity College, Cambridge.[21] Futurism, with its more dramatic visions of the end times, was the predominant position in North American premillennialism, whereas in Britain many Anglican evangelicals favoured the more sober approach of historicism. By the turn of the nineteenth century, however, more British premillennialists were becoming attracted to futurism.[22] The hope of the secret rapture was one that promised that believers would be exempt from the sufferings that would follow – the great tribulation. Prophecies about the kingdom of God were, according to the logic of this 'dispensationalist' schema, to be fulfilled in the millennial age that would follow the advent.[23] The expectation of the second advent, especially of an imminent secret rapture, fostered a desire to be in spiritual readiness' for this event.

Premillennial evangelicals also tended to focus on the purposes of God for the Jews. It was thought that Israel would be spiritually 'restored' either at or after Christ's return to set up his millennial kingdom. In 1839 Murray McCheyne and Andrew Bonar wrote a best-selling account of a mission trip they made to Palestine. As part of their trip they also met Jews in Eastern Europe, including Moldova and Poland. They were horrified by the anti-Jewish activity which they encountered in places on their travels. McCheyne was able to communicate with Jews using the Hebrew Bible.[24] While in London they met with another strong supporter of the Jews, the Earl of Shaftesbury, who had been influenced by Edward Bickersteth and had adopted premillennialism. Edwin Hodder, Shaftesbury's biographer, analysed Shaftesbury's inner, spiritual life, and noted that belief in Christ's second coming stimulated him in all his work.[25] Between 1838 and 1840 Shaftesbury, who was Lord Palmerston's step son-in-law, encouraged Palmerston, then British Foreign Secretary, to set up a Protestant bishopric in Jerusalem. The first bishop, appointed in 1841, was the Professor of Hebrew and Rabbinic Studies at King's College London, Michael Solomon Alexander, a Polish-born Jew who had embraced the Christian faith.[26] In the later nineteenth century a few evangelicals such as James Mountain, who went on to found the Baptist Bible Union, espoused British Israelitism, the theory that the Anglo-Saxon races were descended from the 'Lost Tribes' of Israel and had a special place in God's purpose. One advocate of this position was heard to bolster his argument by suggesting that Saxon was an abridgement of 'Isaac's son'.[27] Premillennialism encouraged both spirituality and speculation.

Advent testimony

On 8 November 1917 an important premillennial manifesto
was widely published in the Christian press in Britain. It
affirmed that Jesus might return 'at any moment', that Israel
would be territorially restored and converted by Christ's
appearing, and that under the subsequent millennial reign of
Christ there would be a 'great effusion of the Holy Spirit'.[28]
The origins of the manifesto can be traced to a visit made a
few weeks earlier by two Baptist ministers, J.S. Harrison and
Alfred Bird, who had both studied at Spurgeon's College, to
the respected Keswick Convention speaker F.B. Meyer, in
which they urged him to call the Church to a perception of
prophecy being fulfilled.[29] Meyer, who with the onset of the
First World War had felt that he was living in 'the joint of two
ages', decided that the time was right for a concentration on
the advent hope and on advent testimony. He now believed
that the war was the 'Midnight Cry', the precursor of Christ's
return. Meyer contacted A.H. Burton and E.L. Langston of the
Prophecy Investigation Society, which was the only existing
interdenominational premillennial body in England (and
which dated back to 1842), and then drew together for discussion a group that included household evangelical names,
including a number of Keswick Anglicans such as H.W. Webb-
Peploe and Free Church leaders like G. Campbell Morgan of
Westminster Chapel.[30] After differences between historicist
and futurist schools of premillennial thought within the group
had been ironed out, the manifesto was produced.[31]

The timing of the launch of what was to be called the
Advent Testimony and Preparation Movement (ATPM) was
perfect. On 2 November 1917, within a week of the manifesto
being published, it was announced (in the letter known as the
Balfour Declaration) that the British government was prepar-
ing to support the establishment of a home for the Jews in
Palestine. There was tremendous excitement among students
of the end times. The first public meetings for Advent
Testimony were held at the Queen's Hall in London on 13

December, when 3,000 enthusiasts came together in an atmosphere of euphoria.[32] In the same month General Allenby entered Jerusalem. In accordance with Luke 21, so it seemed, the times of the treading down of Jerusalem were at an end. Surely Christ would soon return. Not all, however, were convinced. P.T. Forsyth, for example, was dismissive of the new movement. The views of Meyer and his associates were, he commented icily, obsolete, and no one holding these opinions, as far as he could recall, 'ever did the New Testament the honour of being a recognised scholar in it'.[33]

Premillennialism has often divided evangelicals. In North America there was a sharp polarisation in this period between those who were broader and those who were narrower in their theology, and the vitriolic Fundamentalist campaigns were to some extent nurtured by premillennialism.[34] If the second advent was preceded by apostasy, then apostates could be identified and attacked. But Fundamentalist attitudes did not flourish in Britain. Like Moody, Meyer was a bridge-builder, and whereas Fundamentalism thrived on opposition, Meyer's agenda was positive.[35]

Criticisms such as those by Forsyth did not, in fact, have much impact on the Advent Testimony leadership. For them spirituality was more important than scholarship. The Advent Testimony movement, Meyer asserted boldly, was the creation of the Holy Spirit. Many saw in it continuity with the spirituality and ministry of Keswick. God was able to use the Advent Testimony movement because it was striking 'a higher note, the note of the Spirit, the note of the Eternal, the note of the Unseen'.[36] Keswick spirituality and adventism were congruent in their expectation of holiness of life on the part of adherents. The fact that Jesus might personally appear at any time was regarded in Advent Testimony circles as an overwhelming incentive for consistent behaviour. Those committed to the doctrine must, in their lives, reflect the Advent glory.[37] Both the Keswick and Advent Testimony movements attracted people primarily from the middle or upper-middle classes. This does not fit the common theory that millenarianism had a special attraction for the deprived, who could project onto it their unfulfilled aspirations in this life.[38] Rather, these movements held devotional meetings and conventions at which those who attended (who had leisure time available to do so) were drawn into a sense of deeper relationship with Christ. Continuity between the holiness and premillennial streams was also underlined by shared leadership. Evangelists and Bible teachers who had been associated with D.L. Moody were the leading speakers at deeper life conferences and at prophetic gatherings like those held in Canada, in the beautiful setting of Niagara-on-the-Lake, Ontario.[39]

The most notable advocate of Adventist thinking to emerge in the inter-war period was Christabel Pankhurst. She had been converted to wholehearted allegiance to the cause of the second advent in 1918, having read a book by a prominent evangelist, Grattan Guinness, who founded the Regions Beyond Missionary Union. She was initially intrigued by its title, *The Approaching End of the Age.* Pankhurst was probably the most influential member of her family in the struggle for women to have the vote and she never abandoned the principles which underlay her vision for equality for men and women.[40] She wrote books on women's rights, such as *The Great Scourge and How to End It* (1913) and *International Militancy* (1915), but from 1918 her focus was on gathering material to write on premillenial issues. F.B. Meyer wrote the introduction to Pankhurst's first book on the second advent, *The Lord Cometh: The World Crisis Explained* (1923), in which she spoke about the growth of her faith in the personal return of Jesus. In his introduction to the book Meyer alleged that the early Church held to the prospect of the Lord's immediate return and did not put its trust in world betterment or in political or social reorganisation.[41] In November 1926 the evangelical public encountered the full force of the Pankhurst passion at London's Queen's Hall. Pankhurst delivered two devastating messages, arguing that Christ's return was the only hope for the world.[42] Other engagements included large meetings in Glasgow and at the Royal Albert Hall in London in 1927. The Moderators of the General Assemblies of the Church of Scotland and the Free Church presided in Glasgow.[43] Advent Testimony seemed to constitute a core element of evangelical spirituality.

A new evangelicalism

The power of premillennialism was not, however, destined to continue, at least within the evangelical constituency in Britain. In part this was due to a reaction against some of the more bizarre pronouncements made by those within the premillennial camp. William Wileman, a contributor to the premillennial journal *Watching and Waiting*, suggested in 1930 that 'the air is delegated to Satan' (the prince of the power of the air), and that air travel, with its attempt to defy gravity, was contrary to Scripture. He pointed out that 'flying machines are welcomed by all nations as promising to be of use in time of war', and asked for those who feared God to give testimony against this madness. The editorial comment in *Watching and Waiting* struck an even more sinister note. It referred to the expectation that was held by some of a revived Roman empire, with ten kingdoms, and linked this specifically with the use of air routes. A 'prophetic map' that had been prepared by B.W. Newton, which showed these ten kingdoms, was reproduced in *Watching and Waiting*, with an air route shown from London to Babylonia. There was an expectation that Zechariah chapter 5 verses 9 to 11, which spoke about 'two women, and the wind was in their wings', who were bound for the Near East, would be fulfilled. 'Babylon', said *Watching and Waiting*, 'may well become the world's air base'.[44]

There was a considerable amount of speculation by pre-millennial writers during the Second World War and much of this had to be re-interpreted with the end of the war, when the political scene in Europe changed dramatically. For instance, a story circulated about Mussolini which some took as suggesting that he might be the Anti-Christ. Mussolini had allegedly been visited in 1931 by a Mr and Mrs Ralph Norton, missionaries in Belgium, who explained to him, from B.W. Newton's map, that the revived empire was certain to come about. Prophecy Investigation Society members in Britain were told that Mussolini had become so excited by the map that he had ordered one to be made which was sixty feet in length, to highlight the extent of the new Roman 'empire' that he believed he would ultimately rule. It was even suggested – without any proof being offered – that this map had been hung in every state school in Italy.[45] With the collapse of Fascism, premillennial attention moved to the European Economic Community as a possible ten-kingdom entity. Increasingly, however, in part as a reaction against a history of failed prediction, amillennialism was embraced by the leaders of the new post-war evangelicalism. Amillennialism eschewed predictions about the 'end times'. W.J. Grier's book *The Momentous Event*, in 1945, was important. The future evangelical leader John Stott read it, and was convinced by its argument for the amillennial view. *Watching and Waiting* accepted in 1946 that amillennial teaching was reviving.[46] Martyn Lloyd-Jones was a convinced amillennialist, as was Ernest Kevan, a Baptist who, with the backing of Lloyd-Jones, became Principal in 1946 of London Bible College. Kevan was determined to open the eyes of students to ways of interpreting the Bible other than those in the Scofield Reference Bible.[47]

Within the ranks of the Brethren, where premillennialism had been particularly strong, some younger leaders embraced a broader spiritual vision.[48] A. Rendle Short, a Bristol surgeon and prominent member of the Brethren, persuaded a medical student called Douglas Johnson, also nurtured in the Brethren, to become the first full-time worker in the Inter-Varsity Fellowship. Douglas Johnson, who was deeply influenced by the Reformed theological thinking of Martyn Lloyd-Jones, in turn shaped the theological direction of the IVF during his long General Secretaryship of the movement. Among the many younger evangelicals who were nurtured in the growing number of IVF Christians Unions from the 1950s onwards, amillennial thinking was widely accepted. Johnson encouraged projects designed to promote evangelical scholarship, such as the establishment in 1945 of Tyndale House, Cambridge, as a centre for evangelicals wishing to do postgraduate research.[49] Within this scholarly evangelical community few proponents of either premillennial or postmillennial thinking were evident. Michael Wilcock's commentary, *The Message of Revelation*, published in 1975 by the Inter-Varsity Press, embodies an amillennial interpretation of Revelation which by that time was the standard position among British evangelical scholars.[50]

Premillennial advocates were, however, still to be found in Britain. One of these, the well-known Baptist minister Geoffrey King, who was president of the Spurgeon's College conference in 1965, took the second advent as his theme and asked the Methodist historian A. Skevington Wood to come and speak on the premillennial position, while Ernest Kevan spoke on amillennialism. The event was good natured: the Spurgeon's students' title for Kevan's address was 'the kingdom of Kevan'.[51] In America, premillennialism has remained strong. Hal Lindsey's premillennial classic, *Late Great Planet Earth* (1970), sold fifteen million copies in two decades.[52] Samuel Escobar criticised it for being 'conditioned by an intensely conservative nationalism which is hostile to Europe, the Arab countries and communism'. He saw it as reflecting a political rather than a Christian viewpoint.[53] Lindsey assumed the growing power of communism, but in fact much of the pessimistic picture painted about communist dominance has proved unfounded. Amillennialists have generally been unwilling to make these kinds of predictions and have advocated a trust in God's purposes, which are currently unknown, being worked out in his own way. They also prefer to speak in terms of believers knowing that when they die they will be with Christ or that they will be with Christ if he returns before their own death. This is the traditional evangelical message of assurance of personal salvation.

The final judgement

How optimistic, however, have evangelicals been about the final destiny of humanity? Jonathan Edwards, although known for his sermon 'Sinners in the Hands of an Angry God' (from Deuteronomy 32:35), believed that the percentage of human beings who would be damned would be tiny.[54] The period in which the Evangelical Alliance was formed was marked by a rise of interest – among evangelicals as well as others – of alternative views on hell and the afterlife.[55] The majority Christian tradition up to the nineteenth century had taken hell to be a place of unending punishment and, with the possible exception of children who die in infancy and those who never hear the gospel, this tradition had assumed hell to be the fate of all who die without faith in Jesus Christ.[56] During debates in 1854 about the Evangelical Alliance's proposed basis of faith, the Americans present insisted on an article on 'the eternal blessedness of the righteous, and the eternal punishment of the wicked'. A number of British delegates were unhappy about this on the grounds that it could lead to 'a grand inquisitorial court' investigating members' beliefs on this issue. The article, which represented the views of most British as well as American evangelicals, was included.[57] For most evangelicals, however, it was important to place stress on the assurance of heaven that could be offered to all who believed in Christ.

In 1867 considerable debate was prompted by the publication by T.R. Birks of a book called *The Victory of Divine Goodness*.[58] Birks, an Anglican clergyman, had served as curate to Edward Bickersteth during the 1830s and succeeded him as Honorary Secretary of the Evangelical Alliance in 1850. During his nineteen years as Alliance Secretary, he wrote extensively on a wide range of theological topics. In 1872 he was appointed Professor of Moral Theology and Philosophy at King's College London. In *The Victory of Divine Goodness*, Birks suggested that 'the lost' might develop in the afterlife to a point where they could eventually share some of the joy of God's re-made cosmos, if not its full blessings. Birks held that this was consistent with the Alliance's theology. He was teaching neither universal salvation nor 'annihilationism' (or 'conditional immortality') which proposes that the unrighteous will ultimately be destroyed. Birks' scheme *did* maintain unbelievers in an eternal realm divided off from heaven. There were those in the Alliance, however, who could not recognise as consistent with the Alliance's statement of faith 'the assertion that there will be mercy in some form or other extended to the souls under the solemn sentence of eternal judgment'. In 1870, after a period of intense debate about this issue, the Alliance's executive formally accepted Birks' resignation from his post as Honorary Secretary.[59]

The questions that were raised about everlasting punishment would not, however, go away. Faced with the enormous loss of life caused by the First World War, F.B. Meyer began to speculate about the possibility of all those who had died, including especially infants and the heathen, still 'moving forward together' in the afterlife.[60] This seems to suggest a hope for salvation after death for those who had not responded to the gospel while on earth. Basil Atkinson, the robust Inter-Varsity Fellowship leader in Cambridge, held to the idea of conditional immortality and committed his views to paper in 1964 in a privately published book, *Life and Immortality*. In 1988 John Stott published a 'Liberal-Evangelical dialogue' with his fellow-Anglican David L. Edwards. The dialogue between them involved a discussion of eschatology, in which Stott showed sympathy for conditional immortality, while finally declaring himself to be 'tentative' about whether it should replace the traditional view of hell.[61] In 1998 the Evangelical Alliance convened a working group to prepare a report on these issues. A theological survey conducted a few months earlier had shown that 14 per cent of Evangelical Alliance member churches inclined towards annihilationism, with 80 per cent holding to the traditional view on final judgement and eternal punishment.[62] The report, edited by David Hilborn, the Alliance's Theological Secretary, was published as

The Nature of Hell. It affirmed the possibility within evangelicalism of holding traditionalist or conditionalist interpretations of hell.[63] Evangelical approaches to the Last Times are the subject of continued debate.

Conclusion

For evangelicals an understanding of the Last Times has been not only a theological issue but one which has affected their spiritual outlook. The early commitment to postmillennialism inspired great efforts in world mission. As premillennialism became more prominent, however, the postmillennial view came to be widely seen as a product of a rather naïve optimism. Writing in 1919, F.B. Meyer summarily dismissed the postmillennial view that evil would be 'cleansed out of the world' before Christ returned, as an evolutionary theory which was condemned by the condition of the world after nineteen centuries of Christianity.[64] To evangelicals trying to discover God's purpose in history, premillennialism, by contrast, appeared to be a realistic creed. It did not hold out any hope of the winning of the nations or the building of the kingdom until the return of Jesus, the King. Although this meant that some evangelicals withdrew from active involvement in society there were those, like the Earl of Shaftesbury, who were spiritually energised by their premillennial beliefs. In the field of mission, premillennialism tended to direct efforts towards the conversion of individuals rather than towards wider social transformation. In Britain both postmillennial and premillennial thinking have declined in the decades since the Second World War, while amillennialism has gained ground. In America, by contrast, premillennial views have remained widespread, as witnessed by the enormous success of the *Left Behind* series of books written by Tim Lahaye. These have captured many evangelicals' imaginations. Evangelicals, as seen in their views of the millennium and also in the debates about the nature of hell, continue to be affected in their present experience by what they believe the future holds. At the same time, their present experience of the presence of Christ shapes their assured hope about the future beyond this world.

11. 'THE FOSTERING OF SPIRITUALITY'

David Gillett, in *Trust and Obey*, recalls speaking at a retreat house on the subject of evangelical spirituality and being faced with puzzlement, apprehension and surprise from his audience. Most had no helpful experience of personal encounters with evangelical spirituality. Some were surprised that there was such a thing. But the isolation of evangelicalism from other traditions has given way, Gillett suggests, through 'a sea change' within evangelicalism, to a new openness. This means that evangelicals, as well as Christians of other traditions, have had new opportunities to examine varieties of spirituality.[1] Given that background, this is an especially good time to explore the story of evangelical spirituality. As this examination is undertaken, it becomes clear that there is much in common between apparently very different streams of spirituality. Bernard L. Manning, at Jesus College, Cambridge, argued in an address to the assembly of the Congregational Union of England and Wales in October 1927: 'For the Calvinist, as for the mediaeval Catholic or for the eighteenth-century Evangelical, the Cross is the centre of his experience of God.'[2] Manning, who was himself a historian of the medieval period, found his roots within a crucicentrism which was at once Calvinistic, catholic and evangelical. These commonalities are likely to be emphasised in the future, although at the same time there is an increasing recognition that different streams need to be examined in their own right.

Distinctives and diversity in evangelical spirituality

There are distinctive features in different spiritual traditions and indeed in sub-traditions, not least in the different strands that make up the evangelical tradition. The strengths of different spiritual traditions, as Richard Foster's writings show so well, are to be celebrated. Foster speaks especially in dealing with evangelical experience of the evangelical stress on conversion, commitment to Christ, mission, and the Bible and biblical teaching.[3] Other features have been examined in the chapters in this volume. At the heart of the evangelical experience, and running through all the aspects that have been discussed, has been a personal relationship with God in Christ. As this central core is explored more fully, it becomes apparent that although evangelicals have often been divided over aspects of theology, their experience has been to a large extent a uniting factor. Evangelicals have sung the hymns of Isaac Watts, of Charles Wesley, of John Newton and of Fanny Crosby, with their affirmation of salvation in Christ, despite the fact that these writers were far from united in all aspects of their beliefs about the divine and human roles in the salvific process. All evangelicals, whatever their views about issues such as predestination to salvation, could sing, in John Newton's words:

How sweet the name of Jesus sounds
In a believer's ear!

The same focus on the experience of Jesus in human life has been evident in the recent history of evangelicalism. The tradition of influential hymnody continues within evangelical spirituality through song-writers such as Graham Kendrick and Matt Redman. Coming to God in worship, for Redman, involves seeing 'the lion and the lamb, the sinless friend of sinners, who terrifies and befriends, thunders and whispers, reveals and conceals ... his footstool is the earth but he bent down and washed the earth off the feet of his disciples'.[4]

Evangelical spirituality, however, has never been entirely

uniform in the way it has been expressed. It has its sub-sets. In his approach to spirituality, John Wesley, although indebted to the Pietist and the Moravian traditions for his understanding of assurance and for aspects of his practice, such as class meetings, never embraced the intensity of Moravian expressions of worship.[5] Another example of a fault-line in early and in later evangelical thinking was over the way in which holiness was achieved. The Wesleyan stream of spirituality, as we have seen, has emphasised the possibility of Christian perfection, the Calvinist stress has been on divinely aided effort, and Keswick spirituality has talked of rest in God. Some lines from the hymn-writer Frances Ridley Havergal that spoke of a deeper experience of grace, and which were often quoted at Keswick in its early years, illustrate the tensions over this area of spiritual experience:

> Holiness by faith in Jesus,
> Not by effort of my own.
> Sin's dominion crushed and broken,
> By the power of grace alone.[6]

A belief in the grace of God and the power of that grace lies at the heart of the evangelical understanding of the experience of conversion, and this is a belief shared by all evangelicals. At the same time there has been and would still be considerable dispute over the phrase 'not by effort of my own'. Some evangelicals, particularly within the Calvinist section of evangelicalism, would see this kind of approach as too passive. Yet Keswick teaching, as it developed from the 1870s, sought to offer to evangelicals a moderate evangelical spirituality, which embraced aspects of Reformed and Wesleyan thinking and which offered a deeper experience of Christ. The increasing interest among some evangelicals in contemplative spirituality suggests that the Keswick emphasis that involved resting in God may have new resonance. New expressions of traditional evangelical diversity may emerge.

Diversity in expressions of spirituality within evangelicalism has owed much to the contribution of its leading figures, as has been evident in this study. Although evangelical leadership has been largely male, women have had a significant influence. Early Methodism gained from women preachers, and the holiness movement of the nineteenth century was shaped by speakers such as Phoebe Palmer, Hannah Pearsall Smith and Catherine Booth, by hymn-writers like Fanny Crosby and Frances Ridley Havergal, and by missionaries of the calibre of Lilias Trotter. When William Booth wished to support the ministry of women he said: 'We employ women, and for this we have the authority of Mr Wesley'.[7] In the period of the Welsh Revival, one of the effective evangelists was Rosina Davies, who had been influenced by the Salvation Army. In her preaching she often witnessed up to fifty conversions in a single meeting.[8] Testimonies of women have also been important. Joseph Jenkins, a minister in Newquay, Cardiganshire, encouraged one of his young people, Florrie Evans, aged twenty, who was seeking peace, to acknowledge the Lordship of Christ and submit to the Holy Spirit. The next Sunday, at a young people's meeting, Jenkins invited testimonies, and Florrie said simply: 'I love the Lord Jesus with all my heart'. The effect was electrifying.[9] In addition, there was a great deal of singing at Welsh Revival meetings, with Annie Davies, aged eighteen, the best-known singer, regularly singing the Revival hymn 'Here is Love, vast as the ocean'. Joseph Jenkins also spoke of young women prophesying.[10] Future investigations of evangelicalism are likely to give more attention to women and spiritual experience.[11] Evangelical spirituality has not been monochrome, but has reflected the varied experiences of women and men.

Changes over time

Not only has there been diversity within evangelical expressions of spirituality from the beginning, there have also been changes in the way evangelical spirituality has been expressed over time. During the first few decades of the twentieth century, Keswick placed less emphasis on the

'deeper life' and greater stress on the Lordship of Christ. This
was in large measure due to the influence of the Baptist
minister Graham Scroggie, who by 1950 was seen as the foremost Keswick teacher.[12] Scroggie said of Keswick: 'It teaches
that spirituality is the key to every situation ... the emphasis
of its message is not on the Saviourship of Christ, but upon his
Lordship; not upon service, but upon character; not upon
organization, but upon the Holy Spirit.'[13] Sometimes the
meaning of certain phrases used to describe spiritual experience could change in more dramatic ways. 'Jesus is here',
announced F.B. Meyer, speaking at the Keswick Convention in
1903, 'who baptises with the Holy Ghost.'[14] This kind of
language was common in the holiness movements of the nineteenth century, but within a few years of 1903 it would be
associated in evangelical thinking with Pentecostal rather
than with Keswick spirituality. Those who look to the past for
some kind of pristine model of evangelical spirituality are
destined to be disappointed. Change has been a constant
characteristic of the expressions of evangelical experience and
this is set to continue.

Some of the ways in which change might be evident in the
future have been touched on earlier. There is likely to be a
greater emphasis on the 'journey' than on the moment of conversion. Evangelical engagement with the Bible is also
changing. In 1995 Alister McGrath wrote *Beyond the Quiet
Time*, in which he offered 'an approach to spirituality, suitable
for individuals or groups, that is firmly rooted in the great
evangelical tradition, yet adapted to our modern needs'.[15]
Against the background of a growing sense of dissatisfaction
within some sections of evangelicalism about the quiet time,
McGrath has offered a range of imaginative ways of engaging
with the biblical text. This kind of fresh thinking is also evident in evangelical preaching. There is considerable evidence
that evangelicals in the future will draw from a number of
Christian traditions – Catholic, Orthodox and non-Western,
especially experiences shaped in Africa, South America and
China – as well as the older European and North American

evangelical traditions examined in this book. It was in the 1990s that Baptists, for example, began to mine more systematically the riches of the different Christian traditions of spirituality. In an American book published in 1994, *Ties That Bind: Life Together in the Baptist Vision*, E. Glenn Hinson wrote on 'The Contemplative Roots of Baptist Spirituality'. Other contributors to the volume included Thomas Turner, whose topic was 'Spiritual Direction and the Baptist Tradition'.[16] Evangelicals are turning to contemplative prayer, Ignatian or Benedictine ways of reading the Bible, and the practice of spiritual direction, an example of this being Jeannette Bakke's *Holy Invitations*.[17]

The more recent attempts to foster understanding between evangelical thinking and other Christian traditions in the American context have stimulated a number of initiatives. In March 1994 an historic 8,000-word declaration was issued entitled 'Evangelicals and Catholics Together: The Christian Mission in the Third Millennium' (ECT). A core group of seven Roman Catholics and eight evangelicals in North America produced the document, which set out areas of common affirmation, hope, action and witness. The document recognised that evangelicals and Catholics 'constitute the growing edge of the missionary expansion at present and, most likely, in the century ahead', affirmed the Apostles' Creed as a uniting credal statement, and included the important soteriological proposition that we are 'justified by grace through faith because of Christ'.[18] A number of further conversations and publications have followed. In one volume, published in Britain in 1996, *Evangelicals and Catholics Together: Working Towards a Common Mission* (which offered responses to ECT), Packer expressed his thankfulness for 'the wisdom, maturity of mind and conscience, backbone and sheer guts, reverence before God, and above all love for my Lord Jesus Christ' which he had seen many times in Catholics.[19] Here was a spiritual basis for ecumenical endeavour. Wider reflection among evangelicals has also produced important books such as Robert Webber's

Ancient-Future Faith, which seeks, as Webber indicates in the sub-title, to re-think evangelicalism, including evangelical spirituality, so that there can be what he calls a classical/postmodern spirituality.[20] In a follow-up book, *The Younger Evangelicals*, Webber notes the increasing interest among younger evangelicals in sacramental spirituality.[21] Increasingly common ground is being discovered between those whose spirituality has been shaped in more Word-centred and more sacramentally based traditions.

Evangelicals in the later twentieth century found themselves in what David Bebbington has termed 'a broad place'.[22] The massive commitment by evangelicals to involvement in social affairs that marked the nineteenth century,[23] a commitment which was largely lost in the early part of the twentieth century, has been recovered by many evangelicals throughout the world, with organisations such as TEAR Fund leading the way in Britain.[24] Evangelical renewal brought about by the charismatic movement, followed by a growing interest in contemplative spirituality, has also done a great deal to open up evangelicals to the spirituality of aspects of the wider Christian tradition. Cardinal Suenens, the Roman Catholic primate of Belgium, who experienced in the 1970s a release of the Spirit and spoke in tongues, appeared according to one Baptist charismatic, Douglas McBain, to be as much at home among Baptists and other evangelicals as he was in his own Church.[25] The continued spread of Pentecostal and charismatic spirituality, not least in terms of the British context the growth of the Black-majority churches, suggests that an openness to the work of the Holy Spirit will continue to be a central feature of evangelical spirituality. Although at times charismatic spirituality has been expressed in narrow forms, for example in some of the churches that have stressed the authority of apostles, charismatic renewal is an example of the way in which evangelicalism embraced a changing cultural landscape.[26] Throughout its history, evangelical spirituality has been able to adapt to differing socio-cultural contexts without losing its core identity. What about evangelicalism's ability to adapt in the twenty-first century to an increasingly pervasive postmodern culture? This question received attention in Britain in the 1990s, with Graham Cray, Principal of the evangelical Anglican Ridley Hall, Cambridge, suggesting the themes of community, journey and spirituality as relevant for evangelism in a postmodern context.[27] New models of church – often under the title 'the emerging church' – are being examined.[28]

Global currents in evangelical spirituality

Although evangelical spirituality from the eighteenth century onwards was largely fostered in countries in Western Europe and in North America, there has been a shift in the centre of gravity of evangelicalism in the twentieth century. At the 1998 Lambeth Conference of the Anglican Communion, 224 of the 735 bishops present were from Africa, compared with only 139 from Britain and the rest of Europe. Anglicans in Nigeria number seventeen million baptised members, compared to fewer than three million in the USA.[29] The strength of more traditional evangelical approaches, for example to the Bible, is found in non-Western countries. In China, as Dana Robert notes, biblically literalist Christianity, dependent on the power of the Holy Spirit and reflecting Chinese religious sensibilities, grew most under communism, after the Western missionaries left. Whereas in 1949 there were approximately 700,000 Protestants, this number grew to (depending on the way figures are calculated) at least twelve and perhaps as many as thirty-six million Protestants by the end of the twentieth century.[30] David Martin has written of the 'explosion of Protestantism' in South America. In 1916, in the whole of Latin America, Protestants were a tiny minority. Evangelical advance has been such that by the 1990s the number of Protestants involved in worship and fellowship may have exceeded Roman Catholics in some Latin American countries.[31]

Evangelical spirituality was exported to these countries by

missionaries, but as this spirituality has been absorbed it has also been transformed. Globally, there has (as David Martin argues) been a fusion of traditional evangelical spirituality with a black spirituality, including the Afro-Brazilian strain, and with other indigenous expressions of spirituality, for example in Korea, where massive evangelical churches have developed.[32] In part these spiritual streams have commonality with the Pentecostal movement that emerged in North America in the early twentieth century, and the world-wide growth of evangelicals has been interpreted by some in Pentecostal terms.[33] But in certain respects the new evangelicalism of the non-Western world has diverged from some traditional Pentecostal emphases. In Latin America, for example, there has been an increasing engagement with issues of social justice. This is in continuity with an older evangelical tradition of social action, but it has been expressed in new ways. In the face of massive social problems, there has been, on the part of at least some evangelicals, 'a creative and active response, a seizing of opportunities and not merely a spiritual consolation for the hapless victims of social change'.[34] As evangelicals have grown in strength they have also grown in confidence. Thus the massive evangelical constituency of Latin America has fostered a powerful new culture which may well prove as influential in its own context as evangelical spirituality was in Victorian England.

Beyond this, the spirituality being nurtured in various parts of the world has the potential to re-shape Western spirituality. 'The globalization of evangelicalism', as Mark Hutchinson puts it, 'means that the traditional locus of power, the First World, no longer has the ability to control the conversation.' Questions of identity, including questions of the nature of evangelical spirituality, can no longer be settled by Northern hemisphere Anglo leaders.[35] Kwame Bediako, a Presbyterian from Ghana, argued in his seminal *Theology and Identity*, on culture and Christian faith in the second century and in modern Africa, for theology as the struggle with culturally rooted questions.[36] Bediako established a centre for mission research and applied theology in Ghana, founded and became secretary of the Africa Theological Fraternity, and was a research fellow of the Edinburgh Centre for the Study of Christianity in the Non-Western World. While those in the Western world can look back to evangelical revivals of the eighteenth and nineteenth centuries, revivals which shaped the evangelical tradition and contributed to evangelical mission, in the twentieth century revival movements were experienced in (for example) Korea, China, Brazil, Indonesia, India and some countries in East Africa. Arguably, the evangelical ferment in Latin America can be seen as an 'awakening', in which large numbers of people have come to a new sense of themselves and of their society.[37] This has also happened elsewhere, for example in the countries of Eastern Europe which were formerly under communism. In countries such as Ukraine the new religious and political situation since the end of communism has seen the emergence of 'communities of choice' and a consequent significant rise in the number of conversions to evangelical (particularly Baptist) expressions of the Christian faith.[38]

Perhaps the most significant development at the beginning of the twenty-first century has been the way in which the churches in China have begun to see themselves as offering something not only to their own country but also to the world. The many millions of Chinese Christians who meet in house churches are characterised by all the traditional evangelical distinctives. Their spirituality is strongly practical, producing solid families and honest and hard-working citizens. This is often seen as being attractive, and presents a contrast to the problems in the wider society of inter-personal conflict and self-centred consumerism, problems which concern the government.[39] These evangelical Christians, exhibiting the standard evangelical concern for missionary engagement, have begun to speak of a call they feel to preach the gospel and establish fellowships of believers in all the countries, cities and ethnic groups between China and Jerusalem. David Aikman, in *Jesus in Beijing*, explores the spiritual transformation of China during the past few decades.[40] Aikman predicts that within three decades Christians will be one-third of China's population. Whether or not this is realistic, the 'Back to Jerusalem' movement, as it is termed, which has recently been organised by the leaders of the evangelical Chinese Christian churches, has the ambitious aim of sending out a minimum of 100,000 Chinese Christian missionaries over the next ten to twenty years.

The evangelical growth that has been witnessed in China, as well as in Korea and in parts of Africa, is not necessarily explicitly Pentecostal growth. Even where evangelical growth in the non-Western world has been largely Pentecostal, evangelical identity is often clearly evident. Evangelical spirituality has created over the centuries a potent spiritual mix 'capable of combustion on a global scale'.[41] In *Pentecostalism and the Future of the Christian Churches*, Richard Shaull and Waldo Cesar note, with reference to Latin America, that within Pentecostal spirituality it is evangelical doctrines that constitute the centre of the faith of the simplest believers. At the heart of their faith is powerful personal experience. In coming together as believers in communal worship they experience 'not a static solemnity but an unexpected individual and collective happiness', an 'intense spirituality that recalls the life of the early Christians'. It seems clear that Christians in the countries where the evangelical faith was shaped but where the churches are in decline, have something to learn from the way in which new expressions of the evangelical faith, more relevant to an emerging global culture, have blossomed and have increasingly created a non-Western spiritual reality.[42]

Conclusion

Evangelicalism began in the Western world, in the age of the Enlightenment, and was then able to adjust to the Romantic mood of the nineteenth century. Further significant changes have taken place since in the context in which evangelical experiences are to be found and further changes are in prospect. Stanley Grenz envisaged an evangelicalism that returned to a spiritually centred faith. He suggested in 1993 in *Revisioning Evangelical Theology*: 'The renewed emphasis on the practical understanding of theology marks a shift not only to the earlier Pietism but also, in a sense, a move back from modernity to the patristic era, or perhaps a move beyond modernity into the emerging postmodern era.' He wished evangelicals of the future to recapture a theological tradition aimed at 'the fostering of spirituality' and which is 'rooted in spirituality'.[43] Grenz continued to explore these themes, suggesting at the beginning of the twenty-first century that the Bible should be read with a consciousness that 'we are participants in the one faith community that spans the ages'.[44] The faith community to which evangelicals belong is connected with the whole Christian tradition and with the diverse global Christian community, but evangelicals have placed particular stress on an assured relationship with God in Christ. The entry into this trustful relationship is through a process of conversion and the relationship is nurtured by the Bible, the sacraments and prayer. As a spirituality that looks to the cross it recognises that being a disciple of the crucified Jesus will involve suffering, but seeks help in that suffering. The hymn 'What a Friend we have in Jesus' reflects this experience and the way it is turned into prayer.

> Can we find a Friend so faithful,
> Who will all our sorrows share?
> Jesus knows our every weakness –
> Take it to the Lord in prayer.

It is this relationship with Christ which, for evangelicals, is at the core of authentic fellowship between Christians, and it is also this which is the motivation for world mission. Finally, this assurance is central as an evangelical believer looks towards the end of his or her life. Some evangelicals have looked for an imminent second advent, but for all there is the assured expectation of fuller fellowship with Christ beyond this world. Charles Simeon, in Cambridge, at the end of his life, said to someone who was caring for him: 'Soon ... I shall see Him whom having not seen I love; in whom, though now I see Him not, yet believing *I rejoice with joy unspeakable and full of glory.*' Then he added, with classic evangelical assurance: 'Of the *reality* of this I AM AS SURE as if I were there this moment.'[45]

NOTES

Chapter 1. Introduction

1. G. Giles, *The Music of Praise* (Oxford: Bible Reading Fellowship, 2002), pp. 81–5.
2. D.W. Bebbington, *Evangelicalism in Modern Britain: A History from the 1730s to the 1980s* (London: Routledge, 1995), p. 20.
3. J. Kent, *Wesley and the Wesleyans: Religion in Eighteenth-Century Britain* (Cambridge: Cambridge University Press, 2002), pp. 1–2.
4. Cited by K. Hylson-Smith, *Evangelicals in the Church of England* (Edinburgh: T & T Clark, 1988), p. 23.
5. G.M. Ditchfield, *The Evangelical Revival* (London: UCL Press, 1998).
6. For an introduction to the thinking of the Reformation see A.E. McGrath, *Reformation Thought* (Oxford: Blackwell, 1993).
7. J.I. Packer, *Among God's Giants* (Eastbourne: Kingsway, 1991), pp. 236–40.
8. R.T. Kendall, *Calvin and English Calvinism to 1649* (Carlisle: Paternoster Press, 1997), chapter 5.
9. W.R. Ward and R.P. Heitzenrater (eds.), *The Works of John Wesley* (Nashville: Abingdon Press, 1990), Vol. 19, p. 46; cf. A.S. Wood, *The Burning Heart* (Exeter: Paternoster Press, 1978), p. 92.
10. J. Telford (ed.), *The Letters of the Rev. John Wesley, A.M.* (London: Epworth Press, 1931, repr. 1960), Vol. I, p. 286.
11. Jonathan Edwards, 'Concerning the nature of the Religious Affections and their importance in Religion', in *The Select Works of Jonathan Edwards* (Edinburgh: Banner of Truth, 1961), Vol. 3, p. 31.
12. *ibid.*, p. 192.
13. M. Noll, *The Rise of Evangelicalism* (Leicester: Apollos, 2003).
14. See O. Chadwick, *The Victorian Church*, Part 1 (London: A & C Black, 1966), p. 5.
15. I. Bradley, *The Call to Seriousness* (London: Jonathan Cape, 1976), p. 14.
16. J. Wolffe, *God and Greater Britain: Religion and National Life in Britain and Ireland 1843–1945* (London: Routledge, 1994), p. 30.
17. N. Scotland, *John Bird Sumner: Evangelical Archbishop* (Leominster: Gracewing, 1995), pp. 105–7.

18. P. Brierley (ed.), *World Churches Handbook* (London: Christian Research Association, 1997), pp. 13–14. See Harvey Cox, *Fire from Heaven* (London: Cassell, 1996) and W.J. Hollenweger, *Pentecostalism: Origins and Development Worldwide* (Peabody, Mass.: Hendrickson, 1997).

19. V. Synan, *The Holiness-Pentecostal Movement in the United States* (Grand Rapids, Mich.: Eerdmans, 1977); D.W. Dayton, *Theological Roots of Pentecostalism* (Metuchen, NJ: Scarecrow Press, 1987).

20. E.L. Waldvogel, 'The "Overcoming Life": A Study in the Reformed Evangelical Origins of Pentecostalism', Harvard Ph.D thesis (1977); cf. I.M. Randall, 'Old Time Power: Relationships between Pentecostalism and Evangelical Spirituality in England', *Pneuma*, Vol. 19, No. 1 (1997), pp. 53–80.

21. *Redemption Tidings*, May 1933, p. 7. For the British Assemblies of God see W.K. Kay, *Inside Story: A History of British Assemblies of God* (Mattersey: Mattersey Hall Publishing, 1990).

22. Bebbington, *Evangelicalism in Modern Britain*, pp. 2–17.

23. D.K. Gillett, *Trust and Obey: Explorations in Evangelical Spirituality* (London: DLT, 1993), pp. 34–9.

24. I.M. Randall, *Evangelical Experiences: A Study in the Spirituality of English Evangelicalism, 1918–1939* (Carlisle: Paternoster, 1999).

25. D.W. Bebbington, *Holiness in Nineteenth-Century England* (Carlisle: Paternoster, 2000).

26. D.W. Bebbington, 'Holiness in the Evangelical Tradition', in S.C. Barton (ed.), *Holiness Past & Present* (London: T & T Clark, 2003), pp. 298–315.

27. J. Tiller, *Puritan, Pietist, Pentecostalist* (Bramcote: Grove, 1982); P. Adam, *Roots of Contemporary Evangelical Spirituality* (Bramcote: Grove, 1988); J. Cockerton, *Essentials of Evangelical Spirituality* (Bramcote: Grove, 1994).

28. Cockerton, *Essentials of Evangelical Spirituality*, pp. 12–19.

29. P. Seddon, *Gospel and Sacrament: Reclaiming a holistic evangelical spirituality* (Cambridge: Grove, 1994).

30. J. Huggett, *Open to God* (Guildford: Eagle, 1997).

31. A.E. McGrath, *Roots that Refresh: A Celebration of Reformation Spirituality* (London, 1991); A.E. McGrath, *Evangelicalism and the Future of Christianity* (London: Hodder & Stoughton, 1988), chapter 5.

32. McGrath, *Evangelicalism and the Future*, p. 142. See also A.E. McGrath, *Christian Spirituality: An Introduction* (Oxford: Blackwell, 1999).

33. McGrath, *Evangelicalism and the Future*, pp. 137–8; cf. E.H. Peterson, *Working the Angles* (Grand Rapids, Mich.: Eerdmans, 1987); *The Contemplative Pastor* (Grand Rapids, Mich.: Eerdmans, 1993); E.H. Peterson, 'Evangelical Spirituality', in C. Bartholomew,

R. Parry and A. West (eds.), *The Futures of Evangelicalism* (Leicester: InterVarsity Press, 2003), pp. 221–45.

34. D. Willard, *The Divine Conspiracy: Rediscovering our hidden life in God* (London: HarperCollins, 2000).

35. R. Foster, *Celebration of Discipline* (London: Hodder & Stoughton, 1980); *Prayer* (London: Hodder & Stoughton, 1992); *Streams of Living Water* (London: HarperCollins, 1999).

36. D.J. Tidball, *Who are the Evangelicals?* (London: MarshallPickering, 1994), pp. 224–8.

37. P. Sheldrake, *Spirituality and History* (London: SPCK, 1991), p. 52.

38. P. Sheldrake, *Images of Holiness: Explorations in Contemporary Spirituality* (London: DLT, 1987), p. 2.

39. J. Gordon, *Evangelical Spirituality* (London: SPCK, 1991).

40. D. Parker, 'Evangelical Spirituality Reviewed', *The Evangelical Quarterly*, Vol. 63, No. 2 (1991), p. 132.

41. Tidball, *Who are the Evangelicals?*, chapter 11.

42. M.E. Dieter, 'The Wesleyan Perspective', in M.E. Dieter (ed.), *Five Views of Sanctification* (Grand Rapids, Mich.: Zondervan, 1987).

43. *Encountering the Spirit: Charismatic Spirituality* by Mark Cartledge (forthcoming).

44. R.W. Jenson, *America's Theologian* (Oxford: Oxford University Press, 1992), pp. 84–5.

Chapter 2. 'Amazing Grace': Evangelicals and Conversion

1. W.R. Ward and R.P. Heitzenrater (eds.), *The Works of John Wesley* (Nashville: Abingdon Press, 1988), Vol. 18, pp. 249–50.

2. For a full discussion of the meaning of John Wesley's experience see H.D. Rack, *Reasonable Enthusiast: John Wesley and the Rise of Methodism* (London: Epworth Press, 1989), pp. 144–57.

3. For George Whitefield see H.S. Stout, *The Divine Dramatist: George Whitefield and the Rise of Modern Evangelicalism* (Grand Rapids, Mich.: Eerdmans, 1991).

4. See G. F. Nuttall, *The Puritan Spirit* (London: Epworth Press, 1967).

5. D.W. Bebbington, *Evangelicalism in Modern Britain: A History from the 1730s to the 1980s* (London: Routledge, 1995), pp. 37–8. See also A.S. Wood, *The Burning Heart: John Wesley: Evangelist* (Exeter: Paternoster Press, 1978), chapter 3.

6. See D.L. Jeffrey (ed.), *A Burning and a Shining Light* (Grand Rapids, Mich: Eerdmans, 1987), pp. 143, 146.

7. G. Whitefield, *Journals* (Edinburgh: Banner of Truth, repr. 1960), pp. 46–7; A. Dallimore, *George Whitefield* (Edinburgh: Banner of Truth, 1970), Vol. 1, pp. 72–7.

8. P. Toon, *Born Again: A Biblical and Theological Study of Regeneration* (Grand Rapids, Mich.: Baker Book House, 1987), p. 159.

9. The best biography of Jonathan Edwards is G.M. Marsden, *Jonathan*

Edwards: A Life (New Haven and London: Yale University Press, 2003).

10. Jonathan Edwards, 'A Narrative of Surprising Conversions', in C.C. Goen (ed.), *The Works of Jonathan Edwards* (New Haven and London: Yale University Press, 1972), Vol. 4, p. 177.
11. Jonathan Edwards, 'Personal Narrative', in E. Hickman (ed.), *The Works of Jonathan Edwards* (Edinburgh: Banner of Truth, 1974), Vol. 1, pp. xiii-xiv.
12. I.H. Murray, *Jonathan Edwards* (Edinburgh: Banner of Truth, 1987), p. 25.
13. Goen (ed.), *The Works of Jonathan Edwards*, Vol. 4, p. 101.
14. Jonathan Edwards, 'A Faithful Narrative', in *ibid.*
15. M. Noll, *The Rise of Evangelicalism* (Leicester: Apollos, 2003), p. 73.
16. For Zinzendorf see A. J. Lewis, *Zinzendorf: The Ecumenical Pioneer* (London: SCM, 1962).
17. Toon, *Born Again*, pp. 154–5.
18. F.C. Gill, *Charles Wesley: The First Methodist* (London: Lutterworth Press, 1964), pp. 65–71.
19. Goen (ed.), *The Works of Jonathan Edwards*, Vol. 4, pp. 159, 161, 164; cf. Toon, *Born Again*, pp. 144–5.
20. Noll, *Rise of Evangelicalism*, p. 73.
21. *ibid.*, p. 84.
22. L. Tyerman, *Life and Times of John Wesley* (London, 1871), Vol. 1, p. 349, cited by Noll, *Rise of Evangelicalism*, p. 257.
23. For Wesley's understanding of salvation see H.B. McGonigle, *Sufficient Saving Grace: John Wesley's Evangelical Arminianism* (Carlisle: Paternoster Press, 2001).
24. See A.F. Sell, *The Great Debate* (Worthing: H.E. Walter, 1982), p. 68; Noll, *Rise of Evangelicalism*, p. 8.
25. D.K. Gillett, *Trust and Obey: Explorations in Evangelical Spirituality* (London: DLT, 1993), p. 28.
26. D.B. Hindmarsh, *John Newton and the English Evangelical tradition: Between the conversions of Wesley and Wilberforce* (Oxford: Oxford University Press, 1996), chapter 4.
27. *ibid.*, chapter 7, esp. pp. 276–7.
28. For William Wilberforce, see J.C. Pollock, *Wilberforce: God's Statesman* (Eastbourne: Kingsway, 2001).
29. Cited by D.B. Hindmarsh, '"My chains fell off, my heart was free": Early Methodist Conversion Narrative in England', *Church History*, Vol. 68, No. 4 (1999), p. 926.
30. *Arminian Magazine* (London, 1791), pp. 68–70, cited by G.A. Rawlyk and M.A. Noll (eds.), *Amazing Grace: Evangelicalism in Australia, Britain, Canada, and the United States* (Montreal and Kingston: McGill-Queen's University Press, 1994), pp. 16–17.
31. Noll, *Rise of Evangelicalism*, p. 272.
32. J. Gordon, *Evangelical Spirituality* (London: SPCK, 1991), chapter 4.

33. For Robert Murray McCheyne, see D. Robertson, *Awakening: The Life and Ministry of Robert Murray McCheyne* (Carlisle: Paternoster Press, 2004).
34. R.M. McCheyne, *Sermons of M'Cheyne* (London: Banner of Truth, 1961), p. 154: a sermon on conversion, preached 8 May 1842.
35. See R. Brown, *The English Baptists of the Eighteenth Century* (London: Baptist Historical Society, 1986).
36. For more on Andrew Fuller see P.J. Morden, *Offering Christ to the World* (Carlisle: Paternoster Press, 2003).
37. See I.H. Murray, *Revival and Revivalism: The Making and Marring of American Evangelicalism, 1750–1858* (Edinburgh: Banner of Truth, 1994).
38. Toon, *Born Again*, p. 172.
39. *ibid.*, p. 173.
40. L. Wilson, *Constrained by Zeal: Female Spirituality amongst Nonconformists, 1825–1875* (Carlisle: Paternoster Press, 2000), p. 45.
41. C.H. Spurgeon, *Autobiography* (London: Passmore and Alabaster, 1899), Vol. 1, pp. 88–9.
42. See M.K. Nicholls, *C H Spurgeon: The Pastor Evangelist* (Didcot: Baptist Historical Society, 1992).
43. *The Keswick Week* (1921), p. 16.
44. See K. Dix, *Strict and Particular* (Didcot: Baptist Historical Society, 2001), chapters 1 and 2.
45. J.C. Ryle, *Practical Religion* (London: 1900, repr. in Cambridge by James Clarke & Co., 1964), p. 8.
46. Gillett, *Trust and Obey*, p. 42.
47. I.M. Randall, ' "Every Apostolic Church a Mission Society": European Baptist Origins and Identity', in A.R. Cross (ed.), *Ecumenism and History: Studies in Honour of John H. Y. Briggs* (Carlisle: Paternoster Press, 2002).
48. Toon, *Born Again*, pp. 173–4.
49. For the life of Gipsy Smith, see D. Lazell, *Gypsy from the Forest* (Bridgend: Bryntirion Press, 1997).
50. Sunday and Torrey are covered by W.G. McLoughlin, *Modern Revivalism* (New York: The Ronald Press, 1959).
51. *Joyful News*, 15 September 1921, p. 2. For Chadwick, see N.G. Dunning, *Samuel Chadwick* (London: Hodder & Stoughton, 1933).
52. For Billy Graham see W. Martin, *The Billy Graham Story* (London: Hutchinson, 1992).
53. *Moody Monthly,* October 1954, p. 32.
54. *Christianity Today*, Vol. 2, No. 15 (1958), p. 11.
55. B. Hoare and I. Randall, *More than a Methodist: The Life and Ministry of Donald English* (Carlisle: Paternoster Press, 2003), pp. 6–7.
56. M.A. Noll, 'Evangelicalism at its best', in M.A. Noll and R.F.

Thiemann (eds.), *Where Shall My Wond'ring Soul Begin?* (Grand Rapids, Mich.: Eerdmans, 2000), p. 2.

57. Toon, *Born Again*, p. 180.
58. J. Finney, *Finding Faith Today* (Swindon: Bible Society, 1992).
59. S. Hunt, *Anyone for Alpha?: Evangelism in a post-Christian society* (London: DLT, 2001).

Chapter 3. 'O Give Me That Book!' Evangelicals and the Bible

1. M. Noll, *The Rise of Evangelicalism* (Leicester: Apollos, 2003), p. 141.
2. A.C. Outler (ed.), *The Works of John Wesley*, Vol. 1, Sermons, I (Nashville: Abingdon Press, 1984), p. 105; cf. A.S. Wood, *The Burning Heart: John Wesley: Evangelist* (Exeter: Paternoster Press, 1978), p. 211.
3. T. Jackson (ed.), *The Works of John Wesley*, 3rd edn (Kansas: Beacon Hill Press, 1978), Vol. 8, p. 348.
4. J.C. Ryle, *Practical Religion* (London: 1900, repr. in Cambridge, James Clarke & Co., 1964), p. 42.
5. J. Wesley, *Explanatory Notes upon the New Testament* (published 1754, Epworth Press, 1976), Preface, paragraph 10, cited by D.K. Gillett, *Trust and Obey: Explorations in Evangelical Spirituality* (London: DLT, 1993), p. 133.
6. Gillett, *Trust and Obey*, pp. 131, 133.
7. L. Wilson, *Constrained by Zeal: Female Spirituality amongst Nonconformists, 1825–1875* (Carlisle: Paternoster Press, 2000), pp. 116–17.
8. A. Brown, *Recollections of the Conversation Parties of the Revd Charles Simeon* (London, 1863), cited by Gillett, *Trust and Obey*, pp. 134–5.
9. For detail, see D.W. Bebbington, *Evangelicalism in Modern Britain: A History from the 1730s to the 1980s* (London: Routledge, 1995), pp. 86–7; D. Tidball, *Who Are the Evangelicals?* (London: Marshall Pickering, 1994), p. 87.
10. *Christian Observer*, April 1861, p. 256, cited by Bebbington, *Evangelicalism in Modern Britain*, p. 91.
11. For the early years of Princeton Seminary see D.B. Calhoun, *Princeton Seminary. Vol.1: Faith and learning 1812–1868* (Edinburgh: Banner of Truth, 1994); cf. H.A. Harris, *Fundamentalism and Evangelicals* (Oxford: Clarendon Press, 1998), pp. 96–130, 131–42.
12. C. Hodge, *Systematic Theology* (London: James Clarke & Co, 1960 edn), Vol. 1, p. 170.
13. Gillett, *Trust and Obey*, pp. 133–4.
14. H. Venn, *The Complete Duty of Man*, 3rd edn (London, 1779), cited by Gillett, *Trust and Obey*, pp. 140–4.
15. J. Gordon, *Evangelical Spirituality* (London: SPCK, 1991), p. 61.

16. Gordon, *Evangelical Spirituality*, p. 213, citing J.B. Harford and F.C. MacDonald, *Bishop Handley Moule* (London, 1923), pp. 311–14.
17. H.C.G. Moule, *The Call of Lent* (London: SPCK, 1917), p. 74.
18. *The Works of the Late Rev. Robert Murray McCheyne* (New York: Robert Carter, 1848–1850); cf. Gordon, *Evangelical Spirituality*, pp. 139–41.
19. J.C. Zacek, 'The Russian Bible Society and the Russian Orthodox Church', *Church History*, Vol. 35 (1966), pp. 411–37; R. Steer, *Good News for the World* (Oxford: Monarch Books, 2004), pp. 109–14.
20. I.H. Murray, *The Puritan Hope* (Edinburgh: Banner of Truth, 1975), p. 154.
21. C.H. Spurgeon, 'How to Read the Bible', sermon on Matthew 12:3–7, delivered in 1879, *Metropolitan Tabernacle Pulpit*, Vol. 25, No. 1503, p. 634.
22. R. Foster, *Streams of Living Water* (London: HarperCollins, 1999), p. 227.
23. W.R. Ward, *The Protestant Evangelical Awakening* (Cambridge: Cambridge University Press, 1992), p. 57.
24. See J.N. Strom, 'Problems and Promises of Pietism Research', *Church History,* Vol. 71, No. 3 (2002), pp. 536–54.
25. G. and M. Stead, *The Exotic Plant* (Peterborough: Epworth Press, 2003), chapters 2 and 3.
26. N. Curnock (ed.), *Journal of John Wesley*, Vol. 6, p. 100, cited by A. S. Wood, *The Burning Heart: John Wesley: Evangelist* (Exeter: Paternoster Press, 1978), p. 192.
27. R. Dubarry, 'Baptist Work in France and Neighbouring French-Speaking Lands', in J.H. Rushbrooke (ed.), *The Baptist Movement in the Continent of Europe* (London: Carey Kingsgate Press, 1915), p. 114.
28. M. Lindvall, 'Anders Wiberg: Swedish Revivalist and Baptist Leader', *Baptist Quarterly*, Vol. 32, No. 4, p. 173.
29. W. Sawatsky, *Soviet Evangelicals since World War II* (Kitchener, Ont.: Herald Press, 1982), p. 31.
30. J. Russell Howden, for example, in F.D. Coggan, *Christ and the Colleges* (London: IVF, 1934), p. 37.
31. R. Collis, *The Silver Fleece: An Autobiography* (London: T. Nelson, 1936), pp. 111, 114.
32. *The British Weekly*, 18 August 1932, p. 382.
33. Gordon, *Evangelical Spirituality*, p. 63.
34. C. Simeon, *Let Wisdom Judge* (London: InterVarsity Fellowship, repr. 1959), p. 103.
35. Gordon, *Evangelical Spirituality*, p. 95.
36. C.H. Spurgeon, 'The Well-beloved', *Till He Come* (London: Passmore and Alabaster, 1894), pp. 101–2, 111.
37. Spurgeon, 'How to Read the Bible', p. 633.
38. *ibid.*, p. 634.

39. P.T. Forsyth, *Positive Preaching and the Modern Mind* (London: Independent Press, 1907), p. 1.
40. P.T. Forsyth, *The Church and the Sacraments* (London: Independent Press, 1947), p. 144.
41. I.M. Randall, *Evangelical Experiences: A Study in the Spirituality of English Evangelicalism, 1918–1939* (Carlisle: Paternoster Press, 1999), p. 26.
42. W. White, *Revival in Rose Street: A History of Charlotte Baptist Chapel, Edinburgh* (Edinburgh: Charlotte Chapel, n.d.), pp. 48–9.
43. L. and B. Hybels, *Rediscovering church: The story and vision of Willow Creek Community Church* (Grand Rapids, Mich.: Zondervan, 1995).
44. D.M. Lloyd-Jones, *Preaching and Preachers* (London: Hodder & Stoughton, 1971), pp. 97–8.
45. Gordon, *Evangelical Spirituality*, pp. 287–8.
46. D.W. Lambert, *What hath God Wrought* (Calver: Cliff College, 1954), p. 42.
47. P. Sangster, *Doctor Sangster* (London: Epworth Press, 1962), p. 277.
48. P. Smith, 'Donald English – Preacher', in R.W. Abbott (ed.), *Donald English: An Evangelical Celebration* (Ilkeston, Derbys.: Headline Special/Moorley's, 1999), p. 20.
49. T. Dudley-Smith, *John Stott: The Making of a Leader* (Leicester: InterVarsity Press, 1999), p. 188.
50. J.R.W. Stott, *The Preacher's Portrait* (London: Tyndale, 1961), pp. 21–3.
51. Gordon, *Evangelical Spirituality*, p. 297; J.R.W. Stott, *Christ the Controversialist* (Leicester: InterVarsity Press, 1970), p. 165.
52. M. Marty, *Modern American Religion: The Noise of Conflict, 1919–1941* (Chicago: University of Chicago Press, 1991), p. 170.
53. G.M. Marsden, *Fundamentalism and American Culture: The Shaping of Twentieth-Century Evangelicalism, 1870–1925* (New York: Oxford University Press, 1980), pp. 3–8.
54. D.W. Bebbington, 'Martyrs for the Truth: Fundamentalists in Britain', in D. Wood (ed.), *Studies in Church History* (Oxford: Blackwell, 1993), Vol. 30, p. 448.
55. *The Bible League Quarterly,* July–September 1922, insert; D.W. Bebbington, 'Missionary Controversy and the Polarising Tendency in Twentieth-Century British Protestantism', *Anvil*, Vol. 13, No. 2 (1996), pp. 141–3.
56. *The Bible Call,* November 1923, p. 163; April 1924, p. 52; cf. D.W. Bebbington, 'Baptists and Fundamentalism in Inter-War Britain', in K. Robbins (ed.), *Studies in Church History,* Subsidia 7 (Oxford: Blackwell, 1990), pp. 297–326.
57. *The Bible League Quarterly,* July–September 1925, pp. 105–7.
58. *Life of Faith,* 13 May 1931, p. 521.
59. Cited by Harris, *Fundamentalism and Evangelicals*, p. 199.

60. *Joyful News*, 15 January 1920, p. 4.
61. *Joyful News*, 8 September 1921, p. 2; D.H. Howarth, *How Great a Flame* (Ilkeston: Moorley's, 1983), p. 30.
62. Lambert, *What hath God Wrought*, p. 57.
63. See F.F. Bruce, *In Retrospect: Remembrance of Things Past* (London: Pickering & Inglis, 1980).
64. G.M. Marsden, *Reforming Fundamentalism: Fuller Seminary and the New Evangelicalism* (Grand Rapids, Mich.: Eerdmans, 1987).
65. J.R.W. Stott, *Fundamentalism: A Religious Problem: Letters to the Editor of the Times and a Leading Article* (London: n.p., 1955).
66. C. Price and I. Randall, *Transforming Keswick* (Carlisle: Paternoster/OM, 2000), pp. 204–5.

Chapter 4. 'Christ in a Real Presence': The Sacraments

1. P.T. Forsyth, *The Church and the Sacraments* (London: Independent Press, 1947), p. 176.
2. D.K. Gillett, *Trust and Obey: Explorations in Evangelical Spirituality* (London: DLT, 1993), pp. 37–8.
3. A. Chamberlain (ed.), *The Works of Jonathan Edwards* (New Haven: Yale University Press, 2000), Vol. 18, p. 129.
4. R.W. Jenson, *America's Theologian* (Oxford: Oxford University Press, 1988), pp. 56–7.
5. I.H. Murray, *Jonathan Edwards* (Edinburgh: Banner of Truth, 1987), chapters 16 and 17.
6. Cited by G. Rowell, *The Vision Glorious* (Oxford: Clarendon Press, 1983), p. 17.
7. J.C.S. Nias, *Gorham and the Bishop of Exeter* (London: SPCK, 1951), pp. 11, 14.
8. G. Carter, *Anglican Evangelicals* (Oxford: Oxford University Press, 2001), p. 354.
9. K. Hylson-Smith, *Evangelicals in the Church of England, 1734–1984* (Edinburgh: T & T Clark, 1988), p. 124.
10. J.W. Grant, *Free Churchmanship in England, 1870–1940* (London: Independent Press, [1940]), pp. 106–8.
11. Cited by N.A.D. Scotland, *Evangelical Anglicans in a Revolutionary Age, 1789–1901* (Carlisle: Paternoster Press, 2004), p. 171.
12. J.M. Ross, 'The Theology of Baptism in Baptist History', *Baptist Quarterly*, Vol. 15 (1953–4), p. 100.
13. A. Fuller, 'The Practical Uses of Christian Baptism', in A.G. Fuller (ed.), *The Complete Works of the Rev. Andrew Fuller* (London: William Ball and Co., 1841), p. 728; cf. M.A.G. Haykin, ' "Hazarding all for God at a Clap": The Spirituality of Baptism among British Calvinistic Baptists', *Baptist Quarterly*, Vol. 38, No. 4 (1999), pp. 188–9.
14. Fuller, 'The Practical Uses of Christian Baptism', pp. 728–9.

15. *ibid.,* p. 729.
16. I.H. Murray (ed.), *The Early Years* (Edinburgh: Banner of Truth, 1973), p. 131; cf. T. Grass and I. Randall, 'Spurgeon on the Sacraments', in A.R. Cross and P.E. Thompson (eds.), *Baptist Sacramentalism* (Carlisle: Paternoster Press, 2003), pp. 55–75.
17. Murray, *Early Years,* pp. 147–50.
18. I.H. Murray (ed.), *The Full Harvest* (Edinburgh: Banner of Truth, 1973), p. 37.
19. C.H. Spurgeon, 'Baptismal Regeneration', *Metropolitan Tabernacle Pulpit,* sermon on Mark 16:15–16, Vol. 10, No. 573, 5 June 1864, pp. 313–28.
20. L.A. Drummond, *Spurgeon: Prince of Preachers* (Grand Rapids, MI: Kregel Publication, 1992), p. 490.
21. A.R. Cross, *Baptism and the Baptists: Theology and Practice in Twentieth-Century Britain* (Carlisle: Paternoster Press, 2000), pp. 225–7.
22. Editorial, *The Fraternal,* July 1959, p. 4.
23. G.R. Beasley-Murray, 'Baptism in the Epistles of Paul', in A. Gilmore (ed.), *Christian Baptism: A Fresh Attempt to Understand the Rite in terms of Scripture, History and Theology* (London: Lutterworth Press, 1959), p. 148.
24. *Baptist Times,* 10 December 1959, p. 8.
25. *Baptist Times,* 11 February 1960, pp. 9–10.
26. A.C. Outler (ed.), *The Works of John Wesley,* Vol. 3, Sermon on 'The Duty of Constant Communion', Sermons, III (Nashville: Abingdon Press, 1986), p. 430.
27. *ibid.,* p. 428.
28. F.C. Gill, *Charles Wesley: The First Methodist* (London: Lutterworth Press, 1964), p. 123.
29. C. Simeon, *Memoirs of the Life of the Rev Charles Simeon* (London: Hatchard and Son, 1847), pp. 6, 9.
30. Horton Davies, *Worship and Theology in England, Vol. 1: From Cranmer to Hooker 1534–1603* (London: Oxford University Press, 1961), p. 223.
31. Scotland, *Evangelical Anglicans in a Revolutionary Age, 1789–1901,* pp. 352–4.
32. E. Hodder, *The Life and Work of the Seventh Earl of Shaftesbury, KG* (London: Cassell & Co., 1888), p. 743.
33. H.C.G. Moule, *At the Holy Communion: Helps for Preparation and Reception* (London: Seeley Service & Co., 1914), p. 113.
34. H.C.G. Moule, *Outlines of Christian Doctrine,* rev. edn (London: Hodder & Stoughton, [1890]), p. 242.
35. H.C.G. Moule, *The Call of Lent* (London: SPCK, 1917), p. 82.
36. A. Dutton, *Thoughts on the Lord's Supper, Relating to the Nature, Subjects, and right Partaking of this Solemn Ordinance* (London, 1748), p. 4, cited by M.A.G. Haykin, *One Heart and One Soul*

(Darlington: Evangelical Press, 1994), p. 295; cf. S.J. Stein, 'A Note on Anne Dutton, Eighteenth-Century Evangelical', *Church History*, Vol. 44 (1975), pp. 488–9.

37. J. Sutcliff, *The Ordinance of the Lord's Supper considered* (Dunstable: Circular Letter of the Northamptonshire Association, 1803), pp. 2–4, cited by Haykin, *One Heart*, p. 297.

38. M.J. Walker, *Baptists at the Table. The Theology of the Lord's Supper amongst English Baptists in the Nineteenth Century* (Didcot, Oxfordshire: Baptist Historical Society, 1992), p. 3.

39. See I.M. Randall, *Evangelical Experiences: A Study in the Spirituality of English Evangelicalism, 1918–1939* (Carlisle: Paternoster Press, 1999), chapter 7.

40. D. Robertson, *Awakening* (Carlisle: Paternoster Press, 2004), pp. 70–1.

41. J. Gordon, *Evangelical Spirituality* (London: SPCK, 1991), pp. 144–5, citing H. Bonar, *Hymns by Horatius Bonar* (London, 1904), p. 235.

42. Simeon, *Memoirs of the Life of the Rev Charles Simeon*, p. 120.

43. C.H. Spurgeon, *Till He Come* (London: Passmore & Alabaster, 1894), preface.

44. Spurgeon, 'I will Give you Rest', *Till He Come*, p. 197.

45. C.H. Spurgeon, 'The Witness of the Lord's Supper', *Metropolitan Tabernacle Pulpit*, sermon on 1 Cor. 11:26, Vol. 59, No. 3338, undated, p. 38.

46. C.H. Spurgeon, 'The Lord's Supper: A Remembrance of Jesus', *Metropolitan Tabernacle Pulpit*, sermon on Luke 22:19, Vol. 34, No. 2038, 19 August 1888, pp. 451–2.

47. *The Christian*, 15 July 1920, pp. 1–2.

48. I.M. Randall, *Spirituality and Social Change: The Contribution of F.B. Meyer (1847–1929)* (Carlisle: Paternoster Press, 2003), pp. 49–50.

49. *Baptist Times*, 12 November 1909, p. 811.

50. *The Christian*, 21 July 1938, p. 8.

51. *Life of Faith*, 27 July 1932, p. 846.

52. *Life of Faith*, 26 July 1933, p. 859.

53. *Evangelical Christendom*, 1 October 1855, p. 317.

54. *The Jubilee of the Evangelical Alliance* (London: Evangelical Alliance, 1896), pp. 379–83.

55. *The Christian*, 18 January 1963, p. 1.

56. Spurgeon, 'The Well-beloved', *Till He Come*, p. 113.

57. C.H. Spurgeon, 'The Object of the Lord's Supper', *Metropolitan Tabernacle Pulpit*, sermon published 29 June 1905, delivered 2 September 1877, Vol. 51, No. 2942, p. 317.

58. Forsyth, *The Church and the Sacraments*, pp. 229–32.

59. C. Simeon, *Let Wisdom Judge* (London: InterVarsity Fellowship, repr. 1959), p. 178.

60. C.H. Spurgeon, 'The Blood Shed for Many', *Metropolitan Tabernacle Pulpit*, sermon on Matt. 26:28,Vol. 33, No. 1971, 3 July 1887, p. 377.

Chapter 5. 'Sweet Seasons of Communion': Prayer and Praise

1. M. Noll, *The Rise of Evangelicalism* (Leicester: Apollos, 2003), p. 260.
2. D.L. Jeffrey, *A Burning and a Shining Light: English Spirituality in the Age of Wesley* (Grand Rapids, Mich.: Eerdmans, 1987), pp. 229–30.
3. D.K. Gillett, *Trust and Obey: Explorations in Evangelical Spirituality* (London: DLT, 1993), pp. 34–9.
4. J. Wesley, 'The Character of a Methodist', in T. Jackson (ed.), *The Works of the Rev John Wesley*, 3rd edn (Kansas: Beacon Hill Press, 1978), Vol. 8, p. 404.
5. G. Mursell, *English Spirituality: From 1700 to the Present Day* (London: SPCK, 2001), p. 96.
6. A.C. Outler (ed.), *The Works of John Wesley*, Vol. 3, Sermon on 'On Visiting the Sick', Sermons, III (Nashville: Abingdon Press, 1984), p. 392.
7. J. Telford, *The Letters of the Rev. John Wesley, A.M.* (London: Epworth Press, 1931, repr. 1960), Vol. 6, p. 326.
8. E. Welch, *Spiritual Pilgrim: A reassessment of the life of the Countess of Huntingdon* (Cardiff: University of Wales Press, 1995), p. 185.
9. J. Stoughton, *William Wilberforce* (London: Hodder & Stoughton, 1880), p. 121.
10. *ibid.*, p. 124.
11. J. Gordon, *Evangelical Spirituality* (London: SPCK, 1991), p. 5, citing J. Collingwood and M. Collingwood, *Hannah More* (Oxford, 1990), p. 133.
12. C. Simeon, *Memoirs of the Life of the Rev Charles Simeon* (London: Hatchard and Son, 1847), p. 67.
13. N. Scotland, *John Bird Sumner: Evangelical Archbishop* (Leominster: Gracewing, 1995), p. 158.
14. See A. Bonar, *Memoir and Remains of Robert Murray McCheyne* (Edinburgh: Banner of Truth, repr. 1987).
15. H.C.G. Moule, *Charles Simeon* (London: InterVarsity Press, repr. 1948), p. 66.
16. J.C. Ryle, *Practical Religion* (Cambridge: James Clarke & Co., repr. 1959), p. 64.
17. *ibid.*, p. 50.
18. C.H. Spurgeon, *Autobiography* (London: Passmore and Alabaster, 1899), Vol. 3, p. 319.
19. H.C.G. Moule, *The Call of Lent* (London: SPCK, 1917), pp. 78–9.
20. P.T. Forsyth, *The Soul of Prayer* (London: C.H. Kelly, 1916), p. 77.
21. *ibid.*, p. 118.
22. *ibid.*, p. 105.
23. N.G. Dunning, *Samuel Chadwick* (London: Hodder & Stoughton,

1933), p. 20; D.H. Howarth, *How Great a Flame* (Ilkeley: Moorley's, 1982), pp. 34–5.
24. G. Whitefield, *Sermons on Important Subjects* (London: H. Fisher, Son, and P. Jackson, 1835), p. 52.
25. Moule, *Call of Lent*, p. 80.
26. F.C. Spurr wrote two articles: *Baptist Times*, 26 September 1935, p. 700; 10 October 1935, p. 734.
27. D.M. Lloyd-Jones, *Sermons on Ephesians, The Unsearchable Riches of Christ* (Edinburgh: Banner of Truth, 1979), p. 198.
28. G. Giles, *The Music of Praise* (Oxford: Bible Reading Fellowship, 2002), pp. 81–5.
29. G. Mursell, *English Spirituality: From 1700 to the Present Day* (London: SPCK, 2001), p. 30.
30. C.H. Spurgeon, *Metropolitan Tabernacle Pulpit*, sermon on 1 Chron. 4:10, Vol. 17, No. 994, Year 1871, p. 323.
31. Spurgeon, *Autobiography*, Vol. 3, p. 246.
32. F.B. Meyer, *The Call and Challenge of the Unseen* (London: Morgan & Scott, 1928), p. 166.
33. I. Bradley, *The Call to Seriousness* (London: Jonathan Cape, 1976), p. 180.
34. G.W.E. Russell, *A Short History of the Evangelical Movement* (London: Mowbray and Co., 1915), p. 142.
35. M. Hennell, *Sons of Prophets: Evangelical leaders of the Victorian Church* (London: SPCK, 1979), p. 39.
36. See N.A.D. Scotland, *Evangelical Anglicans in a Revolutionary Age, 1789–1901* (Carlisle: Paternoster Press, 2004), pp. 349–50.
37. W.R. Ward and R.P. Heitzenrater (eds.), *The Works of John Wesley*, Vol. 19: Journals and Diaries, II (Nashville: Abingdon Press, 1990), p. 29.
38. Mursell, *English Spirituality*, p. 28.
39. Spurgeon, *Autobiography*, Vol. 3, p. 168.
40. D.W. Bebbington, *Evangelicalism in Modern Britain: A History from the 1730s to the 1980s* (London: Routledge, 1995), p. 94.
41. M.A.G. Haykin, *One Heart and One Soul: John Sutcliff of Olney* (Darlington: Evangelical Press, 1994), chapter 8.
42. Gordon, *Evangelical Spirituality*, pp. 33–5; Noll, *Rise of Evangelicalism*, pp. 260–9; Mursell, *English Spirituality*, p. 97.
43. Gordon, *Evangelical Spirituality*, chapter 3.
44. Scotland, *Evangelical Anglicans in a Revolutionary Age, 1789–1901*, p. 115.
45. I. Bradley, *Abide with me: The world of Victorian hymns* (London: SCM, 1997).
46. See C. Price and I. Randall, *Transforming Keswick* (Carlisle: OM/Paternoster Press, 2000), chapter 5.
47. J.R.W. Stott, *Understanding the Bible* (London: Scripture Union, 1972), p. 244.

48. R. Foster, *Celebration of Discipline* (London: Hodder & Stoughton, 1980).
49. R.A. Torrey, *How to Succeed in the Christian Life* (London: James Nisbet, 1906), p. 80, cited by Gillett, *Trust and Obey*, p. 172.
50. Gillett, *Trust and Obey*, p. 190.
51. M.R. Hooker, *Adventures of an Agnostic* (London: Marshall, Morgan & Scott, 1959), p. 112.
52. I. Randall and D. Hilborn, *One Body in Christ* (Carlisle: Paternoster Press, 2001), p. 301.
53. Horton Davies, *Worship and Theology in England, Vol. 5: The ecumenical century* (London: Oxford University Press, 1962), p. 350.
54. *ibid.*, p. 380.
55. Forsyth, *The Soul of Prayer*, p. 54.
56. D.J. Fant, *A.W. Tozer: A Twentieth Century Prophet* (Harrisburg, Penn.: Christian Publications, 1964), pp. 143–5; A.W. Tozer, *Whatever Happened to Worship?* (Eastbourne: Kingsway, 1985), comprising sermons Tozer preached in 1962.
57. *Things New and Old,* April 1922, p. 7; October 1922, p. 6.
58. For more on these developments see the volume in this series on charismatic spirituality (forthcoming).
59. P. Hocken, *Streams of Renewal: The Origins and Early Development of the Charismatic Movement in Britain* (Carlisle: Paternoster Press, 1997), p. 108.
60. E.A. Payne and S.F. Winward, *Orders and Prayers for Church Worship* (London: Baptist Union, 1967), p. xii.
61. R.E. Webber, *Ancient-Future Faith* (Grand Rapids, Mich.: Baker Book House, 1999).
62. *Memoir and Remains of Robert Murray McCheyne*, pp. 276–7.

Chapter 6. 'O Lamb of God, I Come': Evangelicals and the Cross

1. D.K. Gillett, *Trust and Obey: Explorations in Evangelical Spirituality* (London: DLT, 1993), p. 78.
2. H.C.G. Moule, *Charles Simeon* (London: InterVarsity Press, repr. 1948), pp. 155–6.
3. Gillett, *Trust and Obey*, pp. 67, 73.
4. A.C. Outler (ed.), *The Works of John Wesley*, Vol. 1, Sermon on 'Justification by Faith', Sermons, I (Nashville: Abingdon Press, 1984), p. 187; cf. M.E. Dieter (ed.), *Five Views of Sanctification* (Grand Rapids, Mich.: Zondervan, 1987), p. 25.
5. J. Owen, *The Death of Death in the Death of Christ* (London. Banner of Truth, repr. 1959).
6. Outler (ed.), *The Works of John Wesley,* Vol. 3, Sermon on 'Free Grace' (1739), Sermons, III, pp. 558–9.
7. A. Dallimore, *George Whitefield* (Edinburgh: Banner of Truth, 1980), Vol. 2, pp. 551–2.

8. C.H. Spurgeon, *Metropolitan Tabernacle Pulpit*, 'The blood of sprinkling', Sermon on Hebrews 12:24, 25, Vol. 32, No. 1888, sermon preached 28 February 1886, p. 127.

9. C.H. Spurgeon, *Metropolitan Tabernacle Pulpit*, 'The three hours' darkness', Sermon on Matt. 27:45, Vol. 32, No. 1896, sermon preached 18 April 1886, p. 223.

10. H.C.G. Moule, *The Call of Lent* (London: SPCK, 1917), p. 103.

11. P.T. Forsyth, *The Work of Christ* (London: Hodder & Stoughton, 1910), p. 170.

12. J. Gordon, *Evangelical Spirituality* (London: SPCK, 1991), p. 232.

13. F.B. Meyer, *Key-words of the Inner Life* (London: Morgan & Scott, [1893]), p. 50; F.B. Meyer, *The Way into the Holiest* (London: Morgan & Scott, [1893]), p. 27.

14. F.B. Meyer, *In Defence of the Faith* (London: S.W. Partridge & Co., 1907), p. 73.

15. F.B. Meyer, *At the Gates of the Dawn* (London: James Clarke, [1910]), p. 74; F.B. Meyer, *The Soul's Wrestle with Doubt* (London: Little Books on the Devout Life Series, 1905), p. 50.

16. F.B. Meyer in the *Baptist Times*, 12 November 1909, p. 811.

17. *The Christian*, 5 January 1929, p. 5.

18. F.B. Meyer, *The Soul's Pure Intention* (London: Samuel Bagster, 1906), p. 28.

19. *Baptist Times*, 12 November 1909, p. 811.

20. M. Noll, *The Rise of Evangelicalism* (Leicester: Apollos, 2003), pp. 268–9.

21. F.C. Gill, *Charles Wesley: The First Methodist* (London: Lutterworth Press, 1964), p. 72.

22. D.W. Bebbington, *Evangelicalism in Modern Britain: A History from the 1730s to the 1980s* (London: Routledge, 1995), p. 39.

23. J.E. Hutton, *A History of the Moravian Church* (London: Moravian Publication Office, 1909), pp. 265, 275–6, 322.

24. Gordon, *Evangelical Spirituality*, p. 73.

25. *ibid.*, pp. 73–5, citing J.D. Baird and C. Ryskamp, *The Poems of William Cowper* (Oxford, 1980), Vol. 1, p. 154, and J. Newton, *Works* (Edinburgh: Banner of Truth, 1984), Vol. 1, p. 463.

26. Gillett, *Trust and Obey*, p. 87; Spurgeon, 'The three hours' darkness', pp. 225–6.

27. J.C. Ryle, *Holiness* (Welwyn: Evangelical Press, repr. 1979), p. 52.

28. F.B. Meyer, *A Holy Temple* (London: S.W. Partridge, [1901]), pp. 4, 9, 15.

29. Gordon, *Evangelical Spirituality*, pp. 105, 110–11, citing W. Roberts, *Memoirs of the Life and Correspondence of Mrs Hannah More*, 2nd edn (4 Vols., London, 1834). See also Anne Stott, *Hannah More: The first Victorian* (Oxford: Oxford University Press, 2003).

30. J. Edwards, 'The Distinguishing Marks of a Work of the Spirit of

God', in C.C. Goen (ed.), *The Works of Jonathan Edwards* (New Haven and London: Yale University Press, 1972), Vol. 4, p. 244.

31. J. Penn-Lewis and E. Roberts, *War on the Saints*, 3rd edn (Leicester: The Overcomer Book Room, 1922).
32. N. Grubb, *Rees Howells: Intercessor* (Cambridge: Lutterworth Press, 1973), pp. 246, 260.
33. D. Watson, *Discipleship* (London: Hodder & Stoughton, 1981), chapter 8.
34. C.H. Spurgeon, *Metropolitan Tabernacle Pulpit*, 'Abraham's prompt obedience to the Word of God', Sermon on Hebrews 11:8, Vol. 21, No. 1242, sermon preached 27 June 1875, p. 379.
35. C.H. Spurgeon, *Metropolitan Tabernacle Pulpit*, 'The unchangeable Christ', Sermon on Hebrews 13:8, Vol. 40, No. 2358, sermon preached 23 February 1888, published 1894, p. 193.
36. Gillett, *Trust and Obey*, pp. 20–1. Gillett reproduces the whole hymn.
37. H.C.G. Moule, *Thoughts on Christian Sanctity* (London: Seeley & Co., 1885), p. 35.
38. *ibid.*, pp. 74, 81.
39. Gillett, *Trust and Obey*, p. 78, citing Julian's *Dictionary of Hymnology*.
40. F.W. Boreham, *A Late Lark Singing* (London: Epworth Press, 1945).
41. For Amy Carmichael see E. Elliot, *Amy Carmichael: Her Life and Legacy* (Eastbourne: Kingsway, 1988).
42. Gillett, *Trust and Obey*, pp. 81–2, citing Amy Carmichael, *If* (London: SPCK, 1938).
43. Gillett, *Trust and Obey*, p. 79.
44. F.B. Meyer, *Moses: The Servant of God* (London: Morgan & Scott, 1893), p. 99; *The Evangelical Alliance Quarterly*, No. 11 (January 1902), p. 206. This was an address given by Meyer to the Annual Evangelical Alliance Conference in November 1901.
45. Introduction by F.B. Meyer to G.W. Robinson, *The Philosophy of the Atonement* (London: Dent, 1912); *Keswick Week*, 1924, p. 156.
46. Meyer, *At the Gates of the Dawn*, p. 74; Meyer, *Pure Intention*, p. 45.
47. Gordon, *Evangelical Spirituality*, pp. 242–3.
48. D.J. Fant, *A.W. Tozer: A Twentieth Century Prophet* (Harrisburg, Penn.: Christian Publcns., 1964), p. 181.
49. See A.E. Smith, *Another Anglican Angle: The History of the AEGM* (Oxford: Amate Press, 1991); I.M. Randall, *Evangelical Experiences: A Study in the Spirituality of English Evangelicalism, 1918–1939* (Carlisle: Paternoster Press, 1999), chapter 3.
50. V.F. Storr, *The Problem of the Cross* (London: John Murray, 1918), p. 96.
51. V.F. Storr, *The Problem of the Cross*, 2nd edn (London: SCM, 1924,), pp. 97, 116, 129, 137.
52. V.F. Storr, *The Splendour of God* (London: SPCK, 1928), pp. 50, 56,

65; A.M. Ramsey, *From Gore to Temple* (London: Longmans, 1960), p. 58.

53. C. Simeon, *Memoirs of the Life of the Rev Charles Simeon* (London: Hatchard and Son, 1847), p. 676.

54. Moule, *The Call of Lent*, pp. 65, 68, 71–2.

55. O. Chambers, *My Utmost for His Highest* (London: Marshall, Morgan & Scott, 1927), p. 310.

56. D.W. Lambert, *Oswald Chambers* (London: n.p., 1968), p. 86.

57. D. McCasland, *Oswald Chambers: Abandoned to God* (Nashville: Discovery House, 1993), p. 106.

58. B. Chambers (ed.), *Oswald Chambers: His Life and Work* (London: Marshall, 1933), p. 331.

59. *ibid.*, pp. 144, 221.

60. See B.P. Jones, *The Trials and Triumphs of Mrs Penn-Lewis* (North Brunswick, NJ, 1997), pp. 260–5.

61. J. Stott, *The Cross of Christ* (Leicester: Intervarsity Press, 1986), pp. 293–4.

62. J.R.W. Stott, *Baptism and Fullness*, 2nd edn (Leicester: Intervarsity Press, 1975), p. 69.

63. See Gordon, *Evangelical Spirituality*, p. 50.

64. P.T. Forsyth, *The Soul of Prayer* (London: C.H. Kelly, 1916), p. 12.

65. Gillett, *Trust and Obey*, p. 92.

66. B.L. Manning, *The Hymns of Wesley and Watts* (London: Epworth Press, 1942), p. 133.

Chapter 7. 'The Highest Beauty': The Holy Spirit and Holiness

1. D.W. Bebbington, *Holiness in Nineteenth-Century England* (Carlisle: Paternoster Press, 2000).

2. J. Coughey, *Earnest Christianity Illustrated*, 1857, p. 103, cited by D.W. Bebbington, 'Holiness in the Evangelical Tradition', in S.C. Barton (ed.), *Holiness Past & Present* (London: T & T Clark, 2003), p. 300.

3. J. Gordon, *Evangelical Spirituality* (London: SPCK, 1991), p. 61, citing G. Whitefield, *Works,* ed. Hickman (Edinburgh repr., 1974), Vol. 1, p. 47.

4. D.W. Dayton, 'Yet Another Layer of the Onion: Or Opening the Ecumenical Door to Let the Riffraff in', *The Ecumenical Review*, Vol. 40, No. 1 (1988), p. 100.

5. Gordon, *Evangelical Spirituality*, p. 44.

6. R.W. Jenson, *America's Theologian* (Oxford: Oxford University Press, 1992), p. 16.

7. For Toplady and Wesley see T. Smith, 'The Holy Spirit in the Hymns of the Wesleys', *Wesleyan Theological Journal*, Vol. 16 (Fall, 1981), p. 38.

8. J.C. Ryle, *Holiness* (Welwyn: Evangelical Press, repr. 1979), pp. 34–7.

9. J.C. Ryle, *Practical Religion* (Cambridge: James Clarke & Co., repr., 1959), pp. 8–9.

10. Ryle, *Holiness*, p. viii.

11. J.I. Packer, *Passion for Holiness* (Leicester: Crossway Books, 1992), pp. 19–22, 113–14, 204–5.

12. J. Telford (ed.), *The Letters of the Rev John Wesley, A.M.* (London: Epworth Press, 1931, repr. 1960), Vol. 8, p. 238.

13. J. Wesley, 'Brief Thoughts on Christian Perfection', in T. Jackson (ed.), *The Works of the Rev John Wesley*, 3rd edn (Kansas: Beacon Hill Press, 1978), Vol. 11, p. 446; A.S. Wood, *Love Excluding Sin*, Occasional Paper No. 1 of the Wesley Fellowship (1986), pp. 5, 8–9.

14. Wesley, 'Brief Thoughts', p. 443.

15. F.C. Gill, *Charles Wesley: The First Methodist* (London: Lutterworth Press, 1964), pp. 66–7.

16. See G. Mursell, *English Spirituality: From 1700 to the Present Day* (London: SPCK, 2001), pp. 3–95; H.D. Rack, *Reasonable Enthusiast: John Wesley and the Rise of Methodism* (London: Epworth Press, 1989), p. 98.

17. A.C. Outler (ed.), *The Works of John Wesley*, Vol. 2, Sermon 37, 'The Nature of Enthusiasm', Sermons, II (34–70) (Nashville: Abingdon Press, 1985), p. 52.

18. J. Wesley, *Letters*, Vol. 3, p. 9 (18 July 1749), to a Roman Catholic.

19. M. McFadden, 'The Ironies of Pentecost: Phoebe Palmer, World Evangelism, and Female Networks', *Methodist History*, Vol. 31, No. 2 (1993).

20. C.W. Hall, *Samuel Logan Brengle: Portrait of a Prophet* (New York: Salvation Army, 1933), pp. 56–71.

21. S.L. Brengle, *The Guest of the Soul* (London: Marshall, Morgan & Scott, 1934), pp. 115–16; Hall, *Samuel Logan Brengle*, pp. 87–8, 91–2.

22. R.D. Rightmire, 'Samuel Brengle and the Development of the Salvation Army', *Wesleyan Theological Journal*, Vol. 27 (1992), p. 112.

23. J.L. Peters, *Christian Perfection in American Methodism* (New York: Abingdon, 1956).

24. I.E. Page (ed.), *John Brash: Memorials and Correspondence* (London: C.H. Kelly, 1912), pp. 2–3.

25. J. Baines Atkinson (ed.), *To the Uttermost* (London: n.p., 1945), p. 14.

26. See R.C. Standing, 'The Relationship between Evangelicalism and the Social Gospel with Special Reference to Wesleyan Methodism', University of Manchester M.Phil. thesis (1992), p. 110.

27. I.M. Randall, 'Southport and Swanwick: Contrasting Movements of Methodist Spirituality in Inter-War England', *Proceedings of the Wesley Historical Society*, Vol. 50 (1995), pp. 1–14.

28. *Joyful News*, 16 February 1921, p. 3.

29. M.E. Dieter, *The Holiness Revival of the Nineteenth Century*

(Metuchen, NJ: Scarecrow Press, 1980), pp. 37–40; D.W. Bebbington, *Evangelicalism in Modern Britain: A History from the 1730s to the 1980s* (London: Routledge, 1995), chapter 5.

30. *The Christian's Pathway of Power*, June 1875, p. 101.
31. For an account see Edna Jackson, *The Life that is Life Indeed* (London: James Nisbet & Co., 1910).
32. J.B. Figgis, *Keswick from Within* (London: Marshall Bros., 1914), p. 19.
33. W.B. Sloan, *These Sixty Years: The Story of the Keswick Convention* (London: Pickering & Inglis, 1935), pp. 9–11.
34. *Account of the Union Meeting for the Promotion of Scriptural Holiness, held at Oxford, August 29 to September 7, 1874* (London: S.W. Partridge, 1875), p. 84.
35. C.F. Harford (ed.), *The Keswick Convention: Its Message, Its Method and Its Men* (London: Marshall Bros., 1907), p. 32.
36. For speakers see *Record of the Convention for the Promotion of Scriptural Holiness held at Brighton, May 29th to June 7th, 1875* (Brighton: W.J. Smith, 1875), pp. 492–3.
37. *Record of the Convention for the Promotion of Scriptural Holiness held at Brighton*, p. 82.
38. C. Price and I. Randall, *Transforming Keswick* (Carlisle: OM/Paternoster, 2000), p. 25.
39. D.W. Bebbington, *Evangelicalism in Modern Britain: A History from the 1730s to the 1980s* (London: Routledge, 1995), p. 168.
40. *The Christian's Pathway of Power*, March 1976, p. 41; A. Smellie, *Evan Henry Hopkins: A Memoir* (London: Marshall Bros., 1921), p. 81.
41. E.H. Hopkins, *The Law of Liberty in the Spiritual Life* (London: Marshall Bros., 1884).
42. Bebbington, *Evangelicalism in Modern Britain*, p. 168; Price and Randall, *Transforming Keswick*, pp. 45–6.
43. H.W. Webb-Peploe writing in Harford (ed.), *The Keswick Convention*, pp. 38–9.
44. *The Life of Faith*, 10 February 1926, p. 14; *Baptist Times*, 21 July 1932, p. 513.
45. N.C. MacFarlane, *Scotland's Keswick* (London: Marshall Bros., [1925]), pp. 151–2.
46. J.C. Pollock, *The Keswick Story* (London: Hodder & Stoughton, 1964), pp. 47–8.
47. J. Morgan, *A Man of the Word: Life of G. Campbell Morgan* (London: Pickering & Inglis, 1951), pp. 169–80.
48. W.Y. Fullerton, *F.B. Meyer: A Biography* (London: Marshall, Morgan & Scott, [1929]), pp. 56–9; I.M. Randall, *Spirituality and Social Change: The Contribution of F.B. Meyer (1847–1929)* (Carlisle: Paternoster Press, 2003), chapter 5.

49. H.C.G. Moule, *Christ and the Christian* (London: Marshall Bros., 1919), pp. 49–58.

50. See I.M. Randall, *Evangelical Experiences: A Study in the Spirituality of English Evangelicalism, 1918–1939* (Carlisle: Paternoster Press, 1999), chapter 2.

51. See A.M. Hay, *Charles Inwood: His Ministry and its Secret* (London: Marshall & Co., 1929).

52. J.K. Maclean, *Dr Pierson and His Message* (London, n.d.), p. 35.

53. See J.E. Church, *Quest for the Highest* (Exeter: Paternoster Press, 1981).

54. Price and Randall, *Transforming Keswick*, p. 122.

55. I.M. Randall, 'The Pentecostal League of Prayer: A Transdenominational British Wesleyan-Holiness Movement', *Wesleyan Theological Journal* (Spring 1998), pp. 185–200.

56. S. Barabas, *So Great Salvation* (London: Marshall, Morgan & Scott, 1952), p. 180.

57. *The Life of Faith*, 12 August 1903, p. 572.

58. For Evan Roberts see B.P. Jones, *An Instrument of Revival: The Complete Life of Evan Roberts, 1878–1951* (South Plainfield, NJ, 1995).

59. Figgis, *Keswick from Within*, p. 151. For more on the Welsh Revival see E. Evans, *The Welsh Revival of 1904* (London: Evangelical Press, 1969, republished by the Evangelical Movement of Wales, Bryntirion Press) and K. Adams, *A Diary of Revival: the outbreak of the 1904 Welsh Awakening* (Farnham: CWR, 2004).

60. F. Bartleman, *How Pentecost Came to Los Angeles* (Los Angeles: n.p., 1925), p. 11. See also C. Brumback, *Suddenly from Heaven* (Springfield, Missouri: Gospel Publishing House, 1961), p. 34. For Meyer's report on his Los Angeles meetings, see *The Christian*, 4 May 1905, p. 23.

61. See J. Creech, 'Visions of Glory: The Place of the Azusa Street Revival in Pentecostal History', *Church History*, Vol. 65, No. 3 (1996), pp. 405–24.

62. *The Christian*, 27 February 1902, p. 19.

63. D. Gee, *Wind and Flame* (Croydon: Assemblies of God, 1967), chapters 3–5.

64. Sloan, *These Sixty Years: The Story of the Keswick Convention*, pp. 49–50.

65. J.E. Orr, *The Flaming Tongue* (Chicago: Moody Press, 1973), chapter 19; H.S. Dyer, *Pandita Ramabai: The Story of Her Life* (London: Morgan and Scott, 1912); G.B. McGee, '"Latter Rain" Falling in the East: Early-Twentieth-Century Pentecostalism in India and the Debate over Speaking in Tongues', *Church History*, Vol. 68, No. 3 (1999), pp. 658–65.

66. Ryle, *Holiness*, pp. 20–1.

67. Price and Randall, *Transforming Keswick*, p. 25.

68. Bebbington, 'Holiness in the Evangelical Tradition', p. 315.

Chapter 8. 'That Mystical Body': The Fellowship of Believers

1. C. Price and I. Randall, *Transforming Keswick* (Carlisle: Paternoster Press/OM, 2000), pp. 28–31.
2. D.J. Tidball, *Who are the Evangelicals?* (London: MarshallPickering, 1994), pp. 159–60.
3. B. Hindmarsh, 'Is Evangelical Ecclesiology an Oxymoron?', in J.J. Stackhouse Jnr (ed.), *Evangelical Ecclesiology: Reality or Illusion?* (Grand Rapids, Mich.: Baker Book House, 2003), pp. 31–4.
4. Hindmarsh, 'Is Evangelical Ecclesiology an Oxymoron?', p. 33, citing J. Gillies (ed.), *The Works of ... the Revd. George Whitefield* (London: n.p., 1771), Vol. 1, p. 126.
5. R.E. Olsen, 'Free Church Ecclesiology and Evangelical Spirituality', in Stackhouse Jnr (ed.), *Evangelical Ecclesiology*, pp. 161–78.
6. 2 Corinthians 6:14–18.
7. H.H. Rowdon, *The Origins of the Brethren, 1825–1850* (London: Pickering & Inglis, 1967), pp. 53, 99.
8. See A. Kinnear, *Watchman Nee: Against the Tide* (Eastbourne: Kingsway, 1990).
9. Evangelical Alliance, *Unity in Diversity: The Papers Given at the National Assembly of Evangelicals at Westminster, London, in October, 1966* (London: Evangelical Alliance, 1967), 9. For further details see I.H. Murray, *D. Martyn Lloyd-Jones: The Fight of Faith, 1939–1981* (Edinburgh: Banner of Truth, 1990), pp. 513–33; J. Brencher, *Martyn Lloyd-Jones (1899–1981) and Twentieth-Century Evangelicalism* (Carlisle: Paternoster Press, 2002), pp. 83–115; D.W. Wright, 'A Review Article [of] *Evangelicalism Divided* ... [by] Iain H. Murray', *Reformation and Revival*, Vol. 10, No. 2 (Spring 2001), pp. 121–36.
10. Murray, *D. Martyn Lloyd-Jones: The Fight of Faith*, pp. 523–5; E. Davies, '18 October 1966: Its context, message and significance', *Foundations*, No. 37 (1996), p. 11.
11. *Crusade,* January 1981, p. 22.
12. *Restoration,* November/December 1981, pp. 9–12.
13. Cited by K. Hylson-Smith, *Evangelicals in the Church of England* (Edinburgh: T & T Clark, 1988), p. 23.
14. F. Baker, *John Wesley and the Church of England* (London: Epworth Press, 1970), pp. 183, 191, 196.
15. J. Bennett, *Memoirs of the Life of the Revd David Bogue DD* (London, 1827); cf. R.H. Martin, *Evangelicals United: Ecumenical Stirrings in Pre-Victorian Britain, 1795–1830* (Metuchen, NJ, and London: The Scarecrow Press, 1983), p. 43.
16. See R. Steer, *Good News for the World* (Oxford: Monarch Books, 2004).

17. N.M. Railton, *No North Sea: The Anglo-German Evangelical Network in the Middle of the Nineteenth Century* (Brill: Leiden, 2000), p. 2.

18. R. Rouse and S.C. Neill (eds.), *A History of the Ecumenical Movement* (London: SPCK, 1954), p. 318.

19. *Conference on Christian Union; Being a Narrative of the Proceedings of the Meeting held in Liverpool, October 1845* (London: J. Nisbet & Co., 1845), p. 6; J.W. Massie, *The Evangelical Alliance* (London, 1847), pp. 115, 120.

20. *Baptist Times*, 8 April 1926, p. 262.

21. G. Bray, 'What is the Church? An Ecclesiology for Today', in M. Tinker (ed.), *Restoring the Vision* (Eastbourne: MARC, 1990), pp. 195–6.

22. *John Wesley the Methodist: A Plain Account of his Life and Work* by a Methodist Preacher (New York: Methodist Book Concern, 1903), Chapter 9.

23. A.C. Outler (ed.), *The Works of John Wesley*, Vol. 3, Sermon on 'On obedience to pastors', Sermons, III (Nashville: Abingdon Press, 1986), p. 380.

24. R. Brown, *The English Baptists of the Eighteenth Century* (London: Baptist Historical Society, 1986), p. 81.

25. *English Baptist Records, Vol. 2: Church Book: St. Andrew's Street Baptist Church, Cambridge, 1720–1832* (Didcot: Baptist Historical Society, 1991), pp. 23, 26.

26. C.H. Spurgeon, *Metropolitan Tabernacle Pulpit*, sermon on Hebrews 13:8, Vol. 40, No. 2358, preached on 23 February 1888, p. 194.

27. B.L. Manning, *Essays in Orthodox Dissent* (London: Independent Press, 1953), pp. 72–3.

28. G.F. Nuttall, *Visible Saints* (Oxford: Blackwell, 1957).

29. *The British Weekly*, 28 January 1932, p. 354.

30. E.A. Payne, *The Fellowship of Believers* (London: Carey Kingsgate Press, 1952), pp. 101–6.

31. N. Wright, *Challenge to Change: A Radical Agenda for Baptists* (Eastbourne: Kingsway Publications, 1991).

32. N.A.D. Scotland, *Evangelical Anglicans in a Revolutionary Age, 1789–1901* (Carlisle: Paternoster Press, 2004), pp. 161–3.

33. *ibid.*, p. 390.

34. D.W. Bebbington, *Evangelicalism in Modern Britain: A History from the 1730s to the 1980s* (London: Routledge, 1995), p. 249.

35. P. Crowe (ed.), *Keele '67: The National Evangelical Anglican Congress Statement* (London: Falcon, 1967), p. 37.

36. C.O. Buchanan, *Is the Church of England Biblical?* (London: DLT, 1998), pp. 6–7.

37. C.O. Buchanan, E.L. Mascall, J.I. Packer, and The Bishop of Willesden, *Growing into Union: Proposals for Forming a United Church* (London: SPCK, 1970).

38. For the Christian Library see G. Rupp, 'Introductory Essay', in R.

Davies and G. Rupp (eds.), *A History of the Methodist Church in Great Britain* (London: Epworth Press, 1965), Vol. 1, p. xxxff. Rack is not so convinced of the Eastern influence. H.D. Rack, *Reasonable Enthusiast: John Wesley and the Rise of Methodism* (London: Epworth Press, 1989), p. 102.

39. H.B. McGonigle, *Sufficient Saving Grace: John Wesley's evangelical Arminianism* (Carlisle: Paternoster Press, 2001), pp. 207–10.

40. Evangelical Alliance, *Report of the proceedings of the Conference held at Freemason's Hall London, from August 19th to September 2nd, 1846* (London, 1847), p. 44; cf. I. Randall and D. Hilborn, *One Body in Christ* (Carlisle: Paternoster Press, 2001), chapter 3.

41. G. Carlyle (ed.), *Proceedings of the Geneva Conference of the Evangelical Alliance* (Edinburgh, 1862), p. 7.

42. P.D. Jordan, *The Evangelical Alliance for the United States of America, 1847–1900* (New York: Edwin Mellen, 1982), p. 75. See also N.M. Railton, *No North Sea: The Anglo-German Evangelical Network in the Middle of the Nineteenth Century* (Leiden: Brill, 2000), pp. 183–4. For Philip Schaff see G. Schriver, *Philip Schaff: Christian Scholar and Ecumenical Prophet* (Macon, Ga.: Mercer University Press, 1987).

43. *Evangelical Christendom*, 1 November 1878, p. 346; 1 December 1881, p. 367; 1 October 1884, p. 316.

44. For background to this development, see R. Rouse and S.C. Neill (eds.), *A History of the Ecumenical Movement, 1517–1948*, 2nd edn (London: SPCK, 1967).

45. *Evangelical Christendom* (April–June 1946), 50.

46. *Evangelical Christendom* (July–September 1947), 79.

47. See D. McBain, *Fire over the Waters: Renewal among Baptists and others from the 1960s to the 1990s* (London: DLT, 1997), pp. 63–4.

48. F. Baker, *John Wesley and the Church of England* (New York: Abingdon Press, 1970), 137.

49. F. Baker (ed.), *The Works of John Wesley* (Nashville: Abingdon Press, 1984), Vol. 26, p. 206. This is part of John Wesley's very important correspondence with 'John Smith' in the mid 1740s.

50. Jordan, *The Evangelical Alliance for the United States of America*, pp. 34–5.

51. For John Mott see C.H. Hopkins, *John R. Mott: 1865–1955: A Biography* (Grand Rapids, Mich.: Eerdmans, 1979).

52. Hopkins, *John R Mott, 1865–1955*, pp. 70–1.

53. A.J. Mason, *Memoir of George Howard Wilkinson* (London: Longmans, Green and Co., 1909), Vol. II, p. 10.

54. V. Smith, D. Hilary and M. Melrose, *St. Peter's Eaton Square (1827–1998)* (London: St. Peter's, 1998), p. 10.

55. D. Voll, *Catholic Evangelicalism* (London: The Faith Press, 1963), pp. 72–3, citing *The Standard*, 19 January 1883.

56. A.J. Mason, 'The Ministry of Conversion', in A.W. Robinson (ed.),

Handbooks for the Clergy (London: Longmans & Co., 1902), p. 115, cited by Voll, *Catholic Evangelicalism*, pp. 81–2.

57. D.M. Howard, *The Dream That Would Not Die* (Exeter: Paternoster Press, 1986); Randall and Hilborn, *One Body in Christ*, pp. 230, 237–41.
58. *Idea*, June/July/August 1997, p. 22.
59. T. Jackson (ed.), *The Works of the Rev John Wesley*, 3rd edn (Kansas: Beacon Hill Press, 1978), Vol. 6, p. 397.
60. S.J. Grenz, *Created for Community* (Grand Rapids, Mich.: Baker Book House, 1998).
61. J.I. Packer, 'A Stunted Ecclesiology? The Theory & Practice of Evangelical Churchliness', www.touchstonemag.com Touchstone magazine, Copyright © 2002 the Fellowship of St. James.

Chapter 9. 'Expect Great Things, Attempt Great Things': A Missionary Spirituality

1. A.C. Outler (ed.), *The Works of John Wesley*, Vol. 3, Sermon on 'Of the Church', Sermons, III (Nashville: Abingdon Press, 1986), p. 49.
2. J. Gordon, *Evangelical Spirituality* (London: SPCK, 1991), p. 21, citing F.C. Gill, *John Wesley's Prayers* (London, 1951).
3. D.O. Moberg, *The Great Reversal* (London: Scripture Union, 1972).
4. G. Whitefield, *Journals* (Edinburgh: Banner of Truth, repr. 1960), p. 87.
5. A. Dallimore, *George Whitefield* (Edinburgh: Banner of Truth, 1970), Vol. 1, p. 256.
6. *ibid.*, pp. 258–9.
7. H.S. Stout, *The Divine Dramatist* (Grand Rapids, Mich.: Eerdmans, 1991).
8. F. Lambert, 'The Great Awakening as Artifact: George Whitefield and the Construction of Intercolonial Revival, 1739–1745', *Church History*, Vol. 60, No. 2 (1991); cf. F. Lambert, *Pedlar in Divinity* (Princeton: Princeton University Press, 1994).
9. Stout, *Divine Dramatist*, pp. 147–55.
10. F.C. Gill, *Charles Wesley: The First Methodist* (London: Lutterworth Press, 1964), p. 75.
11. H.D. Rack, *Reasonable Enthusiast: John Wesley and the Rise of Methodism* (London: Epworth Press, 1989), pp. 300–2.
12. P.W. Chilcote, *John Wesley and the Women Preachers of Early Methodism* (Metuchen, New Jersey: Rowman and Littlefield, 1991).
13. D. Guy, 'The Influence of John Wesley on William and Catherine Booth', in P. Taylor (ed.), *Wesley Pieces* (Ilkeston, Derbys: The Wesley Fellowship, 1996), p. 17.
14. I.H. Murray, *Revival and Revivalism: The Making and Marring of American Evangelicalism, 1750–1858* (Edinburgh: Banner of Truth, 1994), pp. 165–6.

15. D.W. Bebbington, *Evangelicalism in Modern Britain: A History from the 1730s to the 1980s* (London: Routledge, 1995), p. 116; cf. J.E. Orr, *The Second Evangelical Awakening in Britain* (London & Edinburgh: Marshall, Morgan & Scott, 1949).

16. M.R. Watts, *The Dissenters, Vol II; The Expansion of Evangelical Nonconformity* (Oxford: Clarendon, 1995), p. 657. On Caughey's work in Britain see R. Carwardine, *Transatlantic Revivalism* (Westport, Conn.: Greenwood, 1978), pp. 97–133.

17. D.W. Bebbington, 'Moody as a Transatlantic Evangelist', in T. George (ed.), *Mr Moody and the Evangelical Tradition* (London: T & T Clark, 2004), pp. 75–92.

18. K.S. Jeffrey, *When the Lord Walked the Land: The 1858–62 Revival in the North East of Scotland* (Carlisle: Paternoster Press, 2002).

19. N.T.R. Dickson, *Brethren in Scotland, 1838–2000* (Carlisle: Paternoster Press, 2002), chapter 3.

20. J.B.A. Kessler, *A Study of the Evangelical Alliance in Great Britain* (Goes, Netherlands: Oosterbann and Le Cointre, 1968), pp. 60–1.

21. *Evangelical Christendom,* October 1859, pp. 368ff.; I. Randall and D. Hilborn, *One Body in Christ* (Carlisle: Paternoster Press, 2001), pp. 108–9, 141.

22. Randall and Hilborn, *One Body in Christ,* p. 108; cf. J. Edwards, *The Distinguishing Marks of the Spirit of God* (1741), in *Jonathan Edwards on Revival* (Edinburgh: Banner of Truth Trust, 1965); *The Religious Affections* (1746) (Edinburgh: Banner of Truth Trust, 1961).

23. The story of Protestant mission in this period is covered in S. Neill, *A History of Christian Missions* (Harmondsworth, Middlesex: Penguin Books, 1964), chapters 9 and 10.

24. For the Baptist Missionary Society, see B. Stanley, *The History of the Baptist Missionary Society, 1792–1992* (Edinburgh: T & T Clark, 1992).

25. For William Carey see T. George, *Faithful Witness* (Leicester: InterVarsity Press, 1992).

26. For Hudson Taylor and the Faith Missions see D.W. Bacon, *From Faith to Faith* (Singapore: OMF, 1984).

27. B. Stanley, *The Bible and the Flag* (Leicester: InterVarsity Press, 1990), p. 172.

28. For A.T. Pierson, see Dana L. Robert, *Occupy until I come: A.T. Pierson and the evangelization of the world* (Grand Rapids, Mich.: Eerdmans, 2003).

29. Blanche A.F. Pigott, *I. Lilias Trotter* (London: Marshall, Morgan & Scott, [1928]); M.H. Rockness, *A Passion for the Impossible* (Wheaton, Ill.: Harold Shaw Publishers, 1998).

30. W. Wilberforce *A Practical view of the prevailing Religious System of Professed Christians in the Higher and Middle Classes in this coun-*

try contrasted with Real Christianity, ed. V. Edmunds (London: Hodder & Stoughton, 1989).

31. J. Telford (ed.), *The Letters of the Rev John Wesley* (London: Epworth Press, 1931, repr. 1960), Vol. 8, p. 265.

32. See J.C. Pollock, *Wilberforce: God's Statesman* (Eastbourne: Kingsway, 2001).

33. Cited by Bebbington, *Evangelicalism in Modern Britain*, p. 12.

34. R. Steer, *Good News for the World* (Oxford: Monarch Books, 2004).

35. For more on these developments see D.W. Smith, *Transforming the World* (Carlisle: Paternoster Press, 1998).

36. K. Heasman, *Evangelicals in Action* (London: Geoffrey Bles, 1962), p. 14.

37. E. Hodder, *The Life and Work of the Seventh Earl of Shaftesbury* (London: Cassell, 1888), p. 519.

38. D.M. Lewis, *Lighten Their Darkness: The Evangelical Mission to Working-Class London, 1828–1860* (Carlisle: Paternoster Press, 2001).

39. For George Muller see R. Steer, *Delighted in God* (London: Hodder & Stoughton, 1975).

40. S.J. Brown, *Thomas Chalmers and the Godly Commonwealth in Scotland* (Oxford: Oxford University Press, 1982), chapter 3.

41. H. Begbie, *The Life of William Booth* (London: Macmillan & Co., 1920), Vol. 2, p. 181.

42. M.G. Fawcett and E.M. Turner, *Josephine Butler* (London: Association for Moral & Social Hygiene, 1927), pp. 99–100.

43. See F.B. Meyer, *The Bells of Is: Or Voices of Human Need and Sorrow* (London: Morgan & Scott [1894]).

44. H.A. Snyder, 'The Marks of Evangelical Ecclesiology', in J.J. Stackhouse Jnr (ed.), *Evangelical Ecclesiology: Reality or Illusion?* (Grand Rapids, Mich.: Baker Book House, 2003), pp. 99–101.

45. Reinhold Niebuhr, *An Interpretation of Christian Ethics* (New York: Seabury, 1935), p. 2. For a biography see: P.M. Minus, *Walter Rauschenbusch: American Reformer* (New York: Macmillan Publishing Company, 1988).

46. See D.M. Thompson, 'The Emergence of the Nonconformist Social Gospel in England', in K. Robbins (ed.), *Protestant Evangelicalism: Britain, Ireland, Germany and America c1750–c1950: Essays in Honour of W.R. Ward* (Oxford: Blackwell, 1990), pp. 255–80.

47. K. Adams, *A diary of revival: the outbreak of the 1904 Welsh Awakening* (Farnham: CWR, 2004), pp. 65–71.

48. From the Winter 2004 Evangelical Alliance Wales *Bulletin*: articles by Kevin Adams, Elfed Godding, Evangelical Alliance General Secretary, and Dan Boucher, National Assembly Liaison Officer.

49. See E. Evans, *The Welsh Revival of 1904* (London: Evangelical Press, 1969, republished by the Evangelical Movement of Wales' Bryntirion Press); B.P. Jones, *Voices from the Welsh Revival 1904–1905* (Bridgend: Evangelical Press of Wales and Bryntirion Press, 1995).

50. G. Lean, *Frank Buchman: A Life* (London: Collins, 1985).
51. *Evening Standard*, 8 December 1933, p. 5.
52. T. Spoerri, *Dynamic out of Silence* (London: Grosvenor, 1976), p. 87.
53. A. Jarlert, The Oxford Group, *Group Revivalism, and the Churches in Northern Europe, 1930–1945* (Lund, Sweden: Chartwell Bratt, 1995), pp. 225–6.
54. *British Weekly*, 16 January 1936, p. 332.
55. D.W. Lambert (ed.), *The Testament of Samuel Chadwick, 1860–1932* (London: Epworth Press, 1957), p. 52.
56. H.H. Rowdon, *London Bible College: The First Twenty-Five Years* (Worthing; Henry E. Walter, 1968), p. 66.
57. *The Christian*, 10 April 1947, p. 9.
58. *FC Magazine*, February 1947, p. 51; April 1947, pp. 5, 24, 25.
59. *The Record*, 18 September 1924, p. 591.
60. D.W. Bebbington, 'Decline and Resurgence of Social Concern', in J. Wolffe (ed.), *Evangelical Faith and Public Zeal* (London: SPCK, 1995), pp. 175–97.
61. P. Crowe (ed.), *Keele '67: The National Evangelical Anglican Congress Statement* (London: Falcon, 1967), p. 23.
62. C.F.H. Henry, *The Uneasy Conscience of Modern Fundamentalism* (Grand Rapids, Mich.: Eerdmans, 1947).
63. See, for example, C. Rowland, 'Anabaptism and Radical Christianity', *Mennonite Quarterly Review*, Vol. LXXIV, No. 4 (October 2000), pp. 549–54. For Anabaptist spirituality see C. Arnold Snyder, *Following in the Footsteps of Christ* (London: DLT, 2004).
64. Bebbington, 'Decline and Resurgence of Social Concern', pp. 185–8.
65. P. Conlan, 'Incurable Fanatic – Unshakeable Friend', in D. Greenlee (ed.), *Global Passion* (Carlisle: Authentic Lifestyle, 2003), p. 193.
66. *Crusade*, September 1974, p. 26.
67. *Baptist Times*, 12 March 1998, p. 1; 21 May 1998, p. 1.
68. *Jubilee of the Evangelical Alliance* (London: Evangelical Alliance, 1896), p. 497.
69. Reproduced in M.K. Nicholls, *C.H. Spurgeon – The Pastor Evangelist* (Didcot: Baptist Historical Society, 1992), p. 65.
70. G. Verwer, 'The Lordship of Christ', in Greenlee (ed.), *Global Passion*, p. xxix.

Chapter 10. 'The Lord Cometh': Evangelicals and the Last Times

1. R.G. Clouse (ed.), *The Meaning of the Millennium: Four Views* (Downers Grove, Ill.: InterVarsity, 1977) usefully draws together apologists for the various traditions.
2. See I.H. Murray, *The Puritan Hope* (Edinburgh: Banner of Truth Trust, 1975).
3. See L. Boettner, *The Millennium* (Philadelphia: Presbyterian and Reformed Publishing Co., 1957).

4. Jonathan Edwards, *A History of the Work of Redemption*, ed. J.F. Wilson (New Haven and London: Yale University Press, 1989), p. 480.
5. Murray, *The Puritan Hope*, pp. 152–3.
6. V. Reasoner, *The Hope of the Gospel* (Evansville, IN: Fundamental Wesleyan Publishers, 1999).
7. Murray, *The Puritan Hope*, pp. 133–4.
8. *ibid.*, p. 132.
9. J.C.S. Mason, *The Moravian Church and the Missionary Awakening in England, 1760–1800* (Woodbridge: The Boydell Press, 2001), p. 189.
10. Murray, *The Puritan Hope*, p. 154.
11. D.W. Bebbington, *Evangelicalism in Modern Britain: A History from the 1730s to the 1980s* (London: Routledge, 1995), p. 62.
12. N.A.D. Scotland, *Evangelical Anglicans in a Revolutionary Age, 1789–1901* (Carlisle: Paternoster Press, 2004), pp. 178–9.
13. Evangelical Alliance, *Report of the Proceedings of the Conference held at Freemasons' Hall, London, From August 19th to September 2nd Inclusive, 1846* (London, 1847), p. 234.
14. Bebbington, *Evangelicalism in Modern Britain*, pp. 102–3.
15. J.F.C. Harrison, *The Second Coming: Popular Millenarianism, 1780–1850* (London: Routledge, 1979), p. 7.
16. See D.W. Bebbington, 'The Advent Hope in British Evangelicalism since 1800', *Scottish Journal of Religious Studies*, Vol. 9, No. 2 (1988); for America see T.P. Weber, *Living in the Shadow of the Second Coming: American Premillennialism, 1875–1982* (Chicago: University of Chicago Press, 1987).
17. H.H. Rowdon, *The Origins of the Brethren, 1825–1850* (London: Pickering & Inglis, 1967), pp. 53, 99. For Darby the different dispensations were periods in which God dealt with his people in different ways. God's dealings with the Jews were quite different from those with the Church.
18. H.H. Rowdon, 'Secession from the Established Church in the early Nineteenth Century', *Vox Evangelica*, Vol. 3 (1964), p. 83. For Philpot see *Letters of J.N.D.*, Vol. 3 (London, n.d.), p. 474; I.M. Randall, '"The Things which shall be Hereafter": Strict Baptist Views of the Second Coming', *The Strict Baptist Historical Society Bulletin*, No. 27 (2000).
19. S.R. Maitland, *An Enquiry into the Grounds on which the Prophetic Period of Daniel and St. John has been supposed to consist of 1,260 years* (London, 1826). Maitland's view that the book of Revelation spoke of future events helped to shape premillennial futurism.
20. Bebbington, *Evangelicalism in Modern Britain*, p. 86.
21. *ibid.*, p. 85.
22. Bebbington, 'Advent Hope', pp. 105, 108; Bebbington, *Evangelicalism in Modern Britain*, p. 192.
23. See F.R. Coad, *Prophetic Developments with Particular Reference to*

the Early Brethren (Pinner: CBRF, 1966), pp. 22, 27, 28; D.W. Frank, *Less than Conquerors: How Evangelicals Entered the Twentieth Century* (Grand Rapids, Mich.: Eerdmans, 1986), p. 94; E.R. Sandeen, *The Roots of Fundamentalism: British and American Millenarianism, 1800–1930* (Chicago: University of Chicago Press, 1970), p. 67.

24. D. Robertson, *Awakening: The Life and Ministry of Robert Murray McCheyne* (Carlisle: Paternoster Press, 2004), pp. 102–6.

25. E. Hodder, *Life and Work of the Seventh Earl of Shaftesbury* (London: Cassell, 1888), p. 523.

26. Scotland, *Evangelical Anglicans*, pp. 175–7.

27. *The Bible Call*, April–June 1927, p. 25; Bebbington, *Evangelicalism in Modern Britain*, p. 62.

28. For the full manifesto, see, for example, *Christian World*, 8 November 1917, p. 7; cf. I.M. Randall, *Spirituality and Social Change* (Carlisle: Paternoster Press, 2003), chapter 3.

29. *The Monthly Bulletin of the Advent Preparation Prayer Union*, June 1919, p. 1.

30. W.Y. Fullerton, *F.B. Meyer: A Biography* (London: Marshall, Morgan & Scott, [1929]), pp. 157–9.

31. *Advent Witness*, December 1923, pp. 135–6; January 1925, p. 1.

32. *Life of Faith*, 19 December 1917, pp. 1451–2; *The Christian*, 20 December 1917, p. 12.

33. *Christian World*, 15 November 1917, p. 7.

34. See D.W. Bebbington, 'Baptists and Fundamentalism in Inter-War Britain', in K. Robbins (ed.), *Protestant Evangelicalism: Britain, Ireland, Germany and America c1750–c1950: Essays in Honour of W.R. Ward* (Oxford: Blackwell, 1990), pp. 309–10; Sandeen, *The Roots of Fundamentalism*, p. 207; G.M. Marsden, *Fundamentalism and American Culture: The Shaping of Twentieth-century Evangelicalism 1870–1925* (Oxford: Oxford University Press, 1980), p. 5.

35. *Life of Faith*, 20 October 1926, p. 1189. For British/American contrasts, see G.M. Marsden, 'Fundamentalism as an American Phenomenon: A Comparison with British Evangelicalism', *Church History*, Vol. 46, No. 2 (1977), pp. 215–32.

36. Randall, *Spirituality and Social Change*, p. 134.

37. *Advent Witness*, December 1922, p. 134; October 1927, p. 158.

38. Bebbington discusses this in 'Advent Hope', pp. 109–10. As with Keswick, the leisured classes were able to attend the requisite conferences.

39. Marsden, *Fundamentalism*, pp. 37, 72, 79; Sandeen, *The Roots of Fundamentalism*, pp. 132–44.

40. See T. Larsen, *Christabel Pankhurst: Fundamentalism and Feminism in Coalition* (Woodbridge: Boydell & Brewer, 2003).

41. C. Pankhurst, *The Lord Cometh: The World Crisis Explained* (London: Morgan & Scott, 1923), pp. iii, 8–9.

42. *Life of Faith*, 24 February 1926, p. 208; 10 November 1926, p. 1262; *Advent Witness*, March 1926, p. 33.
43. *Advent Witness*, February 1927, p. 20; *Christian*, 27 January 1927, p. 11; *Life of Faith*, 2 February 1927, p. 116.
44. *Watching and Waiting*, December 1930, pp. 92–3.
45. *Watching and Waiting*, March–April 1941, p. 219.
46. *Watching and Waiting*, January–March 1946, p. 16.
47. I.M. Randall, *Educating Evangelicalism: The Origins, Development and Impact of London Bible College* (Carlisle, 2000), p. 108.
48. See R. Shuff, *Searching for the True Church: Brethren and Evangelicals in Mid-Twentieth-Century England*, (Carlisle: Paternoster Press, 2005).
49. O. Barclay, *Evangelicalism in Britain, 1935–1995* (Leicester: InterVarsity Press, 1997), chapters 3 and 4.
50. M. Wilcock, *The Message of Revelation* (Leicester: IVP, 1975).
51. *The Christian*, 18 June 1965, p. 14.
52. D. Tidball, *Who are the Evangelicals?* (London: MarshallPickering, 1994), p. 145.
53. S. Escobar, 'The Return of Christ', in C.R. Padilla (ed.), *The New Face of Evangelicalism* (London: Hodder & Stoughton, 1976), p. 259.
54. Jonathan Edwards, 'Apocalyptic Writings', ed. S.J. Stein (New Haven and London: Yale University Press, 1977), pp. 341–3; cf. G.M. Marsden, *Jonathan Edwards: A Life* (New Haven and London: Yale University Press, 2003), pp. 335–7.
55. For background see G. Rowell, *Hell and the Victorians* (Oxford: Clarendon Press, 1974).
56. See R.A. Peterson, *Hell on Trial: The Case for Eternal Punishment* (Phillipsburg: P&R Publishing, 1995), pp. 97–117; D. Powys, 'The Nineteenth and Twentieth Century Debates about Hell and Universalism', in N.M. De S. Cameron (ed.), *Universalism and the Doctrine of Hell* (Carlisle: Paternoster Press, 1993), pp. 93–138.
57. *The Nonconformist*, 26 August 1846, p. 575; I. Randall and D. Hilborn, *One Body in Christ* (Carlisle: Paternoster Press, 2001), pp. 59–60.
58. T.R. Birks, *The Victory of Divine Goodness* (London: Rivingtons, 1867).
59. Evangelical Alliance Executive Council Minutes, 26 January 1870, pp. 52–3; cf. Randall and Hilborn, *One Body in Christ*, pp. 119–32.
60. F.B. Meyer, *Where are our Dead?* (London: National Free Church Council, [1918]), pp. 79–80. See also Meyer's views in F.B. Meyer, *Our Sister Death* (London: NCEFC, 1915), pp. 23–4.
61. D.L. Edwards and J.R.W. Stott, *Essentials: A liberal-evangelical dialogue* (London: Hodder & Stoughton, 1988).
62. Randall and Hilborn, *One Body in Christ*, pp. 337–43.
63. ACUTE, *The Nature of Hell* (Carlisle: Paternoster Press, 2000), pp.134–5.

64. *The Monthly Bulletin of the Advent Testimony and Prayer Union,* December 1919, p. 50.

Chapter 11. 'The Fostering of Spirituality'

1. D.K. Gillett, *Trust and Obey: Explorations in Evangelical Spirituality* (London: DLT, 1993), pp. 1–3.
2. B.L. Manning, *Essays in Orthodox Dissent* (London: Independent Press, 1939), p. 18.
3. R. Foster, *Streams of Living Water* (London: HarperCollins, 1999), chapter 6.
4. *Christianity and Renewal,* July 2004, p. 13.
5. J. Walsh, 'Religious Societies, Methodist and Evangelical, 1738–1800', *Studies in Church History,* Vol. 23 (1986), and H.D. Rack, 'Religious Societies and the Origins of Methodism', *Journal of Ecclesiastical History,* Vol. 38 (1987).
6. J. Mountain, *Hymns of Consecration and Faith* (London: Marshall Bros., 1895).
7. D. Guy, 'The Influence of John Wesley on William and Catherine Booth', in P. Taylor (ed.), *Wesley Pieces* (Ilkeston, Derbys: The Wesley Fellowship, 1996), p. 17.
8. E. Evans, *The Welsh Revival of 1904* (London: Evangelical Press, 1969, republished by the Evangelical Movement of Wales, Bryntirion Press), pp. 28–9.
9. *ibid.,* p. 58.
10. *ibid.,* p. 46.
11. Linda Wilson's *Constrained by Zeal: Female Spirituality amongst Nonconformists, 1825–1875* (Carlisle: Paternoster Press, 2000) is an example of the work that can be done.
12. *Keswick Week* (1950), p. 43.
13. W.G. Scroggie, *What Meaneth This? A Brief Interpretation of the Keswick Movement* (London: privately published, n.d.), p. 9.
14. For such statements see the *Life of Faith,* 10 March 1897, p. 117; 10 April 1901, p. 220; 16 September 1903, p. 630.
15. A.E. McGrath, *Beyond the Quiet Time* (London: SPCK, 1995), p. ix.
16. G.A. Furr and C.W. Freeman (eds.), *Ties That Bind: Life Together in the Baptist Vision* (Macon, Ga.: Smyth & Helwys, 1994), pp. 69–82.
17. J.A. Bakke, *Holy Invitations* (Grand Rapids: Baker Books, 2000). Bakke teaches at a Baptist seminary, Bethel Theological Seminary.
18. For the full text see *First Things,* Vol. 43 (May 1994), pp. 15–22. *First Things* is the magazine for the American Centre for Policy and Religion.
19. J.I. Packer, 'Crosscurrents among Evangelicals', in C. Colson and R.J. Neuhaus (eds.), *Evangelicals and Catholics Together: Working Towards a Common Mission* (London: Hodder and Stoughton, 1996), pp. 159, 164, 171.

20. R.E. Webber, *Ancient-Future Faith* (Grand Rapids, Mich.: Baker Books, 1999).
21. R.E. Webber, *The Younger Evangelicals* (Grand Rapids, Mich.: Baker Books, 2002), pp. 180–2.
22. D.W. Bebbington, *Evangelicalism in Modern Britain: A History from the 1730s to the 1980s* (London: Routledge, 1995), chapter 8.
23. I.M. Randall, 'The Social Gospel: A Case Study', in J. Wolffe (ed.), *Evangelical Faith and Public Zeal* (London: SPCK, 1995), chapter 8.
24. Bebbington, *Evangelicalism in Modern Britain*, chapter 7.
25. D. McBain, *Fire over the Waters: Renewal among Baptists and others from the 1960s to the 1990s* (London: DLT, 1997), p. 64.
26. T. Chester, *Awakening to a world of need: The recovery of evangelical social concern* (Leicester: InterVarsity Press, 1993).
27. D. Tidball on postmodernism, citing Graham Cray, in *Mainstream*, January 1996, pp. 11–18.
28. Church of England, *Mission shaped church: Church planting and fresh expressions of church in a changing context* (London: Church House Publications, 2004).
29. 'Background Briefing: Lambeth Conference at a Glance', Anglican Communion News Service, LC014, 18 July 1998; Bob Libby, 'How many Anglicans are there?', *Lambeth Daily*, 8 August 1998, p. 4.
30. Dana L. Robert, 'Christianity in the Wider World', in H. Kee (ed.), *Christianity: A Social and Cultural History,* Part VI, 2nd edn (Upper Saddle River, NJ: Prentice-Hall, 1998), p. 570.
31. D. Martin, *Tongues of Fire* (Oxford: Blackwell, 1993), pp. 49–50.
32. D. Martin, *Pentecostalism: The World is Their Parish* (Oxford: Blackwell, 2002), pp. 4, 160–2.
33. E.g. W. Hollenweger, *Pentecostalism: Origins and Developments Worldwide* (Peabody, MA: Hendrickson Publishers, 1997); Harvey Cox, *Fire From Heaven: The Rise of Pentecostal Spirituality and the Reshaping of Religion in the Twenty-first Century* (Reading, MA: Addison-Wesley Publishing Company, 1994).
34. Martin, *Pentecostalism: The World is Their Parish*, p. 75.
35. Mark Hutchinson, 'It's a Small Church After All', *Christianity Today*, 16 November 1998, pp. 46–9. Hutchinson is one of the leaders of the 'Currents in World Christianity Project', looking at the global spread of evangelicalism.
36. K. Bediako, *Theology and Identity* (Carlisle: Paternoster Press, 1992).
37. D. Stoll, *Is Latin America Turning Protestant?* (Oxford: University of California Press, 1990), pp. 22–3.
38. Martin, *Pentecostalism: The World is Their Parish*, pp. 65–6.
39. See A. Hunter and K-K. Chan, *Protestantism in Contemporary China* (Cambridge: Cambridge University Press, 1993).
40. D. Aikman, *Jesus in Beijing: How Christianity is Transforming China and Changing the Global Balance of Power* (Washington, DC:

Regnery Publishing, 2003). David Aikman, former senior foreign correspondent for *Time* magazine and Beijing bureau chief, speaks Chinese and has covered China for over thirty years.

41. Martin, *Pentecostalism: The World is Their Parish*, p. 167.
42. R. Shaull and W. Cesar, *Pentecostalism and the Future of the Christian Churches* (Grand Rapids, Mich.: W.B. Eerdmans, 2000), pp. 92–3.
43. S.J. Grenz, *Revisioning Evangelical Theology* (Downers Grove, Ill.: InterVarsity, 1993), pp. 57–9.
44. S.J. Grenz, 'Conversing in Christian Style: Toward a Baptist Theological Method for the Postmodern Context', *Baptist History and Heritage*, Vol. 35, No. 1 (2000), p. 91.
45. W. Carus, *Memoirs of the Life of the Rev. C. Simeon* (London, 1847), pp. 822–3.

SELECT BIBLIOGRAPHY

Adam, P, *Roots of Contemporary Evangelical Spirituality* (Bramcote: Grove, 1988)

Bebbington, D.W., *Evangelicalism in Modern Britain: A History from the 1730s to the 1980s* (London: Routledge, 1995)

Holiness in Nineteenth-Century England (Carlisle: Paternoster, 2000)

Bradley, I., *Abide with me: The world of Victorian hymns* (London: SCM, 1997)

Cockerton, J., *Essentials of Evangelical Spirituality* (Bramcote: Grove, 1994)

Dieter, M.E., *The Holiness Revival of the Nineteenth Century* (Metuchen, NJ: Scarecrow Press, 1980)

(ed.), *Five Views of Sanctification* (Grand Rapids, Mich.: Zondervan, 1987)

Ditchfield, G.M., *The Evangelical Revival* (London: UCL Press, 1998)

Elliot, E., *Amy Carmichael: Her Life and Legacy* (Eastbourne: Kingsway, 1988)

Forsyth, P.T., *The Work of Christ* (London: Hodder & Stoughton, 1910)

The Soul of Prayer (London: C.H. Kelly, 1916)

The Church and the Sacraments (London: Independent Press, 1947)

Foster, R., *Celebration of Discipline* (London: Hodder & Stoughton, 1980)

Prayer (London: Hodder & Stoughton, 1992)

Streams of Living Water (London: HarperCollins, 1999)

Frank, D.W., *Less than Conquerors: How Evangelicals Entered the Twentieth Century* (Grand Rapids, Mich.: Eerdmans, 1986)

Furr, G. A., and C. W. Freeman (eds.), *Ties That Bind: Life Together in the Baptist Vision* (Macon, Ga.: Smyth & Helwys, 1994)

Giles, G., *The Music of Praise* (Oxford: Bible Reading Fellowship, 2002)

Gill, F.C., *Charles Wesley: The First Methodist* (London: Lutterworth Press, 1964)

Gillett, D.K., *Trust and Obey: Explorations in Evangelical Spirituality* (London: DLT, 1993)

Gordon, J., *Evangelical Spirituality* (London: SPCK, 1991)

Greenlee, D. (ed.), *Global Passion* (Carlisle: Authentic Lifestyle, 2003)

Heasman, K., *Evangelicals in Action* (London: Geoffrey Bles, 1962)

Hindmarsh, D.B., *John Newton and the English Evangelical tradition:*

Between the conversions of Wesley and Wilberforce (Oxford: Oxford University Press, 1996)

Kent, J., *Wesley and the Wesleyans: Religion in Eighteenth-Century Britain* (Cambridge: Cambridge University Press, 2002)

Lewis, A.J., *Zinzendorf: The Ecumenical Pioneer* (London: SCM, 1962)

Lewis, D.M. (ed.), *Christianity Reborn: The Global Expansion of Evangelicalism in the Twentieth Century* (Grand Rapids, Mich.: Eerdmans, 2004)

Lloyd-Jones, D.M., *Preaching and Preachers* (London: Hodder & Stoughton, 1971)

Manning, B.L., *The Hymns of Wesley and Watts* (London: Epworth Press, 1942)

Marsden, G.M., *Jonathan Edwards: A Life* (New Haven and London: Yale University Press, 2003)

McBain, D., *Fire over the Waters: Renewal among Baptists and others from the 1960s to the 1990s* (London: DLT, 1997)

McCasland, D., *Oswald Chambers: Abandoned to God* (Nashville: Discovery House, 1993)

McGonigle, H.B., *Sufficient Saving Grace: John Wesley's Evangelical Arminianism* (Carlisle: Paternoster Press, 2001)

McGrath, A.E., *Evangelicalism and the Future of Christianity* (London: Hodder & Stoughton, 1988)

Christian Spirituality: An Introduction (Oxford: Blackwell, 1999)

Mursell, G., *English Spirituality: From 1700 to the Present Day* (London: SPCK, 2001)

Noll, M., *The Rise of Evangelicalism* (Leicester: Apollos, 2003)

Noll, M.A., and R.F. Thiemann (eds.), *Where Shall My Wond'ring Soul Begin?* (Grand Rapids, Mich.: Eerdmans, 2000)

Packer, J.I., *Passion for Holiness* (Leicester: Crossway Books, 1992)

Peterson, E.H., *Working the Angles* (Grand Rapids, Mich.: Eerdmans, 1987)

Price C., and I. Randall, *Transforming Keswick* (Carlisle: Paternoster/ OM, 2000)

Rack, H.D., *Reasonable Enthusiast: John Wesley and the Rise of Methodism* (London: Epworth Press, 1989)

Randall, I.M., *Evangelical Experiences: A Study in the Spirituality of English Evangelicalism, 1918–1939* (Carlisle: Paternoster, 1999)

Spirituality and Social Change: The Contribution of F.B. Meyer (1847–1929) (Carlisle: Paternoster Press, 2003)

and D. Hilborn, *One Body in Christ* (Carlisle: Paternoster Press, 2001)

Ryle, J.C., *Practical Religion* (Cambridge: James Clarke & Co., repr. 1959)

Holiness (Welwyn: Evangelical Press, repr. 1979)

Scotland, N.A.D., *Evangelical Anglicans in a Revolutionary Age, 1789–1901* (Carlisle: Paternoster Press, 2004)

Seddon, P., *Gospel and Sacrament: Reclaiming a holistic evangelical spirituality* (Cambridge: Grove, 2004)

Sheldrake, P., *Spirituality and History* (London: SPCK, 1991)

Stackhouse, J.J. Jnr (ed.), *Evangelical Ecclesiology: Reality or Illusion?* (Grand Rapids, Mich.: Baker Book House, 2003)

Stott, J.R.W., *The Preacher's Portrait* (London: Tyndale, 1961)

Stout, H.S., *The Divine Dramatist: George Whitefield and the Rise of Modern Evangelicalism* (Grand Rapids, Mich.: Eerdmans, 1991)

Tidball, D.J., *Who are the Evangelicals?* (London: MarshallPickering, 1994)

Toon, P., *Born Again: A Biblical and Theological Study of Regeneration* (Grand Rapids, Mich.: Baker Book House, 1987)

Walker, M.J., *Baptists at the Table. The Theology of the Lord's Supper amongst English Baptists in the Nineteenth Century* (Didcot, Oxfordshire: Baptist Historical Society, 1992)

Watson, D., *Discipleship* (London: Hodder & Stoughton, 1981)

Webber, R.E., *Ancient-Future Faith* (Grand Rapids, Mich.: Baker Book House, 1999)

Welch, E., *Spiritual Pilgrim: A reassessment of the life of the Countess of Huntingdon* (Cardiff: University of Wales Press, 1995)

Willard, D., *The Divine Conspiracy: Rediscovering our hidden life in God* (London: HarperCollins, 2000)

Wilson, L., *Constrained by Zeal: Female Spirituality amongst Nonconformists, 1825–1875* (Carlisle: Paternoster Press, 2000)

Wood, A.S., *The Burning Heart* (Exeter: Paternoster Press, 1978)